"Many books that advance comm[unity engagement focus on] a narrow aspect of practice in hope [of capturing a tota]lly complex body of work. *Refram[ing Community Engagement in Hig]her Education* honors the multiplicity [of forms and forums of appropri]ate engagement practice but returns, again and again, to the central role of relationship-oriented changemaking. This book provides valuable portraits of varied practice but keeps the endeavor of seeking a more democratic, inclusive, and thriving world as its center point. In doing so, the chapters combine to provide a cogent, compelling explanation of current-day community engagement in higher education."

Lina Dostilio, *Vice Chancellor of Engagement and Community Affairs, University of Pittsburgh, USA*

"California is a world leader in both higher education and service. This book describes the ways in which #CaliforniansForAll College Corps advances state and national priorities by connecting Californians of different backgrounds with enriching service opportunities while making college more affordable for our future leaders. *Reframing Community Engagement in Higher Education* illustrates California Volunteers' years of impact and shows how programs like the College Corps can be replicated across the nation."

Gavin Newsom, *Governor of California, USA*

"Civic-minded undergraduates with community service encoded into their DNA will have a very positive impact locally, regionally, and around the globe. *Reframing Community Engagement in Higher Education* provides us with many examples of programs and tools we can use to help these young people in their efforts. I can hardly wait to see the positive change they will create."

Walter R. Jacobs, *Provost and Vice President for Academic Affairs, California State University East Bay, USA; Author of* Sparked: George Floyd, Racism, and the Progressive Illusion

REFRAMING COMMUNITY ENGAGEMENT IN HIGHER EDUCATION

This timely book addresses assumptions and challenges inherent within community engagement as a catalyst for developing students' sense of civic responsibility at a time of rampant social polarization.

Promoting academic development and life skills through the high-impact practice of service-learning, the book explores a new ecological framework for reflecting on and improving practice. This book describes new models such as the #CaliforniansForAll College Corps, offers advice on coalition building, and presents the narratives of community-engaged professionals and faculty, offering a sense both of tensions inherent in this work and examples of initiatives in local contexts. Chapters primarily reflect on what action is required for fulfilling our public purpose and what's holding us back.

This book provides guidance, examples, and benchmarks for best practices in community engagement that are particularly relevant to this time of crises and unrest and will be relevant to community-engaged professionals, higher education faculty, and college administrators.

Elena Klaw is Professor of Psychology and the Faculty Director of the Center for Community Learning and Leadership at San José State University, USA.

Andrea Tully is Assistant Director of the Center for Community Learning and Leadership at San José State University, USA.

Elaine K. Ikeda is Executive Director of LEAD California, USA.

REFRAMING COMMUNITY ENGAGEMENT IN HIGHER EDUCATION

Edited by Elena Klaw, Andrea Tully, and Elaine K. Ikeda

Routledge
Taylor & Francis Group
NEW YORK AND LONDON

Designed cover image: © Getty Images

First published 2024
by Routledge
605 Third Avenue, New York, NY 10158

and by Routledge
4 Park Square, Milton Park, Abingdon, Oxon, OX14 4RN

Routledge is an imprint of the Taylor & Francis Group, an informa business

© 2024 Taylor & Francis

The right of Elena Klaw, Andrea Tully, and Elaine K. Ikeda to be identified as the authors of the editorial material, and of the authors for their individual chapters, has been asserted in accordance with sections 77 and 78 of the Copyright, Designs and Patents Act 1988.

All rights reserved. No part of this book may be reprinted or reproduced or utilised in any form or by any electronic, mechanical, or other means, now known or hereafter invented, including photocopying and recording, or in any information storage or retrieval system, without permission in writing from the publishers.

Trademark notice: Product or corporate names may be trademarks or registered trademarks, and are used only for identification and explanation without intent to infringe.

ISBN: 978-1-032-58143-9 (hbk)
ISBN: 978-1-032-58170-5 (pbk)
ISBN: 978-1-003-44852-5 (ebk)

DOI: 10.4324/9781003448525

Typeset in Galliard
by Newgen Publishing UK

I dedicate this book to my parents, Hal and Luisa Smith, who have made all things possible, to my husband, Oliver Pohland, who has been by my side throughout my journey from graduate student to full professor, and to my children, Amanda and Nathaniel, who continually give me new lenses through which to see the world and its inhabitants. I am grateful to my supportive colleagues, to my mentors, and to my students. It is young people that give me hope and resolve for a kinder and more just future.
- Elena Klaw

I dedicate this book to my son, Cooper, and baby on the way, whom I love beyond measure and to their generation, for whom I hope this world is left a better place, to my husband, Patrick, who chose to live this wild life by my side, and to my parents, Anne and Allan, who are my steadfast support system. I am thankful for the strong female mentors I have had throughout my life, two of whom I had the honor of coediting this book with. I am grateful for the community partners with whom I collaborate, the colleagues with whom I commiserate, and the students who have always been and always will be my motivation for working in higher education.
- Andrea Tully

This book is dedicated to my outstanding colleagues in the community engagement field, who, over the years, have become dear friends and mentors. Their commitment to students, faculty, community partners, and the principles of social justice and equity have inspired me throughout my career in community engagement. A special shout out to my support crew who are always in my corner: Nadinne Cruz, Kathleen Yep, and Marisol Morales. I also dedicate this to my mentors Alexander (Sandy) and Helen (Lena) Astin, who encouraged me to say yes to this job offer 22 years ago. Sandy passed away while we were writing this book, but he is always with me. And finally, I am grateful to my family and my ancestors, upon whose shoulders I stand, and who suffered greatly so that I may thrive and live freely.
- Elaine K. Ikeda

CONTENTS

Foreword   *xii*
David M. Donahue
Acknowledgments   *xvi*

1   Introduction   1
    Elena Klaw, Andrea Tully, and Elaine K. Ikeda

PART 1
Enacting Social Justice: Current Contexts and
Community Engagement   **9**

2   Community Engagement Strategies for Responding
    to Sociopolitical and Racial Challenges Facing
    American Society and Higher Education   11
    Glenn A. Bowen, Courtney A. Berrien, and
    Roni Bennett

3   Mapping Our Capacities to Facilitate Change:
    Applying the Ecosystem of Critical Feminist
    Praxis for Community Engagement Professionals   30
    Star Plaxton-Moore

4 Reclaiming the Mission of the Community College: Civic, Community, and Political Equity Reimagined   57
Patricia D. Robinson and Verdis LeVar Robinson

5 Social Media and Youth Climate Activism: Community-Engaged Learning for the 2020s   76
Ellen Middaugh, Mark Felton, and Henry Fan

PART 2
Building a Movement: Establishing Infrastructure for Community Engagement   99

6 Coalition Building for Transformation and Change in Higher Education   101
Elaine K. Ikeda

7 And So Goes the Nation: California Gets to Work   120
Josh Fryday, Elena Klaw, and Andrea Tully

8 A Presidential Perspective: Place-Based Community Engagement in Faith-Based Higher Education   134
Erica K. Yamamura, Kent Koth, and Chris Nayve

PART 3
Reconceptualizing Roles: Faculty, Staff, and Partnerships in Community Engagement   155

9 Community Engagement Professionals and Transformational Education   157
Andrea Tully, Pilar Pacheco, Andrea Tafolla, Bryant Fairley, and Daniel Fidalgo Tomé

10 The Tensions and Rewards of Community Engagement for Faculty Members   177
Elena Klaw, Anh-Thu Ngo, Angie Mejia, Marie Sandy, and Jon A. Levisohn

11 Community-Engaged Partnerships When Healthy
   Relationships Are the Priority   213
   Jamilah Ducar and Daren Ellerbee

12 Ode to Education That Lifts Us Higher   233
   Shandela Contreras

13 Conclusion   237
   Elena Klaw, Andrea Tully, and Elaine K. Ikeda

About the Contributors   *241*
Index   *244*

FOREWORD

David M. Donahue

As I read the chapters in *Reframing Community Engagement in Higher Education*, I kept thinking what a gift this book is to those of us looking for new frameworks, innovative models, and inspiring stories to understand the potential of community engagement in higher education. It provides new ways of seeing ourselves, our work, and our contexts. Like the classic book *Ways of Seeing* (Berger, 1972), the authors of this book challenge how we look at the world and provide insight into how and what we might see in community engagement with new perspectives. Drawing on Berger's focus on visual imagery, I will use three images to ignite your own engagement with this book.

Reading the first section, Enacting Social Justice: Current Contexts and Community Engagement, I was reminded of a certain optical illusion, *Kaninchen und Ente* (1892). You have probably seen it at some point. Depending on how you look at the picture, you might see a duck or a rabbit. Some people can only see one thing, the duck or the rabbit, but others can see both animals. I have read that those who can see the duck and the rabbit when they look at this picture are more creative, better problem solvers, and more adept at using tools. Once you see both the rabbit and the duck, you are able to understand that images do not necessarily have inherent meaning, but instead are interpreted, and that understanding is not fixed and independent of context, but fluid and dependent on context including prior knowledge and experience.

I was reminded of this image because the authors of the chapters in the first section help us see community-engaged teaching and learning in new ways. If we thought we knew what community engagement meant (the equivalent of seeing only the duck) before reading this book, these chapters now help us reframe what we thought (providing a vision of the rabbit along with the duck). That kind of reframing is paradigm shifting, and I found this kind of transformative perspective-taking throughout the book. Glenn Bowen, Courtney Berrien, and Roni Bennett provide a vision of how community-engaged learning can promote racial justice, truth-telling, and reconciliation—processes that serve to counter the hegemony of colonial perspectives in the epistemology and ontology of higher education. Star Plaxton-Moore provides a much-needed feminist perspective and helps us rethink the founding stories of service and community-engaged learning, providing a valuable corrective about the role that civil rights activists and advocates of ethnic studies have played. Patricia Robinson and Verdis LeVar Robinson provide a valuable outlook on the potential of community colleges to revitalize civic life in the United States and remind us that these institutions are "democracy's colleges." In an era where we often fear digital spaces' influence on society, Ellen Middaugh, Mark Felton, and Henry Fan provide perspective on how online platforms can be generative arenas to frame and build critical inquiry and productive political discourse through deliberative dialogue.

Reading the second section, Building a Movement: Establishing Infrastructure for Community Engagement, I thought of Anish Kapoor's sculpture, *Cloud Gate* (2006), more familiarly known as *The Bean*. If you have ever visited Chicago, you have probably seen this giant reflective piece of art in Millennium Park. About the size of a three-story building, the piece's mirrored surface reflects the surrounding skyscrapers, the sky and clouds above, and the people all moving around and underneath the sculpture. Moving around the sculpture, we see ourselves in relation to the world around us.

The authors in this section not only help us understand how to build a movement and the structures for community engagement; but like *Cloud Gate* (2006), they help us reflect and see ourselves in relation to those structures. Elaine K. Ikeda's chapter serves as a powerful reminder about the importance of coalition building across an individual campus and across multiple institutions to harness diverse wisdom, experiences, and perspectives. Her chapter invites us to reflect on our positionality and provides numerous questions to spark our reflection about what we bring, where we are, and where we are heading. Josh Fryday, Elena Klaw, and Andrea Tully provide a picture of creating a state-wide service corps that is inspiring and grounded in reality. They invite us to see how service benefits multiple constituencies and how those constituencies can come together in the process. Erica Yamamura, Kent Koth, and Chris Nayve shed light on the role of mission and faith in building engaged campuses. Their analysis of interviews with two experienced college presidents of faith-based institutions helps us reflect on the role of leadership, presidential and otherwise, to institutionalize community engagement and connect it to efforts at diversity, equity, and inclusion. Interacting with *Cloud Gate* (Kapoor, 2006) brings so much joy as well as reflection, and in that sense, I also thought of the chapters in this section.

Reading the final section, Reconceptualizing Roles: Faculty, Staff, and Partnerships in Community Engagement, brought to mind a kaleidoscope. Kaleidoscopes rely on mirrors to create patterns through reflection. You may have been fascinated with kaleidoscopic images as a child, looking and turning the kaleidoscope tube to create new patterns and multiple perspectives. The authors in the final section provide a kaleidoscope of stories about community engagement and multiply our perspectives. These chapters are all about those stories. Andrea Tully and colleagues tell the stories of community engagement professionals and identify the ways in which their knowledge, wisdom, and experience—from life and from work—are essential to the success of the field. Elena Klaw and colleagues write about their experiences as faculty committed to community-engaged teaching and learning. They provide valuable insight into how other faculty can navigate the institutional obstacles to community-engaged teaching and scholarship. Jamilah Ducar and Daren Ellerbee share their stories and perspectives as community AND campus insiders on campus-community partnerships. They help us to prioritize reciprocal relationships for the benefit of all over transactional bargains to do research that most benefits those engaged in the tenure process. The poem "Ode to Education" by Shandela Contreras, a Los Angeles Youth Poet Laureate Ambassador, adds a student perspective. In this section's chapters and in almost every chapter of the book, authors share stories with the reader that not only establish the authors' positionality but also provide exemplars of reflection on experience. The authors help us see what is unique in each story and where the patterns across stories can make us smarter in our own work.

Readers are privileged to see these stories here together because so often they exist in silos. Faculty members share stories with each other about their experiences with community-engaged coursework. Community-engaged professionals on campus share their stories of programming in and with community among each other. Similarly, those in the foundation and nonprofit sectors often keep their stories in those circles. Here, the reader is fortunate to see how their experiences compare to the experiences of others in similar and different roles and to develop greater understanding of the entire ecosystem of community engagement in higher education. These stories are also an invitation to reflect on the reader's experiences, and as you read these chapters, I encourage you to reflect on your own stories as you read those of others and then consider the possibilities for your own community-engaged work.

Together, these chapters are like guides to seeing more and seeing differently, allowing us to reframe the work of higher education. And this new vision is needed in our time of multiple pandemics. Most obviously, we are and will always live in a world of COVID-19, a disease experienced differentially by race and class. We are living in a time of racial reckoning, of needing to face the anti-Blackness and white supremacy that is part of US history and current reality. We see climate change at a pace that is accelerating and alarming. We see assaults on democracy, not only from those who stormed the Capitol building on inauguration day but also from those who are elected to office and promote lies about the 2020 presidential election being stolen. I write these words within days of grocery shoppers gunned down in a Buffalo supermarket and children murdered in a Texas elementary school, and sadly, I suspect you will be reading these words just days after a mass shooting somewhere in our nation, perhaps close to home. We hear words like polarization and political paralysis to describe our current civic context. Given those challenges, we need new ideas about what preparation for meaningful engagement in civic and political life looks like. Thankfully, these authors point the way.

Not only do these chapters help us see more and reflect, though. They also provide us with tools and models for action—inside the classroom and in the community. The authors have provided ideas for the design of reciprocal, authentic community-engaged learning experiences, as well as strategies for reflection on those projects and for dialogue across the differences that can become explicit in community-engaged learning. Together, they provide a trove of inspiring exemplars for what community-engaged learning and scholarship can look like. As colleges and universities move from a paradigm of service-learning to a more expansive, inclusive, and equity-minded focus on community-engaged learning, these examples arrive just in time.

References

Berger, J. (1972). *Ways of seeing*. Penguin.
Kaninchen und Ente. (1892). *Fliegende Blätter*. https://digi.ub.uni-heidelberg.de/diglit/fb97/0147/image,info
Kapoor, A. (2006). *Cloud Gate*. www.choosechicago.com/articles/tours-and-attractions/the-bean-chicago/

ACKNOWLEDGMENTS

We would like to acknowledge the vision and support provided by LEAD California, Stylus Press, and Taylor & Francis. The fruition of this book would not have been possible without the support of the San José State University Center for Community Learning & Leadership team, specifically Peggy Arana and Joanna Solis, whose commitment to our Center, students, and service is unparalleled. We are grateful for the formatting and proofreading assistance provided by SJSU students, Sally Huynh, Nazanin Ghavami and Laura Schletewitz.

1
INTRODUCTION

Elena Klaw, Andrea Tully, and Elaine K. Ikeda

Introduction to This Book

Across the country and even the globe, institutions of higher education and the students we serve confront unparalleled health, economic, and social challenges. When we started this project, California, the state where we, the editors, all live and work, was literally ablaze. Smoke and particulates from wildfire saturated the air and obstructed sunlight, threatening our ability to envision a landscape past the horizon and making it difficult to breathe. Across the country, climate disasters such as tornadoes and catastrophic floods besieged our cities and our communities. Over the past several years, fundamental inequities in the United States have been exposed by the COVID-19 pandemic. As the nation confronted inadequate infrastructure to provide protection from disease and poverty (Centers for Disease Control, 2020), thousands of people died weekly from the virus. Our national conversation focused again on systemic racism as the Black Lives Matter movement exposed the horrors of racial profiling and police brutality (Kendi, 2019). Amid this period of isolation and unrest, we witnessed extreme political polarization in our country, exemplified by a violent attack on the United States Capitol following the results of our presidential election.

As academics and higher education professionals, it is our mandate to focus our gaze on impinging threats to our planet, to our social contracts, to the wellbeing of individuals and families, and to democracy itself (Daniels, 2021; Flores & Rogers, 2019; Kennedy, 1997; Roth, 2014; Tierney, 2021). As educators, we are tasked with enabling a generation of adults to critically analyze information, understand science and data, assume responsibility as members of the workforce, and participate effectively in the democratic process. Community engagement is a strategy that is uniquely suited to meet this mandate.

In his foundational book, *Academic Duty*, Stanford University President Donald Kennedy (1997) argued that community involvement by universities plays a key role in creating civically minded citizens who contribute to the public good. In the current project, we rely on the term "community engagement" because we believe it captures the equity-minded and inclusive model of collaboration between communities and institutions of higher education that we aim to explore, describe, and illustrate. On the basis of the definition provided by the Carnegie Elective Classifications (2022), we conceptualize community engagement as "a collaboration between institutions of higher education and their larger communities (local, regional/state, national, global) for the mutually beneficial exchange of knowledge and resources in a context of partnership and reciprocity." The purpose of community engagement, according to the Carnegie Elective Classification (2022), is "to enrich scholarship, research, and creative activity; enhance curriculum, teaching, and learning; prepare educated, engaged citizens; strengthen democratic values and civic responsibility; address critical societal issues; and contribute to the public good." In this book, we aim to honor the multiple influences, cultures, and perspectives that determine the language that colleges and universities employ to describe their community engagement.

We recognize the fundamental role that course-based curricular service-learning has played in this movement and we appreciate that it is considered a high-impact practice with demonstrated efficacy in retaining college students (Pascarella & Terenzini, 2005). According to the American Association of Colleges and Universities (2022), a key element in course-based service-learning programs is the opportunity students have to both apply what they are learning in real-world settings and reflect in a classroom setting on their service experiences. These programs model the idea that experiential learning draws on the knowledge and wisdom of community partners, providing good preparation for citizenship, work, and life. A growing body of scholarship, including our own, suggests that participating in service-learning classes is correlated with increased academic engagement, career skills, and leadership and civic involvement (Astin et al., 2000; Bringle & Clayton, 2012; Klaw et al., 2019; Ramnani et al., 2017).

Reflecting the multiplicity of community-engaged perspectives and approaches in higher education, each chapter discusses specific types of community-engaged practices within the distinct context of specific institutions. A Foreword by leading community engagement scholar David Donahue outlines the tensions and challenges involved in enacting community engagement within different institutions and contexts in higher education. In the first section, Enacting Social Justice, Bowen et al. discuss community engagement strategies for responding to sociopolitical and racial challenges, Plaxton-Moore provides a feminist framework for community engagement, Robinson and Robinson explore a vision for reclaiming democracy through experiential education and dialogue implemented at community college and Middaugh et al. explore harnessing students' engagement with social media to facilitate action regarding climate change.

In the second section of this compendium, Building a Movement, Ikeda shares her longstanding efforts in leading a coalition to forward community engagement within California's institutions of higher education. Moving to a statewide and national perspective, California's Chief Service Officer, Josh Fryday et al., discusses the College Corps, a groundbreaking initiative implemented by the Office of the Governor to create a pathway to graduating with less debt by offering funded service opportunities to college students. Yamamura et al. explore the role of college presidents in place-based institutionalization of engagement.

The third section of the book, Reconceptualizing Roles, explores the experiences and perspectives of the different stakeholders involved in campus community engagement. Tully et al. offer an in-depth view of the key role of community engagement professionals in transformational education, Klaw and her colleagues explore the tensions and rewards of engagement for faculty members, and Ducar and Ellerbee discuss partnerships that center healthy relationships with local communities.

Bringing the community engagement movement into the current era is a primary goal of this book. As the nation faces a cascade of unprecedented crises, it is simply not possible for higher education institutions (HEIs) to proceed with business as usual. Broadly, a recent report by Selingo (2021) from the Chronicle of Higher Education on "The Future of Generation Z" noted, "There's no doubt ... the pandemic is prompting a great reassessment of higher education among students and their families." The report asserts that current students seek value from their higher education experiences both in terms of building career skills and building relationships. As a cohort affected by the pandemic, climate change, the insurrection, and the nation's racial reckoning, they prioritize both a sense of purpose and a sense of belonging. Thus, more so than prior generations, the report suggests, they recognize and consider injustice, and see themselves as agents of change (Selingo, 2021, p. 25).

In a related report by the Chronicle on "The Post Pandemic College" (Alexander et al., 2020), Flower Darby (2020, p. 15), building on work by Beth Zemsky (see bethzemsky.com), reminds us to "never waste a crisis." Karen Stout (2020) outlines lessons derived from the pandemic for the community college system that, we believe, apply across higher education. She notes that understanding our students' experiences and their intersectionality is necessary for us to reach them, and that current examples of "faculty resilience and innovation abound" (p. 54). She concludes that to effectively support students, we must "focus on engaging and culturally responsive pedagogy" and "link civic learning to community development." She goes so far as to state that "the pandemic makes our mission urgent and clear" (Stout, 2020, p. 55) and suggests that colleges reach out to local residents through partnerships with school districts, county agencies, and social service providers as we shift our focus to prioritize student wellbeing, career preparedness, and just civic leadership.

In sum, a significant body of research suggests that community engagement approaches provide a path forward as we seek to address worsening inequities, divisiveness, and an overall sense of outrage about the status quo (Selingo, 2021). Through the experiences, case examples, suggestions, and concrete guidance provided in this book, we and the expert contributors encompassing a variety of roles, backgrounds, and institutions make the case that community-engaged learning approaches are essential to preparing students to address the many challenges of our decade (California Campus Compact, 2020). Within the pages of this book, we aim to provide guidance, examples, and benchmarks for best practices in community engagement, especially during times of crises and unrest. We hope that readers will derive encouragement to develop, implement, evaluate, and institutionalize community engagement within all different higher education institutional contexts, ranging from private selective and faith-based colleges to research-focused universities to comprehensive public institutions and community colleges. We hope that this book will encourage critical and reflective conversations across stakeholders about the role of university–community partnerships in improving social welfare and generating social change. We hope the writing of our contributors will inform institutional practices that respect the unique positions of college students, faculty and staff members, community partners, and administrators in building an effective democracy.

As editors, we represent multiple perspectives of community engagement in higher education. Together, the different lenses through which we engage and lead in our work reflect the richness, contextuality, and diversity of the field. Elena Klaw, PhD, is a tenured Professor of Psychology at San José State University (SJSU), an urban comprehensive public institution that is part of the California State University system. She serves as the Faculty Director of the Center for Community Learning & Leadership. Andrea Tully, MEd, holds a unionized staff position as the Assistant Director of the SJSU Center for Community Learning & Leadership. Elaine K. Ikeda, PhD, is the Executive Director of LEAD California, a nonprofit organization that builds the collective commitment and capacity of colleges, universities, and communities to advance civic and community engagement for a healthy, just, and democratic society.

This book was designed to explore the unique roles that individual stakeholders play in implementing, supporting, and promoting community-engaged learning in higher education, recognizing that the geographical and institutional contexts of our work vary greatly. We believe that the multiple vantage points contained in the volume complement each other and we hope that by exploring the different perspectives included, readers will formulate and articulate their own distinct role in this work. The different types of collaboration, dialogue, research, and action that are explored in these pages point the way to creating a better future.

Who We Are

Elena Klaw

Elena was born and raised in the New York metropolitan area. Her maternal grandparents survived the Holocaust genocide despite losing many family members. Her mother was born in Siberia, arriving at Ellis Island with her sister and parents in 1951 as refugees. As a result of her family's background, Elena's career path has been characterized by a devotion to education, a passion for peace and social justice, and a fascination with the role of social support in resilience. She holds a BA from Cornell University and a PhD in Clinical and Community Psychology from the University of Illinois Urbana–Champaign. She has been a tenure track faculty member in Psychology at SJSU for 23 years. At SJSU, she serves as the Faculty Director of the SJSU Center for Community Learning & Leadership and directly supports student leadership groups that provide community education regarding the effects of violence, including the Veterans Embracing Transition (VET) Connect Project and the SJSU chapter of Students Demand Action for Gun Sense in America (SDA). She and her husband, Oliver, have two children.

Andrea Tully

In February 2020, the SJSU Center for Community Learning & Leadership celebrated its 20th anniversary. The party was one of the last days Andrea was on campus before maternity leave. In keeping with the team's penchant for fun, the party was held in SJSU's bowling alley, based on the theme "we can't bowl alone" (Putnam, 2000). Little did we know that we soon would be bowling alone in the hallways of our own homes for months on end. Andrea and her husband welcomed their first child three weeks before the first COVID-19 shelter-in-place orders in California. Needless to say, maternity leave was not the mom and baby yoga classes of her dreams. During the first few months of the pandemic, she didn't leave a half-mile radius of her home. She felt isolated and lonely and spent far too much time doomscrolling through COVID cases and death rates while her son was snoozing. As someone who values community and connection, she needed to do something. While others sewed masks, delivered food to homebound seniors, and donated meals to hospital workers, she got back to work as a community-engaged professional earlier than planned.

Andrea grew up in a very small farming community in central California and had to go "to town" 15 miles away to get gas and groceries. Her first job, at 15, was at a farm stand off the local highway. She was one of few in her high school graduating class to go on to a four-year college. At the University of California, Santa Barbara, she majored in Global Studies, which required that she think critically about the complex problems facing industries, cities, states, nations, and the planet. Her most memorable classes were those with applied experiences, including serving and developing curriculum for high school English language learners. She went on to earn a master's degree in Higher and Post-Secondary Education from Arizona State University and launched a career as a community engagement professional. At time of publication, Andrea is expecting her second child and has no plans to slow down her community-engaged efforts.

Elaine K. Ikeda

Elaine K. Ikeda is the granddaughter of Japanese immigrants who came to the United States around the turn of the 20th century. The experience of being rounded up and interned in "relocation camps" during World War II deeply affected her grandparents and parents (who were young children at the time). Although they did not speak often of their experiences of living behind barbed wire fences for nearly 5 years, being seen as a threat or "the other" in the United States caused them to believe that education (in particular a college degree) was a way of legitimizing their presence as citizens in this country.

Fulfilling her parents' expectations, Elaine obtained a bachelor's degree. She then obtained a master's degree, and after working for several years, returned to graduate school to obtain a second master's degree and a doctoral degree. She began her professional career in community and public health for a county health department, then worked for a year at a branch of a national nonprofit health agency, and then returned to higher education to work in student affairs. She has been an employee at six higher education institutions, four of which are public four-year institutions, one a private institution, and one a public research institution. Elaine obtained her PhD in Higher Education and Organizational Change at the University of California, Los Angeles (UCLA), and while there, she was on a team that conducted the first and largest national study exploring the outcomes of service-learning pedagogy on college students. This launched her current career, promoting service-learning and community engagement in higher education.

References

Alexander, B., Darby, F., Fischer, K., Jack, A. A., Staisloff, R., LeSane, C. B., & Stout, K. A. (2020). *The post-pandemic college: And the future of.* The Chronicle of Higher Education.

American Association of Colleges and Universities. (2022, June 28). *High-impact practices.* AAC&U. www.aacu.org/trending-topics/high-impact

Astin, A. W., Vogelgesang, L. J., Ikeda, E. K., & Yee, J. A. (2000) *How service learning affects students. Executive summary.* Higher Education Research Institute, UCLA.

Bringle, R. G. & Clayton, P. H. (2012). Civic education through service learning: What, how, and why? In L. McIlrath, A. Lyons, & R. Munck (Eds.), *Higher and Civic Engagement* (pp. 101–124). Palgrave Macmillan.

California Campus Compact. (2020, June 27). *The urgency and relevance of community engagement: How institutional values are manifested through commitment to the public good.* https://leadcalifornia.org/the-urgency-and-relevance-of-community-engagement/

Carnegie Elective Classifications. (2022, July 13). *The 2024 elective classification for community engagement.* https://carnegieelectiveclassifications.org/the-2024-elective-classification-for-community-engagement/

Centers for Disease Control and Prevention. (2020, July). *CDC COVID-19 response health equity strategy: Accelerating progress towards reducing COVID-19 disparities and achieving health equity.* www.cdc.gov/coronavirus/2019-ncov/downloads/community/CDC-Strategy.pdf

Daniels, R. J. (2021). *What universities owe democracy.* Johns Hopkins University Press.

Darby, F. (2020). *The post-pandemic college: And the future of.* The Chronicle of Higher Education.

Flores, W. V., & Rogers, K. S. (2019). *Democracy, civic engagement, and citizenship in higher education: Reclaiming our civic purpose.* Lexington Books.

Kendi, I. X. (2019). *How to be an antiracist.* One world.

Kennedy, D. (1997). *Academic duty.* Harvard University Press.

Klaw, E., Tully, A., Maciel, M., & Cerasaro, E. (2019, April). *The effects of service-learning participation on alumni career trajectories.* Poster presented at the annual meeting of the Western Psychological Association, Pasadena, CA.

Pascarella, E. T., & Terenzini, P. T. (2005). *How college affects students: A third decade of research. Volume 2.* Jossey-Bass.

Putnam, R. (2000) *Bowling alone: The collapse and revival of American community.* Simon & Schuster.

Ramnani, A., Lopez, A., & Klaw, E. (2017). Application: A Social Psychology Experiment on Learning by Social Immersion. In S. Randal (Ed.) *Social psychology: How other people influence our thoughts and actions [2 volumes]* (pp. 409–454). ABC: CLIO. Kindle Edition.

Roth, M. S. (2014). *Beyond the university: Why liberal education matters*. Yale University Press.

Selingo, J. J. (2021). *The future of Gen Z: How Covid-19 will shape students and higher education for the next decade*. The Chronicle of Higher Education.

Stout, K. (2020). *The post-pandemic college: And the future of*. The Chronicle of Higher Education.

Tierney, W. G. (2021, December 6) *Academe's neglected responsibility*. Inside Higher Ed. www.insidehighered.com/views/2021/12/06/colleges-are-shirking-their-responsibility-support-democracy-opinion

PART 1
Enacting Social Justice
Current Contexts and Community Engagement

PART 1

2
COMMUNITY ENGAGEMENT STRATEGIES FOR RESPONDING TO SOCIOPOLITICAL AND RACIAL CHALLENGES FACING AMERICAN SOCIETY AND HIGHER EDUCATION

Glenn A. Bowen, Courtney A. Berrien, and Roni Bennett

The social injustice, political strife, and systemic racism currently confronting the nation have created a sharp inflection point for American higher education institutions. As an increasing number of colleges and universities accept that the day of reckoning has come, many have embarked on equity, inclusion, and antiracism initiatives. Furthermore, some institutions have situated such initiatives squarely within a community engagement framework. Strategies pursued by colleges and universities include placing new emphasis on critical, social justice-oriented service-learning; instituting civic learning and democratic engagement (CLDE) programs; and creating campus centers focused on racial healing and transformation. Contextualized as community engagement, the strategies require intentional collaboration between institutions and partners in the wider community.

The twofold purpose of this chapter is to (a) share strategies for responding to the prevailing challenges and (b) discuss community engagement as the basis for effective measures that move institutions well beyond platitudes and rhetoric regarding racism, exclusion, and injustice. The chapter is organized as follows: First, we briefly explore the current context of racial violence and social injustice. Next, we assess the landscape of new and renewed efforts to address issues of diversity, equity, and inclusion (DEI) through higher education. Then we describe some specific strategies and practices for confronting structural racism and inequities and for promoting inclusion that benefits both higher education institutions and the communities they serve.

DOI: 10.4324/9781003448525-3

Racial Violence and Social Injustice

Social injustice is a perennial problem in American society. It is manifested in the wage gap between men and women; in the discriminatory treatment of persons identified as LGBTQ (lesbian, gay, bisexual, transgender, and queer/questioning); and in anti-Semitic acts. We find it in situations where homeowners association boards reject housing applications from prospective homeowners with "Black-sounding" names. It is found in health and education disparities in our communities and in the brutality meted out to Black and Brown folk by police officers. The coronavirus (COVID-19) pandemic made the disparities in healthcare access more pronounced and exacerbated the social and economic hardships experienced by people of color, including Blacks and Indigenous population groups.

In recent years, numerous killings of unarmed Black Americans—notably Breonna Taylor and George Floyd in 2020—at the hands of law enforcement officers led to public protests and to the reinvigoration of the Black Lives Matter movement. Black Lives Matter was born out of the killing of a teenager named Trayvon Martin in 2012 in Sanford, Florida. The young man was racially profiled, surveilled, and killed by a self-appointed neighborhood watch captain turned vigilante.

Higher education has not been immune to the racial tensions and barefaced incidents of injustice affecting our society. To be sure, in higher education institutions across the United States, minoritized groups have been subjected to racial discrimination, diminishing any sense of belonging that some members of those groups once felt. In some cases, faculty members and students of color have experienced campus climates characterized by open hostility. Arguably, when it comes to institutionalized racism, some university campuses are a microcosm of the nation.

In the national arena, racial violence reared its ugly head in an unprecedented manner on January 6, 2021. An insurrection at the United States Capitol in Washington, D.C., was perpetrated by a violent mob with ties to white nationalist and anti-Semitic movements attempting to prevent the certification of the 2020 presidential election results. Although the seditious act did not achieve its goal, it represented an alarming threat to American democracy. In the wake of the insurrection, higher education leaders joined in condemning the mayhem, with many issuing lofty statements regarding the assault on democracy. Their statements were similar to those prompted by the senseless killing of Black Americans and, in some cases, included an express commitment to move their institutions toward racial equity.

The insurrection as well as the present resurgence of white supremacy and racial conflict in the United States is a wake-up call to higher education. One university leader, bluntly declaring that colleges should share the blame for the rioting, offered an incisive analysis of higher education institutions' failure to address racism and to provide appropriate education to students (McGuire, 2021). According to McGuire, racism undergirds many institutions' policies and practices, and those institutions had failed to educate future lawmakers on the kinds of policies that a just society should welcome. College and university leaders themselves had remained silent while lies about the 2020 election were being told. As McGuire argued, by remaining silent, the institutional leaders allowed an "insidious force to spread through the body politic—the racial animus and embrace of white supremacy that gave so much energy to the mob" (para. 6).

American democracy remains at risk; across the nation, democratic rules and traditions are still being cast aside. Recognition of this is now at the forefront of national consciousness. There is also a troubling trend pertaining to race-related education: Across the United States, people occupying seats of power have been enacting laws and instituting policies meant to shape how students discuss the nation's racist past, and its racist present as well. Nearly 40 states have introduced or passed legislation restricting teaching about race and racism in public schools. More specifically, legislators are attempting to ban critical race theory, an academic framework that examines how policies and the law perpetuate systemic racism.

Emphasis on Diversity, Equity, and Inclusion

Higher education institutions responded to the threats to democracy and the spate of racial violence in various ways. The most noticeable response was the issuing of statements condemning racial violence and affirming their commitment to diversity, equity, and inclusion (DEI). However, some statements seemed like in-the-moment platitudes rather than concrete commitments to act against inequity and exclusion. A number of institutions appointed taskforces, charging them with conducting DEI audits and developing DEI plans (or adding DEI elements to strategic plans), while others immediately set about creating campus-based structures to house DEI personnel and programs. Besides, a few issued public apologies for their support of slavery, and a few others renamed campus buildings that previously honored racists.

Diversity Training

Many institutions have increased or expanded diversity training for their staff. Diversity training has been a constant in organizations of all kinds since the early 1980s and is treated by some as sensitivity training focused on understanding racial differences. *Diversity training* is defined simply as "organizational initiatives designed to develop skills needed to work with people from diverse backgrounds" (Hughes & Byrd, 2015, p. 112). A diversity training program aims to make employees knowledgeable and appreciative of differences among coworkers and to support them in developing interpersonal skills that will contribute to a positive, more inclusive work environment. Hughes and Byrd have suggested that, as it builds a harmonious workplace and helps to change organizational cultures, diversity training can reduce prejudice and discrimination.

Nevertheless, diversity training nowadays has considerable shortcomings, the main one being the limited attention to issues related specifically to race. Diversity training programs typically cover the "Big 10+" elements of social identity—age, gender identity/expression, race, ethnicity, religion, ability, sexual orientation, physical appearance, education, socioeconomic status, and nationality/immigration status—and, in the process, give race-related issues short shrift. Colleges and universities cannot afford to continue settling for run-of-the-mill diversity training conducted at the expense of a more deliberate antiracism education.

A new practice among US colleges and universities is the public acknowledgment of the legacy of Indigenous peoples. They acknowledge that the land on which their campuses are located belonged to Indigenous peoples. The University of Colorado, for example, issued an official systemwide Lands Recognition Statement in October 2020. Colleges and universities in the United States are following the example set in Canada, where the tradition of land acknowledgment statements began through that nation's Truth and Reconciliation Commission and is seen as a sign of gratitude and respect (Schacter, 2018).

Some strategies and programs that address racism are rooted in community engagement. As described below, the strategies encompass curricular and cocurricular programs and events. Before community engagement strategies are described, it is important to look at the levers of the current antiracism momentum as well as to examine the place and functions of truth-telling, racial healing, and reparations.

Antiracism Imperative

At a time when colleges and universities throughout the United States are awash in DEI activities, key players are beginning to understand that diversity, equity, and inclusion must be complemented by justice—social justice broadly and racial justice specifically. Indeed, some colleges and universities are responding well to the antiracism imperative—their accepted obligation to tackle racism frontally, on campus for a start, and in the community as well. For those institutions, attention to pervasive racial justice issues has become a priority. Reports indicate an acceleration of efforts to develop strategies, institute programs, and implement actions to address racism. Colleges and universities have begun to acknowledge that, as influential scholar Angela Y. Davis has been quoted as saying, "in a racist society it is not enough to be non-racist; we must be anti-racist." Evidence of this acknowledgment is found in strategies and programs that carry an "antiracism" label—strategies and programs that suggest an acceptance of higher education's role as a leader of the active, sustained effort required to dismantle racism.

Although targeting individual attitudes, assumptions, and biases is a long-standing strategy for dealing with racism, this approach is incomplete. Other strategies are needed if assumptions endemic to American culture are to be challenged and the broader racialized structures are to be torn down. To confront institutional and systemic racism, higher education institutions are engaging themselves and their communities in projects that emphasize coming to terms with the past, amplifying the voices of marginalized community members, and demonstrating accountability for acts that have caused harm to people of color.

Current strategies and programs designed to address racism include campus centers working toward racial equity and healing. The Racial Equity and Justice Institute (REJI), for example, has developed data-informed strategies to help eliminate racial equity gaps on college and university campuses (Gentlewarrior, 2021). Piloted by Bridgewater State University, REJI brings together teams from several colleges and universities to pursue "equity-minded inquiry." In particular, they identify racial equity gaps on campuses and then design, implement, and assess strategies to make their educational practices more racially equitable.

A strategy that has been put forward is the decolonization of the curriculum. This includes disrupting imperialist, colonial, and hegemonic modes of knowledge (Shahjahan et al., 2022). Establishing a systematic process to reform a curriculum shaped by colonialism so as to make it more accurate, inclusive, and interculturally responsive makes complete sense. However, if the curriculum is "that which power and privilege have decided should be taught because it is in the interests of the powerful and privileged to teach it" (Lindsay, 2020, p. 450), decolonization will be hugely challenging. It stands to reason that if the established curriculum serves the interests of the powerful at everyone else's expense, whether intentionally or not, change will not come easy at all.

Surely, as Lindsay (2020) maintained, decolonizing the curriculum is more than merely replacing John Stuart Mill with Ta-Nehisi Coates on required reading lists. Doing so, however, may be one step in implementing inclusive pedagogy. Fundamentally, decolonizing the curriculum requires the interrogation of curricular and pedagogical practices with a view to making the necessary changes. Gradually, whiteness can be decentered, and the histories, knowledges, and experiences of Black Americans, Indigenous peoples, and other people of color can become centered and celebrated.

Some strategies and programs that address racism are rooted in community engagement. As described below, the strategies encompass curricular and cocurricular programs and events. Before community engagement strategies are described, the place and functions of truth-telling, racial healing, and reparations are summarized.

Truth-Telling, Racial Healing, and Reparations

Since the mid-1990s, truth-telling and reconciliation processes have been used in national efforts in many countries to deal with human rights abuses. South Africa's Truth and Reconciliation Commission played an important role in the transition from apartheid to full democracy in that country. In the United States, the Greensboro Truth and Reconciliation Commission (2004–2006) investigated the deadly events of November 1979 in that North Carolina community.

The truth and reconciliation movement is grounded in the restorative justice tradition, which emphasizes repair of relationships, truth-telling processes, and accountability for harmful actions (Llewellyn, 2012). Truth and reconciliation systems include tribunals and commissions as well as indigenous justice traditions that use various methods based on the concept of restorative or reparative justice. Auerbach's (2009) "Reconciliation Pyramid" is included as a method, as is "re-storying." The Reconciliation Pyramid functions as an analytical framework for studying the psycho-political processes involved in reconciliation, which Auerbach defined as "changing attitudes from denial and resentment to acceptance and trust" (p. 303). The seven stages are as follows:

1. *Acquaintance* with clashing narratives
2. *Acknowledgement* of the other's narratives without necessarily accepting them as true
3. Expressing *empathy* for what the other has experienced
4. Assuming (at least partial) *responsibility* for the other's experience or plight
5. Expressing readiness for *restitution* or reparation for past wrongs
6. Offering *public apology* and asking for forgiveness for past wrongs
7. Working toward the *incorporation of opposite narratives* into accepted mutual accounts of the past

With regard to re-storying, research suggests that the efficacy of truth and reconciliation processes is dependent on the ability to deconstruct dominant narratives and reconstruct narratives that move marginalized voices to the center (e.g., Auerbach, 2009; Berrien, 2020; Sonn et al., 2013). Narratives are deeply embedded in culture and identity, and they both capture and shape the human experience. Further, metanarratives play a role in upholding the unjust structures that inflict collective harm, but they can also be a powerful force for challenging and reframing the narratives that perpetuate such harm (Hill, 2016; Sonn et al., 2013). Narrative regeneration, or the ability to recast narratives so that previously suppressed voices are heard loud and clear, is therefore regarded as an effective method of shaping public opinion and institutional action in the pursuit of social justice.

Narrative change is one of the pillars of the Truth, Racial Healing & Transformation (TRHT) Campus Centers launched by the W.K. Kellogg Foundation and administered under the auspices of the American Association of Colleges and Universities (formerly Association of American Colleges and Universities, AAC&U). The main purpose of the TRHT Campus Centers is "to prepare the next generation of leaders to break down systemic racism and dismantle belief in a hierarchy of human value" (AAC&U, n.d.). As part of their work, the Campus Centers seek to deconstruct and reconstruct narratives, and institutions hosting such centers engage with community partners in regenerating local narratives that address specific harms done to those communities.

Community Engagement Strategies

The current situation demands that racism be tackled concertedly. It also demands that higher education institutions prepare students not only for antiracist actions after their graduation but also for immediate participation with others in such actions. Demonstrating that they are responsive to such demands, colleges and universities have begun to leverage community engagement to tackle racism and related forms of injustice. The Carnegie Foundation for the Advancement of Teaching defines *community engagement* broadly as reciprocal collaboration between institutions of higher education and communities at various levels, from local to global, for the mutually beneficial exchange of knowledge and resources (Saltmarsh & Johnson, 2018). According to the Carnegie Elective Classification (2023), community engagement can "enrich scholarship, research, and creative activity; enhance curriculum, teaching, and learning; prepare educated, engaged citizens; strengthen democratic values and civic responsibility; address critical societal issues; and contribute to the public good".

A recent community engagement initiative known as Project H.E.R.E. (Higher Education Reparations Engagement) provides resources to colleges and universities that engage students with communities organizing for racial and social justice. Project H.E.R.E. is described as a resource and networking hub for campuses and local communities that are examining their histories, responsibilities, and commitments to restorative justice and repair for the historical and current injustices of slavery and colonialism. Resources are curated for use in addressing injustices at the institutional, local, and national levels (Project H.E.R.E., n.d.).

The community engagement strategies described in what follows include CLDE; social justice-oriented service-learning; and community-engaged scholarship focused on racial justice. Another strategy being implemented concerns truth-telling and racial healing. These community engagement strategies are exemplified at Barry University, a Catholic institution whose main campus is located in Miami, Florida. Barry attained the Carnegie Foundation's Community Engagement Classification in 2015. The university's core commitments are knowledge and truth, inclusive community, social justice, and collaborative service (Barry University, n.d.). Founded in 1940 as a women's college, Barry is a coeducational, Hispanic-serving institution with a diverse student population of approximately 7,000. Among the 3,500 undergraduates, there is a heavy dependence on Pell Grants and other forms of financial aid.

In mid-2020, Barry's president, Dr. Mike Allen, announced that an antiracism and equity coalition would be established to make the dismantling of systems that perpetuate racial injustice the university's responsibility and a critical institutional priority. A university-wide group, the coalition draws on the expertise and experiences of community partners engaged in antiracism work, and the university's main campus has become the temporary home of the Miami Center for Racial Justice, which was founded by a community leader. Notable among the university's community partners are South Florida People of Color, a racial healing organization, and Dream Defenders, the group who staged the historic occupation of the Florida Capitol in Tallahassee to agitate for justice after Trayvon Martin was killed. Through its Center for Community Service Initiatives (CCSI), Barry also partners with the management of Miami's Virginia Key Beach Park (Virginia Key was called the "Colored Beach" during segregation); and the CCSI is coordinating institutional support for the development of a civil rights museum on the property.

Civic Learning and Democratic Engagement Programs

A growing number of colleges and universities have been instituting civic learning and democratic engagement (CLDE) programs primarily to foster the development of students as active community members. A national organization named NASPA—Student Affairs Administrators in Higher Education has been championing CLDE, which includes educating students on democratic participation, centering the value of dialogue across difference, and nurturing social responsibility. Students are offered opportunities to gain and apply the requisite knowledge, skills, and abilities to make a difference in their communities.

At Barry University, for example, CLDE is demonstrated exemplarily through two programs: the Campus Democracy Project (CDP) and the Barry Service Corps (BSC). A nonpartisan initiative, the CDP promotes CLDE by means of presentations and discussions, voter registration drives, and get-out-the-vote activities. Every year, the CDP Committee invites local legislators to campus for discussions and also hosts a forum focused on the bills (proposed laws) before the Florida Legislature. The BSC is a cocurricular experiential learning program aimed at developing students as civic-minded graduates with the agency to become changemakers in the community. A select group of BSC members receive specialized training for civic leadership roles targeted to social justice outcomes (Bowen & Berrien, 2021). Known as BSC Fellows, the emerging student leaders are mostly students of color and are often first-generation college students in the sophomore, junior, and senior classes. They engage intentionally in year-round activities through which they learn to appreciate diversity, value varied worldviews, and become aware of their own biases. CCSI administrators, who organize and facilitate the program, introduce BSC Fellows to such concepts as *social identity, positionality,* and *intersectionality;* they learn that intersectionality is "a way of understanding and analyzing the complexity in the world, in people, and in human experiences" (Collins & Bilge, 2016, p. 2; see also Crenshaw, 2016). The complexity becomes evident as students consider events and conditions of social life shaped by social identity factors such as race, class, gender, and socioeconomic status. Students come to understand how differences in social position and power shape identities and access in society, and, moreover, they learn to work across difference wherever it is manifested.

Further, BSC Fellows receive guidance and support in developing and implementing projects that address social (justice) issues and promote democratic engagement. Among the issues they have addressed over the years are educational disparities and health inequities, farmworker exploitation, food insecurity, negative public attitudes toward refugees, and the poor treatment of incarcerated women as well as the disenfranchisement of previously incarcerated community members (Bowen & Berrien, 2021). Viewing social issues through a structural/systemic change lens, the students go beyond providing direct service to community members by exploring the root causes of the issue and then engaging in advocacy and sometimes public action. Before taking public action, the program participants take part in issue exploration, coalition building, and direct-action organizing. The positive outcomes of their efforts are found in new procedures and programs that meet at least some of the needs of underserved communities and marginalized population groups such as farmworkers and imprisoned women in Florida. For example, BSC Fellows have staged public demonstrations against fast-food chains that have refused to support the Coalition of Immokalee Workers' (CIW's) Fair Food Program, and the students have also been in the vanguard of a CIW campaign to end modern-day slavery in the fields.

Discussions of Books and Films

As part of a community engagement strategy, books and films are valuable resources for antiracism education. South Florida People of Color, an award-winning nonprofit organization that partners with universities, regularly organizes discussions of selected books and films. Among the books discussed are Ibram X. Kendi's *How to Be an Antiracist*, Isabel Wilkerson's *Caste: The Origins of Our Discontents*, and Carol Anderson's *White Rage: The Unspoken Truth of Our Racial Divide*. Kendi's book helps readers recognize racism and understand its consequences, at once challenging and guiding readers to help in building a just and equitable society. A book discussion also featured *A World More Concrete: Real Estate and the Remaking of Jim Crow South Florida* by N. D. B. Connolly. In addition, South Florida People of Color's Critical Race Film Series has explored the messages of several films. They include *Get Out*, *Green Book*, *Hidden Figures*, and *The Hate U Give* (see Appendix).

Public Forums for Dialogue

Colleges and universities sometimes organize public forums as a method of civic engagement. Forums are opportunities for dialogue around issues of concern to campus and community stakeholders. During academic year 2020–2021, as part of its DEI program, for example, the University of Utah reportedly held "Friday Forums on Racism in Higher Education." The forums covered such topics as "Confronting Our Racism," "Establishing Anti-Racist Policy and Strategy," and "A Call for Racial Healing."

Dialogue with deliberation has been catching on; deliberative dialogues are organized to bring stakeholders together for discussion and shared decisions regarding how to address sociopolitical issues. Deliberative dialogue participants usually include students, faculty members, and stakeholders from the community. The equitable participation of students and community members is important. A few years ago, a scholar-practitioner identified the need for student training in public deliberation as part of the civic role of universities in the face of "wicked problems, hyper-partisanship, and truth decay" (Carcasson, 2019, p. 319). Faculty members may need training in the facilitation of deliberative dialogues, which could be provided by community engagement professionals with expertise in public deliberation. Effective facilitation of public deliberation requires skills in framing the issue, asking thoughtful and probing questions, and encouraging deep reflection by participants.

The Center for Community Service Initiatives at Barry University organizes and hosts an annual Deliberative Dialogue Series, with university and the community stakeholders working toward a shared understanding of specific social issues and practical solutions to those issues. The 2020–2021 Deliberative Dialogue Series on "Race Matters" brought together students and alumni, faculty and staff, and community members in four facilitated forums. The first focused on why race matters; the second examined the impact of COVID-19 on Black and Brown communities; the third was titled "Say Her Name! Working for Social Justice at the Intersection of Race and Gender"; and the fourth drew attention to the disproportionate effects of climate change on communities of color. The forums contributed to a nuanced understanding of minoritized community members' lived experiences in the context of race relations, and the forums also helped to set the stage for the development of an explicit antiracism program at Barry.

Social Justice-Oriented Service-Learning

Service-learning is a teaching and learning strategy that integrates relevant community service with course work and critical reflection to enrich the learning experience, foster social responsibility and civic engagement, and strengthen communities. A distinct approach to community engagement, service-learning has long been viewed as "the skeleton key to unlock the power and potential of postsecondary education as a force for democracy and social justice" (Butin, 2006, p. 476). Critical service-learning has a social justice orientation; it is based on a social change paradigm and aims to foster college students' commitment to promoting fairness and equality. In contrast to traditional service-learning, critical service-learning encourages students to move beyond charity to social change, challenging them to see themselves as social change agents who respond to injustice in communities (Mitchell, 2008). Service-learning without a focus on social justice can perpetuate racist, sexist, or classist assumptions about others and reinforce a colonialist mentality or superiority (O'Grady, 2000, as cited in Bowen, 2014).

Mitchell and her colleagues (2012) criticized service-learning as "a pedagogy of whiteness" (p. 612) that reflects normalized patterns and privileges of the dominant class. Later, Santiago-Ortiz (2019) advocated the decolonizing of service-learning, particularly to challenge the reproduction of colonialist structures in community–university relations and to emphasize the development of horizontal relationships among stakeholders as an expression of solidarity. Guided by antiracist values, decolonized service-learning involves action and reflection aimed at transforming oppressive conditions in community spaces.

Students might look to, and be encouraged by, their professors as social justice/antiracism educators who design the curriculum to include analyses of root causes of specific social problems and the interplay of inequality, powerlessness, and marginalization (Bowen, 2014). Understandably, students of color will have motivations and encounter barriers to social justice engagement that are quite different from those experienced by White students. In a recent study, service-learning students described how their identities shaped engagement. As study participants, the students reflected on their privileged or marginalized identities and how their identities influenced their approach to engaging with a particular social issue (Guerrero et al., 2021).

Professors might guide and support students in conducting research and in participating in discussions that will help them understand social issues and the historical, sociological, cultural, and political contexts from which those issues emerge. Students could learn skills in navigating race-related issues and in advocating antiracist policies and practices on campus and in their community. The students' service might be in the form of research-informed advocacy (e.g., through letters or petitions to campus, local and national leaders) or social action (e.g., public protests), or both.

Scholarship Focused on Racial Justice

University professors who teach service-learning courses may pursue the scholarship of engagement (Boyer, 1996), or community-engaged scholarship, which "incorporates reciprocal practices of civic engagement into the production of knowledge" (Baker, 2011, p. 124). Such practices, as Baker pointed out, cut across disciplinary boundaries as well as research and teaching through which scholars communicate and work with communities.

Concentrating community-engaged scholarship on racial justice is a way to facilitate the inclusion of voices that might otherwise remain muffled or unheard. Faculty members, students, and community partners could take part together in research projects that throw light on the lived experiences of marginalized community members and contribute to the building of knowledge and understanding in an effort to address race-related issues at the local level. Intentionally creating racially diverse research teams would signal attention to inclusion and could support the efficacy of the research. The findings of community-engaged scholarship are best disseminated in multiple outlets and especially in public venues that are accessible to community members. Done well, with a clear purpose and strategic planning, community-engaged scholarship has utility in advancing an antiracism agenda.

Truth, Education, and Reconciliation Initiative

The truth-telling and reconciliation approach has gained traction across the country as community leaders ramp up efforts to overcome racial ills and create a new national discourse (Berrien, 2020). Some higher education institutions have adopted that approach to addressing racial injustice, and a few have emphasized the need for reparations. Those institutions have a shared commitment to interrogating historical narratives, providing outlets for suppressed voices, and naming and challenging power structures.

Recently, with leadership expertise from Barry University, racial justice proponents and community activists in Florida's Miami-Dade County launched their Truth, Education, and Reconciliation (TEAR) Initiative. The TEAR Steering Committee is engaging the community in a truth-telling process that calls for acknowledgment of, and accountability for, "the ills of American history," including "the cycle of racial inequity" (Smalls, 2021, para. 18). Inspired by the work of the Equal Justice Initiative (EJI), the TEAR Steering Committee is also planning public remembrances of incidents of racial terror perpetrated against African Americans in Miami-Dade. The community remembrance effort is part of the re-storying process that aims to help the county (and the country) reckon with the lynching of Black Americans. This includes acknowledging complicity in the extrajudicial executions and providing relief from intergenerational trauma that continues to affect community health and well-being.

Constructing narratives for a new collective memory of lynching incidents is considered an important element of antiracism work (Apel, 2008). Public memorials to lynching victims, visual displays, and lynching scholarship are examples of efforts to "activate social memory about lynchings" so as to "create a new kind of popular consciousness about America's racist and violent past in the face of what has been a profound mis-remembering of lynching" (Wood & Donaldson, 2008, p. 6). Wood and Donaldson deliberately write "mis-remember" to indicate that, in present-day situations, the word "lynching" is too often bandied about in a manner that indicates misconceptions and myths about such gross, horrific acts of racist violence during Jim Crow segregation. In cases where a new collective memory of lynching incidents was awakened, the memorializing process instigated a communal reconciliation of sorts through new narratives that promote healing and redemption for communities (Apel, 2008, p. 228).

In addition, TEAR includes a series of public forums held both on campus and in the community. Each forum presents information on incidents of lynching, explains the truth and reconciliation process, and provides opportunities for reflection and dialogue. Forum participants have welcomed a plan by the TEAR organizers to work with county and municipal officials to erect historical markers at the sites where lynching incidents occurred.

On November 29, 2020, community leaders and Barry representatives memorialized the lynching of a young Black man named J. B. Harris, which took place in Miami-Dade County 100 years earlier. The killing of the 19-year-old is one of three well-documented incidents of lynching in Miami-Dade County. Committee members previously collected soil at the site of the Harris lynching on Silver Palm Drive, Miami, to be delivered to the EJI's Legacy Museum in Montgomery, Alabama. Additionally, TEAR was represented at a Black History Month (February 2021) event hosted by the Miami Center for Racial Justice to commemorate the Rosewood (Florida) Massacre of 1923.

Workshops and Awkward Dinners

South Florida People of Color, a community partner with educational institutions and other organizations in the region, offers workshops to guide them toward an inclusive, transformative culture. The workshops draw on the organization's IDEAS (Inclusivity, Diversity, Equity, Accountability, and Sustainability) curriculum, which is situated within an intersectional framework. According to Shin et al. (2017), "The framework of intersectionality is a powerful analytical tool for making sense of how interlocking systems of privilege and oppression are experienced by individuals and groups" (p. 458).

Workshop participants are given the building blocks and vocabulary necessary to engage in meaningful discussions. Moreover, the workshop organizers employ a restorative approach that requires participants to make personal connections toward shifts in empathy and understanding, which become internalized and add to their personal power to help usher in transformative change within their institutions. The *accountability* and *sustainability* elements of the IDEAS curriculum are important; workshop participants are encouraged to hold one another accountable for the ongoing work needed within the institution across pertinent policies, procedures, and practices to create and sustain change toward equity and inclusion.

As a racial healing collective, the organization also hosts Awkward Dinners, its signature event, inviting guests to get comfortable with being uncomfortable. Offered nationally, the event provides "brave spaces" for conversation (as opposed to "safe spaces" for protection) in which 12–25 community members with diverse backgrounds and experiences break bread together. The intimate format invites participants to step outside their comfort zones to share and learn from differing perspectives. As the dinner guests engage in personal storytelling and in deep, authentic conversations on racism and white privilege, they also critically challenge social norms and unlearn racial bias and discrimination.

Fruitful discussions and ownership of white privilege have been a long time coming. It was way back in 1989 that Peggy McIntosh, the women's studies scholar and, latterly, antiracism activist, set about helping people unpack "the invisible knapsack." A White woman, McIntosh (1989) described white privilege as "an invisible package of unearned assets" that she could count on cashing in each day, but about which she was expected to remain oblivious (p. 10). Within the past few years, and especially since the summer of 2020, organizations have become more open to discussions about racism, white privilege, and white supremacy.

South Florida People of Color's Awkward Dinners have become so popular that there is a long waiting list for the event. Participants have shared that their experiences were transformative, causing shifts in understanding that have positively affected the way they engage with others in the community. The outcomes reflect progress in fulfilling the organization's role as a catalyst for dismantling individual, institutional, and systemic racism. As the organization continues its key role in the racial justice-focused community engagement initiatives of South Florida institutions, their leaders have welcomed the willingness of people in the society at large to discuss the effects of white privilege and to work at combatting entrenched racism.

Conclusion

Amid the twin pandemics of COVID-19 and sociopolitical strife, higher education institutions are challenged to take a long, hard look at systems, policies, and practices that have endowed a few groups of people with privilege and power to the detriment of all others. It is incumbent on them to lead the reform of those systems, policies, and practices with a view to creating equitable campus spaces and redressing racial wrongs. In this regard, colleges and universities must consider their crucial role in preparing future generations to take their rightful place in a more just society.

A major shortcoming of their typical DEI (diversity, equity, and inclusion) strategies is the inattention to actions designed for structural or systemic change. Also, articulation of institutional commitment to DEI must not be a box-checking exercise. Further, statements from higher education institutions denouncing racial violence and proclaiming commitment to inclusive, racially equitable practices are clearly not enough. In cases where taskforces have completed DEI audits and developed DEI plans, a racial justice component might be added, and then the real work of implementing those plans must begin.

While workshops can be informative and instructive, one-off workshops usually do not create results. To be effective, workshops should be part of a comprehensive plan to create an institutional culture that values, facilitates, and celebrates equity and inclusivity with special attention to racial justice. A racial justice/antiracism component is necessary if systems of discrimination, inequity, and exclusion are to be dismantled.

Community engagement provides a solid basis for effective measures that move institutions well beyond platitudes and rhetoric regarding racism, exclusion, and injustice. CLDE programs, social justice-oriented service-learning, and community-engaged scholarship focused on racial justice can contribute to lasting social change. So, too, can the truth-telling and racial healing strategy when implemented as a community engagement endeavor.

The call to action in response to the prevailing sociopolitical situation is urgent. It must be understood, however, that the work required for DEI and social/racial justice is slow work with no expectation of quick fixes. It involves time-consuming processes and practices that call for patience and perseverance. The work must begin, and it must go on, if there is to be any hope of creating a more humane and decidedly just society.

References

Apel, D. (2008). Memorialization and its discontents: America's first lynching memorial. *The Mississippi Quarterly, 61*(1/2), 217–235.

Association of American Colleges and Universities. (n.d.). Initiative: Truth, Racial Healing & Transformation (TRHT) Campus Centers. www.aacu.org/initiatives/truth-racial-healing-transformation-campus-centers

Auerbach, Y. (2009). The reconciliation pyramid—A narrative-based framework for analyzing identity conflicts. *Political Psychology, 30*(2), 291–318. https://doi.org/10.1111/j.1467-9221.2008.00692.x

Baker, D. (2011). The scholarship of engagement: A taxonomy of five emerging practices. *Journal of Higher Education Outreach and Engagement, 9*(2), 123–137.

Barry University. (n.d.). About Barry: Mission & core commitments. www.barry.edu/en/about-barry/

Berrien, C. (2020). *The role of narratives in collective violence, collective memory, and truth and reconciliation* [Unpublished manuscript]. Educational and Psychological Studies Department, University of Miami.

Bowen, G. A. (2014). Promoting social change through service-learning in the curriculum. *The Journal of Effective Teaching, 14*(1), 51–62.

Bowen, G. A., & Berrien, C. A. (2021). Implementing an experiential learning program focused on civic leadership to produce social justice outcomes. *Experiential Learning & Teaching in Higher Education, 4*(2), Article 8. https://nsuworks.nova.edu/elthe/vol4/iss2/8/

Boyer, E. L. (1996). The scholarship of engagement. *Journal of Public Service and Outreach, 1*(1), 11–20.

Butin, D. W. (2006). The limits of service-learning in higher education. *The Review of Higher Education, 29*(4), 473–498.

Carcasson, M. (2019). From crisis to opportunity: Rethinking the civic role of universities in the face of wicked problems, hyper-partisanship, and truth decay. In W. V. Flores & K. S. Rogers (Eds.), *Democracy, civic engagement, and citizenship in higher education: Reclaiming our civic purpose* (pp. 319–348). Lexington Books/Rowman & Littlefield.

Carnegie Elective Classifications. (2023, July 13). The 2024 elective classification for community engagement. https://carnegieclassifications.acenet.edu/elective-classifications/community-engagement/

Collins, P. H., & Bilge, S. (2016). *Intersectionality*. Polity Press.

Crenshaw, K. (2016, October). *The urgency of intersectionality* [Video]. TED: Ideas Worth Spreading. www.ted.com/talks/kimberle_crenshaw_the_urgency_of_intersectionality

Gentlewarrior, S. (2021, November 19). The Racial Equity and Justice Institute: A new resource to guide equity-minded campus reform. *Liberal Education Blog*. www.aacu.org/blog/racial-equity-and-justice-institute-new-resource-guide-equity-minded-campus-reform

Guerrero, M., Anderson, A. J., Catlett, B. S., Sánchez, B., & Liao, C. L. (2021). Emerging adults' social justice engagement: Motivations, barriers, and social identity. *American Journal of Community Psychology, 68*(1/2), 73–87. https://doi.org/10.1002/ajcp.12495

Hill, K. K. (2016). *Beyond the rope: The impact of lynching on Black culture and memory*. Cambridge University Press.

Hughes, C., & Byrd, M. Y. (2015). *Managing human resource development programs: Current issues and evolving trends*. Palgrave Macmillan.

Lindsay, J. (2020). Decolonizing the curriculum. *Academic Questions, 33*(3), 448–454.

Llewellyn, J. J. (2012). Restorative justice: Thinking relationally about justice. In J. Downie & J. J. Llewellyn (Eds.), *Being relational: Reflections on relational theory and health law* (pp. 89–108). UBC Press.

McGuire, P. (2021, January 8). Colleges share blame for assault on democracy. *The Chronicle of Higher Education*. www.chronicle.com/article/colleges-share-the-blame-for-assault-on-democracy?cid2=gen_login_refresh&cid=gen_sign_in

McIntosh, P. (1989). White privilege: Unpacking the invisible knapsack. *Peace and Freedom, 49*(4), 10–12.

Mitchell, T. D. (2008). Traditional vs. critical service-learning: Engaging the literature to differentiate two models. *Michigan Journal of Community Service Learning, 14*(2), 50–65.

Mitchell, T. D., Donahue, D. M., & Young-Law, C. (2012). Service learning as a pedagogy of whiteness. *Equity & Excellence in Education, 45*(4), 612–629. https://doi.org/10.1080/10665684.2012.715534

Project H.E.R.E. (n.d.). Project H.E.R.E.: Who we are. https://projecthere.givepulse.com/

Saltmarsh, J., & Johnson, M. (2018). *The elective Carnegie engagement classification: Constructing a successful application for first-time and re-classification applicants*. Campus Compact.

Santiago-Ortiz, A. (2019). From critical to decolonizing service-learning: Limits and possibilities of social justice–based approaches to community service-learning. *Michigan Journal of Community Service Learning*, 25(1) 43–54. https://doi.org/10.3998/mjcsloa.3239521.0025.104

Schacter, A. (2018, August). Traditional land acknowledgements. *Communiqué 2.0*, 6–7. https://lawsociety.mb.ca/wp-content/uploads/2019/07/August-2018v2.pdf

Shahjahan, R. A., Estera, A. L., Surla, K. L., & Edwards, K. T. (2022). "Decolonizing" curriculum and pedagogy: A comparative review across disciplines and global higher education contexts. *Review of Educational Research*, 92(1), 73–113. https://doi.org/10.3102/00346543211042423

Shin, R. Q., Welch, J. C., Kaya, A. E., Yeung, J. G., Obana, C., Sharma, R., Vernay, C. N., & Yee, S. (2017). The intersectionality framework and identity intersections in the Journal of Counseling Psychology and The Counseling Psychologist: A content analysis. *Journal of Counseling Psychology*, 64(5), 458–474. https://doi.org/10.1037/cou0000204

Smalls, C. I. (2021, November 19). "It's just not something we were taught." Three South Dade lynchings brought to light. *Miami Herald*. www.msn.com/en-us/news/us/it-s-just-not-something-we-were-taught-three-south-dade-lynchings-brought-to-light/ar-AAQOZSs

Sonn, C. C., Stevens, G., & Duncan, N. (2013). Decolonisation, critical methodologies and why stories matter. In G. Stevens, N. Duncan, & D. Hook (Eds.), *Race, memory and the apartheid archive: Studies in the* psychosocial (pp. 295–314). Palgrave Macmillan. https://doi.org/10.1057/9781137263902_15

Wood, A. L., & Donaldson, S. V. (2008). Lynching's legacy in American culture. *The Mississippi Quarterly*, 6(1/2), 5–25.

Appendix

Recommended Resources for Antiracism Education

Books	
Between the World and Me	by Ta-Nehisi Coates
Fatal Invention: How Science, Politics, and Big Business Re-create Race in the Twenty-First Century	by Dorothy Roberts
The Fire Next Time	by James Baldwin
Freedom is a Constant Struggle: Ferguson, Palestine, and the Foundations of a Movement	by Angela Y. Davis
Home: A Novel	by Toni Morrison
How to Be an Antiracist	by Ibram X. Kendi

Books

I Know Why the Caged Bird Sings	by Maya Angelou
Just Mercy: A Story of Justice and Redemption	by Bryan Stevenson
Me and White Supremacy: Combat Racism, Change the World, and Become a Good Ancestor	by Layla F. Saad
The New Jim Crow: Mass Incarceration in the Age of Colorblindness	by Michelle Alexander
The Racial Healing Handbook: Practical Activities to Help You Challenge Privilege, Confront Systemic Racism, and Engage in Collective Healing	by Anneliese A. Singh
So You Want to Talk About Race	by Ijeoma Oluo
Stamped From the Beginning: The Definitive History of Racist Ideas in America	by Ibram X. Kendi
Tears We Cannot Stop: A Sermon to White America	by Michael Eric Dyson
White Fragility: Why It's So Hard for White People to Talk About Racism	by Robin DiAngelo

Movies and TV Shows

Dear White People (2017–2021)
Do the Right Thing (1989)
Fruitvale Station (2013)
If Beale Street Could Talk (2018)
Just Mercy (2019)
Loving (2016)
Selma (2014)
The Hate U Give (2018)
When They See Us (2019)

TED Talks

The Danger of a Single Story —Chimamanda Ngozi Adichie	TEDGlobal 2009, July 2009
An Interview With the Founders of Black Lives Matter —Alicia Garza, Patrisse Cullors, and Opal Tometi	TEDWomen 2016, October 2016
Racism Has a Cost for Everyone —Heather C. McGhee	TEDWomen 2019, December 2019
The Urgency of Intersectionality —Kimberlé Crenshaw	TEDWomen 2016, October 2016
We Need to Talk About an Injustice —Bryan Stevenson	TED2012, February 2012

3

MAPPING OUR CAPACITIES TO FACILITATE CHANGE

Applying the Ecosystem of Critical Feminist Praxis for Community Engagement Professionals

Star Plaxton-Moore

Introduction

My purpose for this chapter is to urge community engagement professionals (CEPs) to believe that community engagement can guide our institutions to authentically enact the public purpose of higher education while also advancing social justice outcomes for multiple constituencies, including students, faculty, and community members. Dostilio (2017, p. 1) defines community engagement professionals (CEPs) as "professional staff whose primary job is to support and administer community-campus engagement." Many of us were welcomed into our initial CEP roles with the explicit expectation, as noted in our job descriptions, of administering programs for students and faculty, developing community partnerships, assessing civic learning, and/or implementing faculty development. One could easily stay within these parameters, faithfully running programming, processes, partnerships, and policies that sustain the institution's community engagement initiative. However, based on my own experience and conversations with colleagues in the field, I assert that there comes a time in every CEP's career trajectory when they begin to ponder the following questions: What impact are we really having on our community and students? What more could/should we be doing if we truly want to fulfill our public purpose, and what is keeping us from doing it? Is my work advancing equity and justice, or just making the university look good in promotional materials? Might our programs and initiatives be perpetuating problematic understandings among students about the nature of injustice? How are we complicit in

DOI: 10.4324/9781003448525-4

sustaining inequitable power dynamics between campus and community, even when the institution's rhetoric espouses a public purpose?

These moments of questioning, which usually arise from a dissonance between what we understand the work to be, and how it is perceived and reflected back to us by other constituencies, have the power to galvanize us as change agents and movement builders. We begin to see that the work of community engagement requires institutional transformation to truly fulfill a public purpose and must be focused on systems transformation to advance social justice. What if we could bring new CEPs into the field from a starting point of critically questioning the work of community engagement and seeing themselves as catalysts for institutional change? What if we could offer a coherent set of tools, frameworks, strategies, and support networks for CEPs to do the hard work of pushing our institutions to be accountable for a public purpose and fulfilling social justice outcomes? I assert that this is not only possible but imperative, if the field of higher education community engagement truly wants to realize its espoused aspirations for equity and justice, and if our institutions truly intend to fulfill their public purpose.

I write this from a particular positionality that shapes my perspective on community-engaged work. My career in higher education community engagement has spanned 16 years. I'm currently serving in a director-level position at a West Coast faith-based institution that supports undergraduate students to complete a community-engaged learning course as one of their graduation requirements. I am part of multiple professional associations in the field and have a generous and beloved network of colleagues and friends who have guided me in my professional formation. Prior to entering higher education as a professional, I taught elementary school on the East and West Coasts. I am a White, cis-gender, middle-class woman, first-generation college student, and mother to two children. I recently completed a doctoral program in organizational leadership in (what I would proudly call) a "radically activist" school of education. It is from this standpoint that I offer a framework for CEPs to develop a critical feminist approach to our work, allowing us to tap into our power and capacities to affect positive institutional and systems change at all levels of our professional sphere of influence. The *Ecosystem of Critical Feminist Praxis for Community Engagement Professionals* (ECFP) (Plaxton-Moore, 2021) maps the foundations upon which we might build our practices and illuminates the contexts and dynamics that shape the work of community engagement. The CEP is at the center of the ecosystem, moving through a praxis of clarifying values, reflecting on experiences, analyzing power dynamics, and acting in ways that both disrupt the status quo and create new possibilities for community engagement. The CEPs deploy their praxis to enact tendrils of change in various settings and situations with the purpose of achieving explicit aspirations of transformative justice.

I developed the ECFP framework through my dissertation research process for the primary purpose of facilitating CEP professional development and reflection. The framework emerged from an extensive literature review, qualitative interview process, and qualitative data analysis. The literature review spans across the fields of higher education community engagement, critical feminist theory, and intersections of feminism and engagement. The interviews included seven mid to late-career CEPs, with an added conversation between CEPs and their community partners. Because this was an exploratory study, I used a purposive sample, drawing on my own network and the networks of my dissertation committee to access CEPs whose work I admired and respected. Some scholars argue that this sampling method runs the risk of reinforcing the researcher's biases (Sharma, 2017) and is best considered as a starting point for theory development. The seven CEPs who participated in my study were diverse in multiple ways: geographic locations, institution types, genders, races, ethnicities, etc. They already identified as mid- to late-career professionals, as it was important to my study that they had experience in institutional leadership positions and had accumulated significant professional experiences to draw upon in the interviews. The creative data analysis included both inductive and deductive thematic mapping, which yielded findings that I configured into the *Ecosystem of Critical Feminist Praxis for Community Engagement Professionals* (Plaxton-Moore, 2021). Since creating the framework, I've shared it with multiple colleagues and constituencies, including adapting it for use with community-engaged students. My hope is that field builders use it alongside other well-respected contemporary scholarship to reimagine and reshape the roles, competencies, and commitments of CEPs.

Literature Review

Most scholars trace the roots of higher education community engagement through John Dewey's (1986) experiential progressive education theory, Paolo Freire's (1970) problem-posing education and conscientization, and Ernest Boyer's (1996) scholarship of engagement. I do not debate that these constructs have immensely influenced the trajectory, practice, and purpose of higher education community engagement. However, this "single story" of the origin of engagement is incomplete and limits our understanding of how we can leverage our field in service to broader movements for social justice. Encouragingly, more and more scholars in our field are ensuring that we create a more diverse and inclusive map of the origins of our field, connecting it back to movements for civil rights and Black liberation, the creation of ethnic studies and women's studies, student strikes for open college admissions, and establishment of historically Black colleges and universities (HBCUs). When we understand these more diverse origins of higher education community engagement, we see how our field can have a social change orientation (versus a charity orientation), employ activist tactics (as an alternative to traditional service activities), center the wisdom and power of systematically oppressed communities (instead of the epistemological supremacy of academia), enact higher education's accountability to care for our broader community (instead of just espousing engagement as a PR strategy), and prioritize mutually fulfilling relationships (instead of transactional partnership).

Some community engagement scholars have provided practical frameworks and concepts that draw on a more diversified foundation for our field. Noteworthy among these is Nadinne Cruz's (1990) *Principles for Combining Service and Learning: A Diversity Perspective*, in which Cruz has crafted a series of ten principles aimed at shifting power in the community-engaged learning relationship to ensure that community members/partners and students have a significant voice in determining all aspects of engagement, from defining their expectations for the relationship to how interactions occur and toward what ultimate purpose. Additionally, Tania Mitchell's (2008) critical service-learning framework reorients the pedagogy around social change as a north star for guiding how partnerships are identified and developed, the types of engagement and service students might do, the curricular focus on identity-based power and oppression, explicit attention to examining structural inequities, and fostering student commitment to enact positive and enduring change.

More recently, there's an emerging focus on decolonizing service-learning (Santiago-Ortiz, 2019; Yep & Mitchell, 2017) which entails acknowledgment of settler colonialism as an inherent characteristic of higher education and calls for disruption of dominant norms and narratives in higher education by introducing diverse ways of knowing and being, and radically shifting the campus-community relationship to ensure that power rests with the community. Focusing on the institutional level, Saltmarsh et al. (2015) have proposed a framework for an "engaged campus" that demonstrates a deep, pervasive, and integrated change, moving from higher education's status quo toward a focus on honoring community assets and epistemologies, engaging in transformative collective work with the community to advance equity and justice, and democratizing learning processes to allow for each constituent to be a learner and teacher. The constellation of theories, concepts, and principles for community engagement presented above provides a crucial foundation for how CEPs understand and enact our work, positioning us to develop relationships of solidarity with community and students, guide institutional transformation by disrupting the status quo and integrating diverse epistemologies, and attend to the priorities and needs of systematically marginalized communities through our engagement efforts. This can manifest in so many ways in our daily practice, from prioritizing participation in community and/or student-led events and movement work to advocating for community-centered policies in decision-making to responding to community-identified priorities by leveraging institutional resources (e.g., sharing campus space, access to libraries, etc.).

Further, I recommend that CEPs consider a critical feminist approach to community engagement, though our field has sorely underutilized this theoretical tradition thus far. Very few publications link feminism and community engagement. However, seeds have been planted. Drawing on lessons from the collective contributions of the authors to their edited volume, James and Iverson (2014) encourage the field of community engagement to infuse a more explicitly feminist approach, calling upon educators to invite students to explore their own activist and feminist identities, cultivate authentic relationships across student and community constituencies, attend to the particular contexts of engagement and account for community desires/priorities/needs, embed critical reflection on the intersections of experience and curriculum, and develop students' understanding of pervasive justice issues.

It's possible for CEPs to play a powerful role in shaping the field of community engagement to be more reflective of diverse activist and community-rooted origins, aligned with critical and disruptive frameworks for working with the community and fostering student learning, and inspired by feminist theory. Indeed, within the past decade, scholars in our field have come to theorize and research the possibilities for the role of CEPs, thanks in large part to the efforts of Dr. Lina Dostilio. Her dissertation research and subsequent scholarship have elucidated often unacknowledged and underappreciated intellectual and organizing labor done by CEPs. Her model articulates the nuances of CEPs' practical responsibilities, including program administration and assessment (Farmer-Hanson, 2017), facilitation of students' civic learning (Benenson et al., 2017), stewardship of community-campus partnerships (Martin & Crossland, 2017), and development and support of community-engaged faculty (Chamberlin & Phelps-Hillen, 2017).

However, I assert that the most revolutionary and potentially impactful components of the competency model are focused on CEPs' roles in enacting institutional change for the public good (Hubler & Quan, 2017) and institutionalizing community engagement (Weaver & Kellogg, 2017). In their chapter on catalyzing institutional change, Hubler and Quan (2017) begin by acknowledging the particularity of CEPs' contexts and networks as a starting point for examining their possible paths to enact change. They assert that CEPs must understand methods for fostering change, articulate a shared vision to guide the work, infuse democratic principles into the change process, engage in creative and collaborative organizing methods, and work in good faith with administrators and powerholders. According to Weaver and Kellogg (2017), the competencies for institutionalization are developing political capital, sustaining stakeholder relationships, collecting, analyzing, and disseminating data to support one's work, and deploying communication and marketing strategies. These competencies are used to build four components of institutionalization, including alignment with institutional values and mission, cultivation of infrastructure and leadership, access to resources and support, and collaboration with stakeholders.

The extant scholarship on higher education community engagement origins, critical and disruptive frameworks for engagement, feminist approaches to engagement, and the role of CEPs provide a solid foundation upon which to build our next wave praxis as CEPs. My research is meant to serve as a bridge between the scant but powerful literature on these topics within our field and the way we think about, develop, support, and reflect on the roles of CEPs and the potentiality of community engagement as a strategy for advancing higher education's public purpose and social justice outcomes.

Framework Development

The *Ecosystem of Critical Feminist Praxis for Community Engagement Professionals* (Plaxton-Moore, 2021) evolved from my dissertation research process. My original goal was to understand how CEPs intentionally or unintentionally employ critical feminist praxis to guide their higher education institutions to authentically fulfill a public purpose. I grounded my research in critical feminist theory and praxis, synthesizing a set of guiding principles for critical feminist praxis that shaped my research questions, research design, data collection, and data analysis (Appendix A).

My research questions focused on 1) how CEPs understand higher education community engagement and their roles in their institutions; 2) their practices of partnership, program administration, policy setting, and implementation, etc.; 3) principles, theories, and strategies they employ to enact change; and 4) their shared vision for community engagement at their institutions. I conducted qualitative interviews with seven CEPs representing diverse identities, professional positions, geographic locations, and institution types. In addition to these one-hour structured interviews, I facilitated a series of seven 45-minute "shared visioning" conversations in which each CEP engaged in discussion with a community partner about their critiques and aspirations for community engagement. All interviews and conversations were conducted on Zoom, recorded, and transcribed. In addition, I made notes based on observations of how CEPs interacted with their community partners.

I reviewed and coded the interview transcripts and observation notes using both deductive and inductive themes. The deductive themes connected directly to one particular framework within critical feminist theory, *Emergent Strategy: Shaping Change, Changing Worlds* (2017) by Adrienne Maree Brown. Emergent strategy asserts that social change happens through enactment of multiple intersecting elements that parallel principles shaping the natural world: 1) *Fractals:* practices and habits that individuals enact in their daily lives can set patterns for whole social systems; 2) *Adaptation:* individuals and movements have to be open to changing tactics and strategies while staying true to their purpose; 3) *Interdependence and Decentralization:* social movements require reciprocal relationships, shared leadership, and distribution of power and responsibilities among participants; 4) *Nonlinear and Iterative:* individuals and movements progress along pathways that are wrought with detours, double-backs, accelerations, and forks in the road but repeating grounding practices and actions can help to stay the course; 5) *Resilience:* people and movements demonstrate strength and persistence in the face of challenges and defeats; and 6) *Creating more possibilities:* movements thrive on collective visioning that makes space for multiple futures to become reality.

I also discovered inductive themes, including a metatheme of understanding feminism as an aspirational and contextual praxis, and subthemes of employing intersectional power analysis, disrupting the status quo, honoring community-rooted wisdom, and mentoring. Most participants didn't claim feminism as an identity, noting that they feel that feminism is something that one must constantly practice. However, they described feminist principles as a north star that guides their daily work and their visions for what is possible. CEPs described how power analysis shaped their participation in decision-making spaces, program design, relationships with community partners, interactions with students and staff, etc. They gave examples of situations where they subtly or overtly disrupted the status quo to advance an agenda of equity and social justice on large and small scales in their workplaces. They talked about honoring and compensating community partners and leaders as coeducators and wisdom-holders. They also described the power of mentorship in their own formation, citing not just mentors within academia but also community leaders, family members, and friends.

The resulting framework attempts to balance the reality that CEPs have experiences that can be classified as common across many roles and institutions (e.g., program management, committee participation, etc.), and also that CEPs have unique and distinctive experiences of their work based on their diverse identities, positionalities, and contexts.

Ecosystem of Critical Feminist Praxis for Community Engagement Professionals

Community engagement scholars have lamented the dearth of theoretical and conceptual frameworks needed to help us not only make meaning of our work but also envision a future trajectory for higher education community engagement (Bringle et al., 2013). Because our field is interdisciplinary and practical, scholars and practitioners draw on theoretical traditions from a range of disciplines, such as sociology, psychology, and communication studies, and interdisciplines, such as education, ethnic studies, women's studies, and business. On the other hand, many CEPs come to this work through alternative pathways, bypassing formal educational programs and specialized professional development certifications, and joining the field of higher education community engagement with a wealth of lived experience as community organizers, and nonprofit professionals, or youth educators.

Thus, our theoretical and conceptual frameworks should reflect the diversity of academic and community-rooted traditions we bring into the field, while also organizing information in such a way that we can expand, enhance, and replicate the work that is truly transforming higher education to achieve its public purpose and advance social justice. Toward that end, the *Ecosystem of Critical Feminist Praxis for Community Engagement Professionals* (Figure 3.1) that I developed synthesizes critical feminist theory with my own experience and perspective as a CEP, and the exemplary practices, ideas, understandings, values, and aspirations of seven CEPs influencing the contemporary field of higher education community engagement to help us transform our practice (Plaxton-Moore, 2021).

In this model, the ecosystem situates the CEP on a fertile foundation that supports their work and surrounds them with the systems and structures that influence community engagement. There's a significant focus on elements of the CEP's praxis, which is defined by Freire (1970) as the process of integrating reflection and action to foster a deeper understanding of the world around us. My research and self-reflection revealed that critical feminist CEPs are perpetually analyzing their experiences through the lens of their values and professional competencies, while also attending to power dynamics at the interpersonal, institutional, and systemic levels, to inform actions in any given situation. For example, a CEP described how she engaged in a praxis of power analysis and prioritizing solidarity when she chose how to challenge institutional leadership on their plans for new campus construction in the adjacent community. Given the power

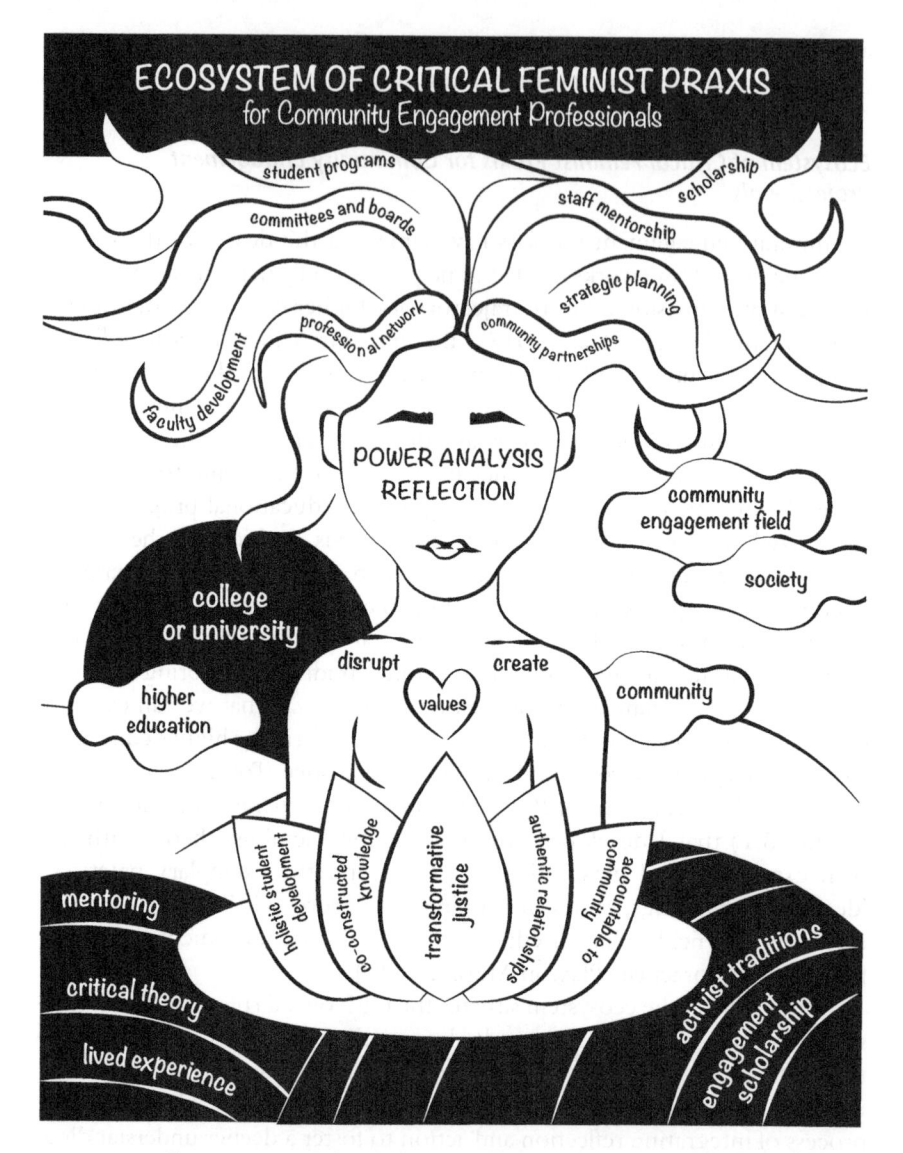

FIGURE 3.1 *Ecosystem of Critical Feminist Praxis for Community Engagement Professionals,* Framework Created by Star Plaxton-Moore, Graphic Design by Natalie Ferrer.

structure present in the room, and the values held by campus leadership, she knew that her best approach was to ask questions, and that through this approach she could best appeal to their concerns about public relations optics and concurrently help them rethink their plans to be more inclusive of, and favorable to, community. Using this approach, CEPs are also invited to consider the ways various aspects of their role might afford them opportunities to enact "tendrils" of change and cultivate critical feminist aspirations for community engagement. The ultimate goal of the model is to enact visionary and transformative outcomes for higher education institutions, the community, and the field of higher education.

Fertile Grounds (Foundations)

Every CEP builds our practice on a foundation of understandings and experiences, whether we do so intentionally or subconsciously. Our foundations include past professional and educational experiences, which signaled information to us about everything from our individual worth in educational and professional spaces to our understanding of what education should entail. As a first-generation college student from a working-class family who attended an elite private university, I felt out of place, unprepared, and unworthy. I struggled quietly to develop study skills and learn how to write so I could pass my classes, working one to two jobs to help me pay for living expenses, feeling too self-conscious to develop meaningful friendships, and avoiding all extracurricular activities because I saw them as a distraction and a luxury I couldn't afford. My mentality was to work hard to get my degree so I could have financial security, but I also had a strong yearning to contribute to the public good, which was why I eventually pursued teaching as my professional path. As a teacher, I felt conflicted about my role, internalizing the message that my job was to deliver curriculum and manage the class, but also feeling that I wanted to support students holistically and care for their emotional and physical wellbeing. Eventually, the restrictions of teaching in the public school system made me feel like a tool of oppression instead of a vehicle for support and liberation, so I moved into higher education where I hoped to have more freedom to be the kind of educator I wanted to be. It was in this career transition that I landed in the community engagement field.

My relationship with work was guided by the same values that shaped my academic experience, meaning I was task oriented, goal driven, eager to please, and fearful of being seen as incompetent. I brought this approach into my first paid job at Dairy Queen and through every professional position, including my first several years as a CEP. I remember coming into my role coordinating a small social justice student leadership program and some public service internships and feeling limited in my understanding of how to do community engagement. It wasn't in my skill sets or aspirations to look for ways to enhance or strengthen programs or to use literature or innovative models to shape curriculum, but rather to keep programs running as they had originally been created. My background did not prepare me to be visionary, relational, or creative. Thus, I had to harness informal mentorship and professional development opportunities to learn new ways of approaching my work. I was able to develop competencies, confidence, and connections that made me a better CEP. Further, through my doctoral program, and friendships with peers working across community engagement, I transformed my professional practice toward a revolutionary pursuit of equity and social justice. Our experiences inform whether we see ourselves as change agents and whether we feel empowered to hold our institutions accountable to a public purpose and social justice outcomes.

Furthermore, we are all influenced by scholarship and resources offered by mentors, supervisors, peers, and educators. I was originally introduced to what Chimamanda Adichie (2009) calls "the single story," in this case, the story of the origin and evolution of higher education community engagement. In other words, I learned of community engagement's origins in John Dewey's (1986) experiential progressive education theory, Paolo Freire's (1970) problem-posing education and conscientization, and Ernest Boyer's (1996) scholarship of engagement. In this story, community engagement began and remains a potent pedagogical tool as well as a category of scholarship for faculty. My belief in this story shaped how I did the work and what I hoped to accomplish through it. Eventually, I had mentors who invited me to connect higher education community engagement to its roots in ethnic studies, women's studies, student strikes and demonstrations, and community-rooted movements for equity and justice. This radically transformed my understanding of my role and our field and has informed my daily practices. The point is that the foundations upon which we build our practices as CEPs might be diverse and expansive, or limited and canonical.

The ecosystem framework I provide guides us toward the former approach, providing specific thematic areas where we might grow our field's foundation, and moves beyond the commonly cited scholarship on/of engagement to attend to the diversity of voices represented in the literature. The model I provide draws from widely referenced germinal texts in our field, but also more recent, revolutionary, and creative texts that infuse critiques and aspirations for how community engagement can be a vehicle for social justice. Similarly, this model values scholarship from the interdisciplines, namely ethnic studies and women's studies, that position community engagement as a tool for advancing racial and gender equity. Relatedly, CEPs have much to gain from considering the canon of critical theory, including foundational texts such as Freire's (1970) *Pedagogy of the Oppressed*, and equally relevant and radical texts like bell hooks' (2014) *Teaching to Transgress* or Eve Tuck's (2009) desire-centered research approach. CEPs would benefit from a working knowledge of global and national social change movements, including the fights for civil rights, farm worker rights, and women's rights, and how their strategies and tactics influence (or should influence) higher education community engagement.

The final component of the ecosystem's fertile foundation is a network of robust and intentional mentoring relationships that include supervisors, peers, academic "veterans," and community leaders. CEPs would benefit from seeking and sustaining relationships with mentors as a crucial part of our professional development. Reflecting on my own practice, I found that taking time to meet with and learn from folks across a range of community engagement constituencies greatly enhanced my understanding and practice. In turn, I have mentored colleagues, including direct reports and other new scholars in our field, by sharing stories, resources, words of wisdom, and connections relevant to their professional challenges and aspirations. I know there are already programs and professional associations that foster mentoring relationships among CEPs and veteran scholars/practitioners, but I am unaware of any formalized or intentional program that connects CEPs directly with community leaders and wisdom-holders to learn from their insights and practice. This is a growing edge for our field to explore.

In the Air (Context)

I came into higher education community engagement from another career (elementary school teacher) at a time when the field wasn't yet "professionalized" in the way it is now. In other words, professional associations and universities weren't offering formalized educational degree/certificate programs or prescribed pathways for developing CEPs, whereas now there are several certificate and degree programs designed to prepare professionals specifically to work in higher education community engagement. Instead, when I entered the field, I found that associations like Campus Compact and the International Association for Research on Service-Learning and Community Engagement (IARSLCE) were providing professional development programming at the time in the form of intensive institutes and conferences. My supervisor connected me to these associations early on to help me begin developing an understanding of the context of our work.

Even so, it took a few years for me to think outside of the silo of our individual institution and realize that not only was similar community engagement work happening at other institutions but that we were all facing a combination of common dynamics rooted in higher education systems and structures, as well as distinct situations emanating from community-campus factors reflecting the political, cultural, economic, social, and historical influences of geographic place. For example, it took me a while to learn that dominant cultural influences of neoliberalism, positivism, and capitalism shape the perceived value of community engagement among institutional leadership, faculty, and students, and therefore, guide resource allocation, faculty commitment, and student approaches to engagement. I also learned hard lessons about how our institution's relationship with the adjacent historically Black neighborhood was perceived by community members as alternating between negligent and exploitative, which made them righteously suspicious and defensive when we approached them about collaborating on a place-based initiative. Residents shared stories of faculty coming to collect data from the community to produce research that they never saw or benefited from. They described how students from our institution came into the community to do service for a day or a semester, but their demeanor and approach were condescending and distant, and their actions provided very little benefit, while the university touted its perceived impact on the community through self-aggrandizing public announcements. They expressed anger and frustration as they questioned why, without any input or advanced notice, the university closed the TRIO program, a retention program for underserved students, that had been operating on the campus with support from the school of education for over 50 years. While I learned so much about the dynamics and factors shaping my institution's community engagement on the job, I would have benefited from a more intentional and robust introduction to the contexts of academia and our community when I began my role as a CEP.

The ecosystem illustration posits these dynamics as being in the air and all around us as we do our work. As CEPs, how do we educate ourselves about the forces that influence community engagement? For starters, we can tap into critical scholarship on higher education, which explores how power, privilege, and oppression manifest in academic structures, pedagogies, and content. Recent publications like Spooner and McNinch's (2018) edited volume, *Dissident Knowledge in Higher Education*, provide insightful critiques from scholars across disciplines, geographies, and identities. For example, there are publications that examine how higher education community engagement is used to accumulate power, resources, and land for colleges and universities (Baldwin, 2021; Paperson, 2017). Knowledge of how institutions of higher education perpetuate inequities can give us a window into where and how community engagement can subvert problematic dynamics, enabling us to move our work in a more justice-oriented direction. Many CEPs are doing this work of disruption. For example, instead of buying property in adjacent underserved neighborhoods, some universities lease space from small business owners or nonprofits to hold classes and/or facilitate community-identified projects. Some universities have established scholarships earmarked for students from adjacent neighborhoods. Other institutions have set up ways to compensate community partners for their role as coeducators and/or provide access to learning opportunities free of charge for partners. These are just some ways CEPs are guiding their institutions to move toward an authentic enactment of their public purpose.

Simultaneously, CEPs have a responsibility to attend to the factors shaping our campus, local, and global communities. The geographies of our campuses might lend themselves to education about place-specific issues like gentrification in urban centers or lack of infrastructure in rural areas. The demographics of communities might signal a need to explore historical and contemporary patterns of migration, displacement, redlining, etc., and how one's college or university fits within those trends. Examination of local politics and policies yields information about who is empowered/disempowered and valued/devalued in the community. We might discover this kind of contextual information about our communities through local news media, historical societies, educational and cultural events, and the oral traditions of community wisdom-holders.

The Source of Light and Heat (the Higher Education Institution)

In the ecosystem framework, the CEP's college or university is represented by the sun, or the source of light and heat. This felt like an apt metaphor because, like the sun, the higher education institution has the power to enlighten or bring light to students and community. This light could be in the form of liberatory education and research, mutually beneficial collaborations, and resource sharing. However, the higher education institution can also "bring the heat" to the community, meaning using its power to control and silence communities in order to advance its own interests. As CEPs, we represent our institutions and are accountable for acting in their best interests. However, we may find this professional expectation at odds with what we know to be ethical and just in our relationships with the community. For example, in response to community outrage about a campus-based youth program being shut down, I was called upon by institutional leadership to provide various statistics on service outputs (e.g., number of students doing community service, number of hours served) to be used in a PR statement about how the university contributes to the community. How do we grapple with the tensions of representing our institutions and pushing them to do right by the communities to which they belong?

As an extension of examining and understanding the context of our community engagement work, CEPs need to turn our critical gaze on our own institutions. We need to be aware of the strengths and opportunities, as well as the limitations that dictate everything from student enrollment to faculty recruitment and retention to resource allocation. We need to have a clear sense of the priorities of the leadership, map the hierarchies of power and decision-making, and be aware of the marketing and messaging about the institution's academic and public purposes. It's important to understand how the type of institution we work within, whether faith based, community college, research focused, or liberal arts centered, influences stakeholders' perceptions of the value of community engagement, what it looks like, and what purpose it serves. For example, at my faith-based institution, community engagement is deeply connected with the institutional mission and values, including the pursuit of social justice and developing students as positive change agents. This means it is valued as an integral part of the student experience. Simultaneously, the faith-based influence on our work can create a challenge because there are particular issues such as reproductive rights, LGBTQ rights, etc. on which the church and school take a conservative stance. Wrapping our heads around the particularities of our institutions allows us to see possibilities for catalyzing institutional change.

Embodied Praxis (Combining Values, Reflection, Power Analysis, and Action)

At the center of the ecosystem, the CEP functions in a perpetual cycle of praxis: clarifying their values, infusing them into processes of reflection and power analysis, and allowing these processes to inform daily actions and interactions, as well as more strategic practices of creation and disruption. When I think back to my years as a K–12 teacher, I can only imagine how much my teaching would have improved if I had explicitly rooted it in values of equity, justice, and love. To be honest, I would have first had to interrogate my core working-class values of productivity, individualism, and obedience to authority, which I was only able to do once I entered the higher education community engagement space and encountered explicit critiques of these otherwise reified dominant cultural norms. These discussions happened in the form of book clubs, professional learning communities, conference sessions, informal conversations with trusted colleagues, and formal education spaces in my doctoral program. Scholars shared perspectives, critiques, and critical frames of analysis, and invited others to engage with, and reflect on their radical ideas. I realize that not all CEPs have access to this kind of critical discourse and assert that it would be beneficial to invite more CEPs into conversations that allow for this sort of analysis, reflection, and learning.

Reflection is a way of synthesizing our foundational knowledge, contextual signals, internalized values, and relevant experiences into an understanding of our work and the roles we play in community engagement as CEPs. In the critical feminist ecosystem, the CEP reflects continuously, recognizing that their understandings and actions have an impact on multiple constituencies, including faculty, students, and community. Reflection is most powerful when it is both individual and collective, structured and pragmatic, purposeful and free flowing. It is crucial for CEPs to learn frameworks for guiding their own and others' reflections, as well as theories on reflection, like Schön's (1983) Reflective Practitioner Model.

Intersectional power analysis is a distinctive process that overlaps with reflection but emanates from the critical feminist scholarship of Kimberlé Crenshaw (1989, 1991). It involves careful examination of how systems of privilege and oppression work together to amplify and multiply experiences of injustice for particular individuals and groups. Specifically, Crenshaw argues that we must attend to systemic racism, sexism, classism, and other forms of oppression to truly understand that landscape of power in any given situation so we can disrupt and redistribute power interpersonally and at the moment, as well as structurally and permanently. I am particularly aware of the imperative for me to engage in consistent intersectional analysis, given my identity as a White, cis-gender, middle-class woman in a mid-level leadership position. For example, CEPs might discuss these key questions. How might intersectional power analysis shape participation in a community-led event versus in a classroom versus a meeting with academic leadership? What understandings and actions might the CEP deploy in each of those situations that attempt to redistribute power among participants more equitably and justly?

In the ecosystem framework, I suggest that these actions fall into two categories: disruption of the status quo and creation of more possibilities. The focus on disruption is inspired by the critical feminist scholarship of Audre Lorde (2007) and Sara Ahmed's (2010) construct of the feminist killjoy. The element of creating more possibilities comes directly from Adrienne Maree Brown's (2017) emergent strategy framework. Based on processes of reflection and power analysis, the CEP might make calculated attempts at disruption. This might look like "gently" naming misconceptions or biases articulated by others during a decision-making process, refusing to take on unpaid labor, or introducing revolutionary texts into a curriculum that is otherwise colonized. Similarly, critical feminist CEPs choose to act in ways that create more possibilities and opportunities, instead of operating from a place of scarcity and limitation. Examples of this might be providing access to renewable university resources for community partners (e.g., library access, use of event spaces), collaborating on grant-funded projects that are mutually beneficial, or inviting multiple constituents to play a role in a decision-making process that affects them.

Tendrils of Change (Change-Making Practices)

Depending on the CEP's role, there are particular responsibilities that lend themselves well to enacting change. Many CEPs facilitate or contribute to some form of educational programming, whether targeted to students or faculty. The structure and content of these programs reflect a critical feminist approach if they are designed to advance inclusion of diverse perspectives, equity, and social justice. At a very practical level, the CEP might ask themself questions like: how does the program structure invite students (or faculty) from diverse backgrounds and circumstances to participate fully and feel a sense of belonging? This might require addressing barriers related to cost, time commitment, prerequisites, etc. It might also mean reimagining classroom teaching and learning dynamics to facilitate the democratic exchange of knowledge across participants. Other important questions are: How does the program content reflect diverse voices and experiences? And how can this content contribute to collective empowerment and liberation from injustice? CEPs might need to expend extra time and thought to replace or supplement existing curricular content with content generated by, for, and with systematically marginalized groups. This content could include scholarly publications, speeches, artistic performances, policy papers, op-eds, oral histories, personal narratives, etc. In my practice, I make a point of bringing in, and compensating, community-wisdom holders as guest speakers. Additionally, I draw heavily from oral history publications, including the ones produced by Voice of Witness, which has published several thematic anthologies related to specific justice issues like incarceration, forced migration, etc.

Most CEPs are also involved in cultivating and sustaining community partnerships, whether in support of community-engaged courses across the institution or for smaller-scale service-learning programs within public service centers. Applying a critical feminist approach to partnership shapes how we identify partners, connect them with institutional resources and constituents, honor and compensate their work as coeducators, and invite them to inform the institution's efforts to fulfill its public purpose. To begin, CEPs might seek out organizations that focus on social change, advocacy, and community empowerment, instead of prioritizing a charity model which involves exclusively addressing the symptoms of systemic injustices without also advocating for equitable policies. When connecting community partners with faculty, students, and/or institutional resources, the critical feminist CEP fosters connections based on an understanding of the community partner's articulated desires, priorities, needs, and limitations. CEPs might use the language of coeducators to reinforce that community partners hold distinct, complementary, and equally valuable wisdom and expertise in relation to the wisdom and expertise held by faculty. We can work toward a common practice of offering honoraria or other nonfinancial gestures of gratitude to demonstrate appreciation and celebration of community-rooted wisdom. Additionally, CEPs can identify opportunities for community voices to inform institutional practices and policies, especially those that have an impact on the community.

For CEPs who are in middle- or higher-level leadership positions, there might be opportunities for staff mentorship, which allows one to cultivate relationships of mutual respect and learning and play a role in the formation of the next generation of engagement professionals to ensure that they espouse and enact community engagement that centers equity and justice. Another part of the advanced/veteran CEP's role might be participation on committees and in strategic planning processes at one's institution, or on boards of nonprofits or professional associations. In most cases, these bodies tend to have functions that include policy setting and implementation, resource allocation, and recruitment and retention. The critical feminist CEP can contribute to these spaces, bringing an important power analysis and commitment to advancing social justice to inform the internal dynamics of the committee or board, as well as what they produce or implement. In my experience, simply naming power dynamics, amplifying comments from participants who might be overlooked by leadership, and ensuring equitable distribution of action items can heavily influence the culture within a group. With regard to what the group produces, inviting folks to consider constituencies that they might otherwise overlook and reminding decision-makers to align policies with the espoused values of the institution can be a useful role for CEPs to play.

The CEP's capacity to enact change can also extend to shape the field of higher education community engagement through building strategic professional networks and producing scholarship. Professional networks foster idea-sharing and systems of support to sustain critical feminist CEPs and keep us accountable to a social justice orientation to the work. Producing scholarship allows us to disseminate our critical feminist approach to community engagement so it can be better understood, adapted, and applied more broadly and effectively in the field.

Bloom of Possibility (Aspirations for Our Work)

At the center of the ecosystem framework, the CEP holds the bloom of possibility, or their aspirations for higher education community engagement.

These aspirations move beyond the commonly articulated definition and purpose of higher education community engagement: "collaboration between institutions of higher education and their larger community for the mutually beneficial exchange of knowledge and resources in a context of partnership and reciprocity" (Carnegie Foundation for the Advancement of Teaching, 2023). Indeed, aspirations rooted in critical feminism are loftier and more transformative in nature, though they still reference the components at the heart of higher education: knowledge, students, relationships, and accountability.

Higher education institutions present themselves primarily as producers and distributors of knowledge, but particular ways of knowing continue to be privileged while others are shut out. When situated in a critical feminist orientation to engagement, we are not just concerned with students' development of cognitive skills, but their holistic development as individuals and community members. Community engagement should attend to fostering strong and healthy cognitive, social, and emotional competencies among students, recognizing that their well-being is deeply intertwined with the strength and vitality of the broader community. Relatedly, I suggest students and all constituencies involved in community engagement understand ourselves as being in relationship with others, with a requisite commitment to authenticity, trust, and accountability for our actions and impacts.

Applications and Implications

The *Ecosystem of Critical Feminist Praxis for Community Engagement Professionals* (Plaxton-Moore, 2021) illuminates myriad forces shaping our work, diverse ways we can position ourselves to be change-makers, and radical aspirations for fulfilling our institution's public purpose and advancing social justice. Reflecting on the dynamics of our ecosystems leads us to realizations about 1) untapped foundations for our professional development, 2) previously unnoticed cultural, social, political, economic, or historical dynamics manifesting at our institutions and/or in the community, 3) the cycle of praxis guiding our actions, 4) ways our professional activities and relationships can affect change, and 5) aspirations for our institutions, the field, and the community. I recommend two strategic approaches to apply the framework, which I will describe below.

Feminist Praxis as the Starting Point

For CEPs who desire to root their praxis in critical feminism or feel that they already do, the ecosystem framework can help them explicitly articulate the particular aspects of their unique praxis. In examining the "fertile grounds" section, CEPs might spend time writing out (or sharing verbally in group facilitation settings) the particular mentors who have influenced them, the critical theories and lived experiences that inform their work, the activist traditions that inspire them or have relevance to their community commitments, and the scholarly texts in the field of community engagement that have contributed to their formation as professionals. When analyzing the "source of light and heat" (the institution), the CEP might describe the type of institution, academic culture, policies and procedures, leadership, and hierarchies of power, etc. that affect their community engagement work. The framework also invites a thoughtful exploration of other contextual factors beyond the institution, including the dynamics of the communities engaged by the institution, the current trends and norms of higher education and the community engagement field, and sociocultural systems and structures in contemporary society. Currently, some of the most salient factors we are facing at our institution are the competitive dynamics among community partner organizations vying for limited city and grant funding, competing ideas and agendas within our institution about how to implement our place-based initiative with integrity and fidelity to our adjacent neighborhood's priorities and needs, and the constraints associated with the COVID-19 pandemic, as we try to balance addressing the most urgent needs of our city while also keeping our students safe.

Turning their reflections inward, CEPs could use the "embodied praxis" component of the framework, which entails the values, reflection, power analysis, and actions, to articulate the values that motivate their work; describe when, how, and why they engage in reflection; examine the power dynamics inherent in relationships across individual and constituent groups with which they engage, and consider how their daily work practices might fall into categories of disrupting the status quo and creating new possibilities. Relatedly, CEPs can specifically describe how they are involved in "tendrils of change," that create positive change at their institutions, in/with the community, and in the field of higher education community engagement. For example, what specific student programs and faculty development programs do they offer, and how do these fulfill the institution's public purpose and advance social justice outcomes? What professional networks do CEPs belong to and how are they participating? How are they influencing the field by producing scholarship (e.g., publications and conference presentations)? What committees, boards, and strategic planning processes might CEPs join and influence? What partnerships and relationships have potential to be transformative?

The culminating component of the reflection process is unpacking the "bloom of possibility," or aspiration for our community engagement praxis. CEPs might write about or discuss what it looks like to achieve holistic student development, produce coconstructed knowledge, sustain authentic relationships, demonstrate accountability to the community, and advance transformative justice at their specific institution at this particular moment in history.

If there are components of the ecosystem that CEPs don't feel equipped to elaborate on, these might be areas for further professional development. CEPs can prioritize opportunities to enhance their learning and/or practices in these areas. The components that yield extensive and thoughtful reflection (or conversation in group facilitation settings) might be considered areas of strength and clarity upon which to build.

Feminist Praxis as Emergence

An alternative way to use the ecosystem framework is to opt for the blank worksheet (Figure 3.2).

The blank worksheet doesn't prescribe specific elements of the ecosystem but rather allows CEPs (or other constituencies like students and community partners) to populate each section with their own ideas. This approach draws on the existing implicit frameworks driving praxis by inviting CEPs to make their understandings, practices, and aspirations visible in a coherent way. In a group reflection setting, a facilitator would distribute the blank worksheet and invite CEPs to fill it in using the following guiding prompts:

- Start by asking CEPs to write down the foundations undergirding their work in the "fertile grounds" section. Prompt CEPs to think of particular theories, articles, scholars, mentors, experiences, etc. that have been crucial to developing their understanding of community engagement and their role in it.
- Next, prompt CEPs to write down the name of their institution and its salient characteristics in the sun (also referred to as the source of light and heat).
- CEPs fill in the clouds and air after that with other dynamics that shape their work. Prompt them to think about the specific forces that they are paying attention to in the community (e.g., gentrification), in the field (e.g., place-based initiatives), and in higher education (e.g., focus on career preparation over liberal arts).
- The next phase of the activity invites CEPs to list their values in the heart and imagine how those values integrate with their own processes of reflection and power analysis. This is where they might articulate understandings of their identities, positionalities, and experiences of power and oppression.

Mapping Our Capacities to Facilitate Change **51**

FIGURE 3.2 Ecosystem of Critical Feminist Praxis Worksheet.

- Then, CEPs can write down (on the body) the verbs that represent their professional actions and commitments day to day, recognizing the extent to which these actions are informed by the interplay of values, reflection, and power analysis. CEPs might write down verbs like teaching, partnering, supporting, etc.

- Next, direct CEPs to the "tendrils of change" section, represented by the hair, and ask them to write down the different things they do that they think contribute to making positive change in their institutions, field, and community.
- Finally, CEPs culminate the individual part of this reflective activity by writing aspirations for the outcomes of community engagement in the petals of the bloom.

The facilitator can allocate time for CEPs to review their completed framework and notice anything that is surprising, exciting, frustrating, etc. Ideally, there would also be an opportunity for CEPs to discuss their frameworks with peers in pairs or small groups so they can learn from each other's reflections. After this processing, the facilitator might show the original *Ecosystem of Critical Feminist Praxis for CEPs* (Plaxton-Moore, 2021) and explain the specific elements featured in it. The reflective activity might wrap up with CEPs noting the overlaps and divergence between the frameworks they created and the ones that emerged from the dissertation research.

Conclusion

The nature of the CEP's role within our institutions positions us as agents of change who can actively drive higher education to fulfill its public purpose and advance justice. CEPs can do this in large and small ways, regardless of our official titles and positions within a hierarchy. First, we can interrogate and resist our own complicity in perpetuating unjust thoughts, actions, interactions, relationships, policies, and practices. For example, at our campus, public service center staff advocated for campus police to revise their policies for handling unhoused people found sleeping on campus property. We can do it by creating new possibilities for our partnerships and programs that center on equity, abundance, and solidarity. At our institution, we revised a student program focused on peer-leadership in service settings to focus instead on placing students as paid interns with organizations conducting grassroots organizing involving advocacy and activism. As we move up the administrative ranks, we can bring a justice-oriented approach to institutional decision-making and policy implementation. As one of the leaders in our public service center, I collaborated with staff to develop an equity-centered approach for considering how and when staff would return to in-person work as we move through the pandemic. Others at our institution, and colleagues at peer institutions, learned of these principles that our staff collectively created and asked us to share so they could adapt them to their offices. In other words, we have power.

I contend that our field has an ethical imperative to intentionally cultivate and leverage CEPs' power to catalyze equitable and just systems change in our institutions, communities, and academia. To accomplish this, we must take a more radical and expansive approach to foster CEPs' capacities for disruption and creation. Critical feminism is one tradition rooted in activism and scholarship that can provide useful theories, concepts, and curricula to guide our individual and collective practices. Relatedly, a feminist approach to community engagement reorients how we build and sustain relationships with a focus on mutual care, respect, and even love. The suggested readings on this model provided in a bibliography in Appendix B provide a foundation for this work. The *Ecosystem of Critical Feminist Praxis for CEPs* (Plaxton-Moore, 2021) is a tool that we can use in combination with existing frameworks for CEP development to move us in this direction.

References

Adichie, C. N. (2009). The danger of a single story [Video]. TED Conferences. www.ted.com/talks/chimamanda_ngozi_adichie_the_danger_of_a_single_story. Source: https://wr1ter.com/how-to-cite-a-ted-talk-in-apa

Ahmed, S. (2010). Feminist Killjoys (and Other Willful Subjects). *Scholar and Feminist Online*. http://sfonline.barnard.edu/polyphonic/print_ahmed.htm

Baldwin, D. L. (2021). *In the shadow of the ivory tower: How universities are plundering our cities*. Hachette UK.

Benenson, J., Hemer, K. M., & Trebil, K. (2017). Supporting student civic learning and development. In L. D. Dostilio (Ed.), *The community engagement professional in higher education: A competency model for an emerging field* (pp. 139–160). Stylus Publishing, LLC.

Bleasdale, J. (n.d.). *Flip the table feminism*. Bleasdale Educational Research and Consulting. https://janebleasdale.com/flip-the-table-feminism/

Boyer, E. L. (1996). The scholarship of engagement. *Bulletin of the American Academy of Arts and Sciences, 49*(7), 18–33.

Bringle, R. G., Hatcher, J. A., & Clayton, P. H. (Eds.). (2013). *Research on service learning: Conceptual frameworks and assessments: Students and faculty* (Vol. 3). Stylus Publishing, LLC.

Brown, A. M. (2017). *Emergent strategy: shaping change, changing worlds*. AK Press.

Carnegie Foundation for the Advancement of Teaching. (2023). *Community engagement elective classification*. https://carnegieclassifications.acenet.edu/elective-classifications/community-engagement/

Chamberlin, J. S., & Phelps-Hillen, J. (2017). Competencies community engagement professionals need for faculty development. In L. D. Dostilio (Ed.), *The community engagement professional in higher education: A competency model for an emerging field* (pp. 179–200). Stylus Publishing, LLC.

Collins, P. H. (1989). The social construction of black feminist thought. *Signs: Journal of Women in Culture and Society, 14*(4), 745–773.

Crenshaw, K. (1989). Demarginalizing the intersection of race and sex: A black feminist critique of antidiscrimination doctrine, feminist theory and antiracist politics. *University of Chicago Legal Forum, 1989*(1), 139–167.

Crenshaw, K. (1991). Mapping the margins: Intersectionality, identity politics, and violence against women of color. *Stanford Law Review, 43*(6), 1241–1299.

Cruz, N. (1990). *Principles of good practice in combining service and learning: A diversity perspective.* Author.

De Saxe, J. (2012). Conceptualizing critical feminist theory and emancipatory education. *Journal for Critical Education Policy Studies, 10*(2), 183–201.

Dewey, J. (1986). Experience and education. *Educational Forum, 50,* 241–252. https://doi.org/10.1080/00131728609335764

Dostilio, L. D. (Ed.). (2017). *The community engagement professional in higher education: A competency model for an emerging field.* Stylus Publishing, LLC.

Farmer-Hanson, A. J. (2017). Program administration and evaluation. In L. D. Dostilio (Ed.), *The community engagement professional in higher education: A competency model for an emerging field* (pp. 79–97). Stylus Publishing, LLC.

Freire, P. (1970). *Pedagogy of the oppressed.* Seabury Press.

hooks, b. (2003). *Teaching community: A pedagogy of hope* (Vol. 36). Psychology Press.

hooks, b. (2014). *Teaching to transgress: Education as the practice of freedom.* Routledge.

Hübler, R., & Quan, M. (2017). Envisioning, leading, and enacting institutional change for the public good. In L. D. Dostilio (Ed.), *The community engagement professional in higher education: A competency model for an emerging field* (pp. 98–117). Stylus Publishing, LLC.

Iverson, S., & James, J. (Eds.). (2014). *Feminist community engagement: Achieving praxis.* Springer.

James, J. H., & Iverson, S. V. D. (2014). Conclusions: Re-visioning community engagement as feminist praxis. In S. Iverson & J. James (Eds.), *Feminist community engagement: Achieving praxis.* Springer.

Lorde, A. (Ed.). (2007). The transformation of silence into language and action. *Sister outsider: Essays and speeches by Audre Lorde* (pp. 40–44). Crossing Press.

Lorde, A., & Rich, A. (1981). An Interview with Audre Lorde. *Signs: Journal of Women in Culture and Society, 6*(4), 713–736.

Martin, L., & Crossland, S. (2017). High quality community–campus partnerships: Approaches and competencies. In L. D. Dostilio (Ed.), *The community engagement professional in higher education: A competency model for an emerging field* (pp. 161–178). Stylus Publishing, LLC.

Mitchell, T. D. (2008). Traditional vs. critical service-learning: Engaging the literature to differentiate two models. *Michigan Journal of Community Service Learning, 14*(2), 50–65.

Paperson, L. (2017). *A third university is possible.* University of Minnesota Press.

Plaxton-Moore, P. S. (2021). *Engaging feminism, transforming institutions: How community engagement professionals employ critical feminist praxis to re-imagine and re-shape the public purpose of higher education* [Doctoral dissertation]. University of San Francisco.

Rich, A. (1977). *Claiming an Education* [Convocation speech]. Douglass College. www.yorku.ca/cvandaal/files/ClaimingAnEducation.pdf

Saltmarsh, J., Janke, E. M., & Clayton, P. H. (2015). Transforming higher education through and for democratic civic engagement: A model for change. *Michigan Journal of Community Service Learning*, 22(1), 122–127.

Santiago-Ortiz, J. D. (2019). From critical to decolonizing service-learning: Limits and possibilities to social justice-based approaches to community service learning. *Michigan Journal of Community Service Learning*, 25(1), 43–54.

Schön, D. A. (1983). *The reflective practitioner: How professionals think in action.* Basic Books.

Sharma, G. (2017). Pros and cons of different sampling techniques. *International Journal of Applied Research*, 3(7), 749–752.

Spooner, M. & McNinch, J. (Eds.). (2018). *Dissident knowledge in higher education* (pp. 235–251). University of Regina Press.

Tuck, E. (2009). Suspending damage: A letter to communities. *Harvard Educational Review*, 79(3), 409–428.

Verjee, B. & Butterwick, S. (2014). Conversations from within: Critical race feminism and the roots/routes of change. In S. Iverson & J. James (Eds.), *Feminist community engagement: Achieving praxis.* Springer.

Ward, E. C. (2010). *Women's ways of engagement: An exploration of gender, the scholarship of engagement and institutional rewards policy and practice.* (Publication No. 3420073). Doctoral Dissertation, University of Massachusetts Boston. Proquest Dissertations and Theses Global.

Weaver, L. & Kellogg, B. T. (2017). Attributes of community engagement professionals seeking to institutionalize community–campus engagement. In L. D. Dostilio (Ed.), *The community engagement professional in higher education: A competency model for an emerging field* (pp. 118–138). Stylus Publishing.

Yep, K. S. & Mitchell, T. D. (2017). Decolonizing community engagement: Reimagining service learning through an ethnic studies lens. In C. Dolgon, T. D. Mitchell, & T. K. Eatman (Eds.), *The Cambridge handbook of service learning and community engagement* (pp. 294–303). Cambridge University Press.

Appendix A
Critical Feminist Principles for Community Engagement

I grounded my research in critical feminist theory and praxis, synthesizing a set of guiding principles for critical feminist praxis that shaped my research questions, research design, data collection, and data analysis

- Commitment to uplift and advance equity for women of diverse identities (Bleasdale, n.d.; Crenshaw, 1991; hooks, 2015a, 2015b)
- Focus on building equitable and mutually fulfilling relationships (Bleasdale, n.d.; hooks, 2015a, 2015b; Lorde, 2007; Lorde & Rich, 1981; Ward, 2010)
- Recognize the importance of context in shaping one's experiences and possibilities (Bleasdale, n.d.; hooks, 2003; Iverson & James, 2014; Lorde & Rich, 1981; Ward, 2010)

- Employ intersectional analysis, or an examination of how systems of power and oppression overlap to disproportionately affect particular identity groups (Collins, 1989, Crenshaw, 1989, 1991, hooks, 2015a, 2015b, Verjee & Butterwick, 2014)
- Seek opportunities to challenge unjust practices, policies, and systems (Ahmed, 2010; Bleasdale, n.d.; de Saxe, 2012; Lorde, 2007; Lorde & Rich, 1981; Rich, 1977; Verjee & Butterwick, 2014)
- Center and value the voices of individuals and groups that have historically been excluded (Ahmed, 2010; Bleasdale, n.d.; Collins, 1989; Crenshaw, 1989, 1991; Lorde, 2007, Verjee & Butterwick, 2014)
- Engage in self-reflection, including a cycle of praxis that involves synthesis of theory and action (Ahmed, 2010; Collins, 1989; hooks, 2003; Lorde, 2007; Verjee & Butterwick, 2014)
- Work in coalition with others to affect change that leads to greater equity and justice, particularly (but not exclusively) for women (Bleasdale, n.d.; Collins, 1989; hooks, 2015a, 2015b; Lorde & Rich, 1981; Ward, 2010)

Appendix B
Bibliography of Suggested Critical Feminist Readings

Ahmed, S. (2010). Feminist Killjoys (and other willful subjects). *Scholar and Feminist Online.* http://sfonline.barnard.edu/polyphonic/print_ahmed.htm

Brown, A. M. (2017). *Emergent strategy: shaping change, changing worlds.* AK Press.

Collins, P. H. (1989). The social construction of black feminist thought. *Signs: Journal of Women in Culture and Society, 14*(4), 745–773.

Crenshaw, K. (1989). Demarginalizing the intersection of race and sex: A black feminist critique of antidiscrimination doctrine, feminist theory and antiracist politics. *University of Chicago Legal Forum, 1989*(1), 139–167.

Crenshaw, K. (1991). Mapping the margins: Intersectionality, identity politics, and violence against women of color. *Stanford Law Review, 43*(6), 1241–1299.

hooks, b. (2003). *Teaching community: A pedagogy of hope* (Vol. 36). Psychology Press.

hooks, b. (2014). *Teaching to transgress: Education as the practice of freedom.* Routledge.

hooks, b. (2015a). *Feminist theory: From margin to center.* Routledge.

hooks, b. (2015b). *Feminism is for everybody: Passionate politics.* Routledge.

Lorde, A. (2007). Sister outsider: Essays and speeches by Audre Lorde. Crossing Press.

Yosso, T. J. (2005). Whose culture has capital? A critical race theory discussion of community cultural wealth. *Race Ethnicity and Education, 8*(1), 69–91.

4

RECLAIMING THE MISSION OF THE COMMUNITY COLLEGE

Civic, Community, and Political Equity Reimagined

Patricia D. Robinson and Verdis LeVar Robinson

Introduction to the Authors

Patty's Story

I am a product of the community college and I believe in its power to shape students and their future goals, aspirations, and accomplishments. I grew up as an only child in a White, middle-class household in the Central Valley of California, a region shaped by agriculture, oil, and the 1930's Dust Bowl Okie migration, guided by my parents' love, desire, and sacrifice to see me succeed. They had experienced the Great Depression, witnessed the atrocities of World War II, and followed the American Dream in the 1940s to California. Like many postwar American families, my parents recognized the importance of being civically involved. My father was a civil servant who took part in voluntary associations, including the Lions, Kiwanis, Masons, and Shriners, not to mention the Navy Reserve, and our church. My mother was more politically engaged, volunteering to work for political campaigns, serving in the women's auxiliary of my dad's work, and actively participating in union work with the telephone company before leaving the workforce to raise me. Neither of my parents went to college, but they believed in American democracy and equality for all–values they instilled in me. Although ardent supporters of education, they had no experience navigating higher education; and, as a result, I entered a community college.

I never realized how much these experiences shaped my perspective of democracy until years later. While waiting for a meeting to begin, I stood with three women who identified as Hispanic, one of whom I was meeting

DOI: 10.4324/9781003448525-5

for the first time. As we introduced ourselves, she asked me how I had gotten into the work of civic engagement and I told my story, much like above. I emphasized the importance of getting involved and giving back, as it was the way I had learned to make a difference through the democratic process. When I finished talking, she asked, "So, democracy worked for your family?" I, of course, provided a resounding, "Yes, it did." Puzzled by her question, I thought, "Why wouldn't it have worked for my family? Democracy works for everyone." It was at that moment that she stated softly, "Democracy didn't work for my family." It was at this moment I realized that my belief and value of democracy existing for all was a myth, not a reality. The need to create a democracy representative of all is my personal priority, while fostering a campus-wide civic engagement initiative is my academic imperative.

College of the Canyons' Civic and Community Engagement Initiative

College of the Canyons (COC) is a 2-year community college in Santa Clarita, California located in North Los Angeles County. It is 1 of 116 colleges which comprise the California Community College (CCC) system. During the 2019–2020 academic year, COC served over 33,000 students, and over 65% of these students belonged to a racial or ethnic minority group of traditionally under represented students (CCCCO, 2022a).

As a result of a 2013–2014 Bringing Theory to Practice Seminar Grant awarded to COC entitled *Civics in Action: Recognizing College of the Canyons' Obligation to Self and Society*, Dr. Dianne G. Van Hook, Chancellor, Santa Clarita Community College District, and President, College of the Canyons, has committed to make civic engagement a campus-wide initiative. The $1,000 grant supported a day-long workshop in spring 2014 examining the concept of civic engagement. I gathered much information from participants (e.g., students, faculty, staff, administrators, and guests), including data collected from a campus Civic Engagement Gap Analysis and Civic Engagement S.W.O.T. Analysis. The strengths, weakness, opportunities, and threats (S.W.O.T.) analysis eventually assisted with the strategic planning of the new initiative. A team visited De Anza College in Northern California that fall and met with students, staff, and the then president, Dr. Brian Murphy. De Anza College was a logical starting point, given its long and accomplished history of addressing civic and community engagement. Based on the resulting report, Dr. Van Hook received a report of the visit, along with a concept paper suggesting the plan to create a campus-wide civic engagement initiative. By spring 2015, our Chancellor, approved establishing a Center for Civic Engagement and creating the position of faculty director, Civic and Community Engagement Initiatives.

As inaugural faculty director, I organized a steering committee and set forth to advance a civic-minded campus culture. After scouring the literature and developing a strategic plan, with little to guide me, I conducted an extensive literature review, combed websites, and examined 2- and 4-year college and university civic engagement departments and programs. I developed a strategic plan, *A Call to Action: An Initiative for Civic Engagement, Self, and Society* (Robinson, 2015), and submitted it to Dr. Van Hook on August 1, 2015, the official start date of the position. The initiative follows the tenets of the seminal work *A Crucible Moment: College Learning and Democracy's Future (2012)* and emphasizes the need to infuse aspects of civic engagement throughout the campus milieu. My decision to attend the 2016 Civic Learning and Democratic Engagement (CLDE) Annual Conference provided a plethora of networking opportunities. This is where I first met Verdis LeVar Robinson, then National Director of The Democracy Commitment, and we instantly formed a personal and professional bond based on our shared values of civic equity.

Verdis' Story

I became a registered voter at the age of 30 years. I was an adjunct instructor of history and African American studies at a large community college in Western New York, and I was finishing a second master's degree in African American Studies. It was 2008 and despite my knowledge in teaching about our democracy, I felt disenfranchised. I believed that my voice did not matter, and my vote did not matter. I was not alone. The majority of my students believed as well that our participation did not matter. Historically, my race has been disenfranchised. With the prospects that in my lifetime I could see a Black president elected, and with my growing role as an educational leader, I was convinced that I was, in essence, disenfranchising myself. In fact, because I did not participate, my voice and vote did not matter.

So, that year, I made an agreement with my students, turning electoral engagement into a service-learning project leading up to the 2008 elections. Using subcommittees and projects, my students and I engaged in the election. We registered ourselves and others; we educated ourselves and others on the ballot and candidate information; we presented what we learned in our history and what we had researched publicly; we rallied for registration and commitments to vote; we hosted a Rock-the-Vote dance party on campus with local candidates; and on election day, we voted—some of us—for the very first time in our lives. The day after the election, we celebrated in class—not just that our candidates were victorious but that we, as voters, most importantly as individuals who had exercised our right to express our views, were victorious. We engaged in the election and overturned our own disenfranchisement. After reflecting on our project, the students asked for what's next as they were empowered to change themselves and the community around them through their own actions instead of being oppressed and depressed in their inactions. Every following semester, I engaged my students in civic learning and civic action, building their civic power. Many of whom continued their engagement beyond my classroom. This journey in finding various ways to engage my students in civic action and building civic power has allowed me to lead these efforts nationally.

The Role of the Community College

Community college students are the face of America today and they represent the voice of America tomorrow. They are the students who live in our communities and witness social, cultural, and economic injustices first-hand and hold established relationships with community partners related to racial, ethnic, religious, sexual orientation, or political affiliation. They reflect the pulse of their communities, which go beyond physical locales, to provide a collective body of change agents. Given the opportunity to problem-solve local issues that most affect them, especially through real-world, project-based learning (PBL), as teams, not as individuals, democratic engagement becomes embedded in the learning process, and an ethos of Diversity, Equity, and Inclusion (DEI) automatically permeates this process. Community colleges are well situated to provide our country's most vulnerable student populations innovative, holistic, and integrative pedagogies that promote active citizens who, through collective action with campus and community, engage in real-world problem-solving of today's most pressing *wicked* problems (Rittel & Webber, 1973) to reimagine American democracy. The community college system can help reimagine American democracy by building a strong, organized civic engagement movement that embeds civic learning and democratic engagement to confront the "civic empowerment gap" (Levinson, 2010, 2012). Through real-world projects associated with local communities, community colleges can redefine teaching and learning to use personal narratives and collective relationship-building to examine social problems.

Democracy's College and Its Civic Mission

The civic health of America is in crisis. Divisiveness and hatred are tearing apart the seams of democracy, as civic learning, and democratic engagement decline. This chapter returns to the moniker "Democracy's Colleges" which quickly identified those academic institutions, especially community colleges, that would advance the 1947 President's Commission's key recommendation following World War II. According to the recommendation, "The first and most essential charge upon higher education is that at all levels and in all fields of specialization, it shall be the carrier of democratic values, ideals, and processes" to a large swath of the American population (Zook, 1947/2015, p. 102). In 2006, writers such as Ira Harkavy again suggested America needs to return to the "core mission" of "effectively educating students to be democratic, creative, caring, constructive citizens of a democratic society" (Harkavy, 2006, p. 5). For those of us in the community college system, this means broadening the mission, purpose, and priority of America's community colleges from access, completion, inclusion, and workforce readiness to include civic learning and democratic engagement. "It is time to bring two national priorities-career preparation and increased access and completion rates together," suggests the National Task Force on Civic Learning and Democratic Engagement, "in a more comprehensive vision with a third national priority: fostering informed, engaged, responsible citizens" (National Task Force on Civic Learning and Democratic Engagement, 2012, p. 13).

Colleges and universities can provide "public spaces" to engage in open dialogue, constructive deliberation, and participatory action in a free and safe environment to help mend our tattered democracy. Community colleges, in particular, are academic settings uniquely embedded in their local communities where collaborative problem-solving of today's issues can take place through "public work" (Boyte & Kari, 1996; Boyte, 2014). Higher education now recognizes the organizational strength of the nation's 1,044 community colleges and understands how they reflect the racial, ethnic, and socioeconomic diversity of the country. Indeed, our almost 12 million students can build back democracy to represent an equitable, just, and representative republic (AACC Fast Facts, 2022; see also CLDE Coalition, 2022).

Community Colleges

California

The California Community College (CCC) system comprises 116 colleges (CCCCO, 2022b); and, of this number, 67% classify as Hispanic Serving Institutions (Federally-Designated HSIs, 2021). CCCs comprise 73 college districts and served 2.2 million students during the 2020–2021 academic year, most of whom were first-generation and students of color. This figure has dropped to 1.8 million in 2022 (CCCCO, 2022c). The racial and ethnic composition of CCC students in 2020–2021 included 45.7% Hispanic, 24.1% White, 11.5% Asian, 5.6% African American, .33% American Indian/Alaskan Native, 2.84% Filipino, .41% Pacific Islander, 4.3% Multi-Ethnic, and 4.1% noted as ethnicity unknown (CCCCO, 2022a).

Democratic Learning, Civic Engagement, and Liberal Education

Democratic learning and civic engagement have depended on the knowledge, skills, and dispositions created from the liberal arts; or what is commonly referred to as a liberal education. The word liberal originates from the Latin word "liber" which means "free" or to "liberate." A liberal education, according to historian William Cronon, "celebrates and nurtures human freedom" (Cronon, 1998, p. 1), as well as emphasizes a broad knowledge of skills, values, and ethics. He lists ten qualities of a liberal education to allow one to listen and hear different voices; to nurture and empower others; and to recognize and understand the intersectionality of people, places, and artifacts, as they provide meaning-making in everyday life (Cronon, 1998).

Unfortunately, in today's neoliberal environment, civic learning and democratic engagement compete with job preparation and the civic mission of higher education often takes a backseat. When recognized, civic learning and democratic engagement are most often associated with voter engagement or volunteerism. Few highlight the importance of building citizenship skills to foster the public good. However, according to Barbara Jacoby and her associates (Jacoby & Associates, 2009, p. 2):

> If civic engagement is to gain real traction in today's higher education, it must be clearly defined, and civic learning outcomes must be established. Opportunities to learn about and practice civic engagement must be embedded throughout the curriculum and the co curriculum.

The traditional model of American higher education fails to meet the demands of a declining democracy riddled with social problems. As Ernest Boyer suggested over two decades ago, many college graduates are ill equipped to serve as democratic citizens, often lacking the basic foundations of citizenship. "The campus is being viewed as a place where students get credentialed and faculty get tenured," he stated and "the overall work of the academy does not seem relevant to the nation's most pressing civic, social, economic, and moral problems" (Boyer, 1996, p. 19). If campus stakeholders can recognize the intersection of civic learning and democratic engagement with the leading initiatives guiding today's community colleges, including workforce/economic development, completion/pathways, access/equity/

inclusion, and assessment/accreditation, campus leaders and civic-minded practitioners can visibly, strategically, and purposefully incorporate civic learning and democratic engagement throughout the campus culture (Robinson, 2020a).

Civic engagement promotes an awareness of today's social problems and encourages action, while civic education provides the tools to foster social change. Thomas Ehrlich, a former Carnegie Foundation Senior Scholar, provides the most widely cited definition of civic engagement in higher education states:

> Civic engagement means working to make a difference in the civic life of our communities and developing the combination of knowledge, skills, values and motivation to make that difference. It means promoting the quality of life in a community, through both political and non-political processes.
>
> *(Ehrlich, 2000:vi)*

The concept of civic engagement remains unrestricted; its knowledge, skills, and activities do not presuppose one academic discipline over another. The term reflects *civic* is not limited to political engagement only, nor to community service or volunteerism. (See the Latin term *Civitas*, relating to citizen, citizenship, and community.) While the definition of civic engagement may encompass a variety of terms, including service-learning, community engagement, political engagement, etc.), it involves an abundance of moving parts, including knowledge, skills, actions, activities, values, and behaviors (Lawry, 2009, pp. 23–24). No matter the term, the goal of civic engagement in education is to engage in skills, attitudes, and actions that foster American democracy.

Civic Gaps and Community College Students

Given the disruptions that continue to affect campuses, communities, and the nation including the COVID-19 pandemic, racial unrest, and economic divides, not to mention the threat to the sanctity of the Supreme Court and potential world war, American democracy is moving toward an untenable state. This is concerning as many, especially the young, express less interest in the fundamental foundations of democracy, as well as the traditional values that have driven American society. Some argue that democracy is at a tipping point, while others suggest a turning point. By revisiting the original mission of Democracy's College, community colleges can foster a "civic minded" campus culture (National Task Force on Civic Learning and Democratic Engagement, 2012, p. 15) and reclaim the voice of democracy for the new generation committed to social change for the public good.

The civic opportunity gap (Levine, 2009); or, specifically, what Harvard educational philosopher Meira Levinson terms the "civic empowerment gap" (Levinson, 2010, 2012) is most pronounced among underserved communities resulting from disparities rooted in systemic inequities that have resulted in groups feeling disillusioned, cynical, and uninterested in civic learning and democratic engagement. Participatory democracy is least understood, valued, and practiced by those individuals whose needs are most ignored and their communities most disadvantaged by decisions not reflective of their collective experiences, perspectives, or opinions. As a result, many community college students who experience the civic empowerment gap, whether entering college for the first time or completing a degree or certificate, lack economic, social, and political capital, all of which disenfranchise them from democracy.

Higher education is now recognizing how community colleges can impact the future of democracy, as well as address issues of "civic equity" and "civic inclusion" by embedding civic learning and democratic engagement into the mission, vision, and strategic plans of 2-year institutions. As Eduardo Padrón, President Emeritus of Miami Dade College, states, "We fail as a society if we treat civic education as a luxury rather than an essential public good." He suggests that today is a "watershed moment for the community college movement, as a new generation can rebuild our democracy" (Padrón, 2021). In their work with DEI, community colleges must address civic equity as the overarching catalyst to accomplish long-lasting social change beyond the confines of the academic institution. In order to remedy the fragility of our democracy, community colleges must teach students, no matter their class, race, ethnicity, gender, religion, or major, how to understand, influence, and engage in social action. By engaging college students in civic equity, especially those marginalized, stigmatized, or disenfranchised from the social and political arena, they will embody the knowledge, skills, behaviors, and attitudes to make a difference.

A Pedagogy of Civic Equity

Civic equity is about empowerment and making long-term, institutional, and structural change. A civic equity model questions privilege and breaks down barriers while asking questions, confronting power relationships, and "calling out" inequitable practices. This model involves recognizing personal and institutional values, missions, and goals and determining whether they reflect civic equity; involves practicing culturally responsive teaching; and creates an equity mindset, including engagement, cultural identity, relationships, vulnerability, assets, and rigor (Stembridge, 2020).

Boyer (1990, p. 6) states that "education for citizenship means helping students make connections between what they learn and how they live." According to Rogers (2019), addressing civic equity "requires closing the book on White-norming" when discussing civic participation and the civic engagement "gap," which assumes that people of color lack civic knowledge, skills, agency, or traditions. Currently, community colleges are not "set up" to listen to individual stories nor to consider holistic approaches that confront a traditional hierarchical system that perpetuates a system of teaching and learning that may no longer best educate a new generation of students. However, if colleges can emphasize completion, DEI, and the workforce within the larger context of civic learning, community participation, and democratic engagement, higher education can address the civic mission of Democracy's College.

Completion, DEI, and Workforce and the Civic Mission of Democracy's College

As California Community Colleges work to increase completion and transfer rates, especially among students of color, Guided Pathways dominates the academic landscape. Campuses across the state are implementing ways to address the four pillars: 1) Clarify the Path, 2) Enter the Path, 3) Stay on the Path, and 4) Ensure Learning (Bailey et al., 2015). Many students from marginalized backgrounds long to realize their passion by exploring their purpose in authentic, real-world curricular and cocurricular learning environments that emphasize their unique identities, talents, and experiences to make a difference. Generation Z students, in particular, want to experience transformation that goes beyond obtaining a degree to create sociopolitical change (Seemiller & Grace, 2018). By aligning DEI with the broader concept of civic engagement, civic learning and democratic engagement can advance. This is especially important as alliances are formed, multicultural centers created, and antiracist policies approved. This alignment encourages what Paulo Freire (2017/1970) termed critical consciousness, whereby one steps back and examines their place within the larger social world as well as identifies the systemic problem. Reflection can lead to action and encourage students from diverse backgrounds, perspectives, and histories to work collectively to address social issues and create a civic-minded campus culture that aspires to diversity, equity, and social justice.

In addition, workforce training is a perfect setting to prepare students for democratic participation. Civic learning is not only "compatible with career preparation and improved graduation rates," but it is the foundation of creating successful employees and citizens (U.S. Department of Education, 2012, p. 21). When aspects of civic learning and democratic engagement are incorporated into workforce training, students understand their social responsibility to the larger good. They became stewards of their campus and community. So, why not aim for "college, career, *and* civic readiness?" (Levine & Kawashima-Ginsberg, 2015)?

A Need to Create an Integrative, Holistic Learning Model

Whether through transfer or career education courses, real-world PBL places students in learning environments that welcome their diverse personal histories, experiences, and identities. Combined with the freedom to problem-solve using design thinking through action teams, students enter situations where they dialogue, deliberate, and find common ground based on opposing opinions, conflicting values, and differing beliefs. Based on the work of the Stanford Design School (also referred to as the Stanford d.School), students learn to work collaboratively to analyze real-world problems using a "maker's mentality," which 1) emphasizes the problem experienced by the group, 2) defines the exact problem of your community, 3) ideates solutions to the problem, 4) creates a prototype of how to solve the problem, and 5) tests a solution (Stanford d.School, n.d.; Provenzano, 2018). This work relates to the Buck Institute's PBL's *Gold Standard: Project Design Elements*, which emphasizes: 1) challenging problem(s) or question(s), 2) sustained inquiry, 3) authenticity, 4) student voice and choice, 5) reflection, 6) critique and revision, and 7) public product (Buck Institute for Education, 2015). This model works well for transdisciplinary teaching and learning and encourages action research, power analysis, social entrepreneurism, and asset-based community development. Expectations include students listen to diverse thoughts, respect opposing viewpoints, and discuss differences in a thoughtful, respectful, and civil manner. In doing so, not only are students taking part in participatory democracy, but they are also addressing civic equity by encouraging all voices to speak and to act.

Impactful DEI change comes from fostering relational connections, especially with those whose life histories, experiences, and identities differ from one's own. Narrative inquiry, storytelling, and story sharing are effective ways to advance social change, especially as students engage in relationship-building based on similarities, not differences, and confront social issues together, not alone. Story sharing is a valuable technique for building relationships for organizing; or, in this case, identifying common values, passions, and purposes. Personal stories build trust and accountability and often lead to sociopolitical action (Avila, 2018).

Two Stories, One Civic Engagement Path

Reimagining Teaching and Learning

Our nation can no longer rely on an outdated, bureaucratic system of higher education that teaches concepts of democracy yet does not engage students in democracy. Our suggestion of a redefined teaching and learning model includes embedding civic learning and democratic engagement throughout the academic experience to align the current priorities of the California Community College System (FCCC, 2017). One way to achieve this goal is to embed inquiry-based learning through curricular and cocurricular integrative pedagogies to help students better master creativity, collaboration, communication, and critical thinking. These are, in fact, the skills desired by employers (Hart Research Associates, 2018; Finley, 2021). The overarching pedagogy of integrative project-based learning (PBL) builds campus community alliances by encouraging students to consult, collaborate, and work with local partners, regional organizations, or national associations to coeducate learning, cocreate solutions, and coproduce outcomes (Wobbe & Stoddard, 2019). Student-centered practices that encourage transdisciplinary responses to America's *wicked* problems (Hanstedt, 2018) strengthen collaborative campus-community partnerships that foster active, coproducers of knowledge, innovation, and change (Mathews, 2020). Intentionally establishing learning spaces that focus on dialogue, deliberation, and collaboration builds trust, which results in problem-solving for the larger whole and transcends outcomes from "me" to "we". This addresses citizenship education and examines concerns posed by Boyer (1996) who suggested that many college graduates are ill equipped to serve as democratic citizens, often lacking the basic foundations of citizenship (Flores & Rogers, 2019).

Reinvesting in Democracy's College

Democracy remains challenged, but community colleges can lead the way in higher education to meet the obligation to foster greater civic learning and democratic engagement. Community colleges offer spaces where students, faculty, and the community work together to collaborate, listen, and learn from each other through public work. When students "co-create" solutions to social problems, they engage in public work that coproduces outcomes for the public good (Boyte, 2014; Boyte & Scarnati, 2014, p. 78). Together, civic actors contribute to the betterment of the campus, community, or nation, reminiscent of the "people's college" that encourages appreciation for the people, but also with the people (Witt, et al., 1994, p. 43). In fact, as Caryn McTighe Musil, lead author of *A Crucible Moment: College Learning and Democracy's Future* (2012), states, "Community colleges have the potential to be civic dynamos" (Musil, 2021).

We reject models in which students bank knowledge that is imparted by the faculty "experts"; and, as a result, student voices remain unheard, life experiences unshared, and talents unexplored (Freire, 2017/1970). Thus, we look forward to codeveloping modes of engagement grounded in student's own lived experiences. Unlike conventional teaching and learning models, those of us who adhere to a pedagogy of liberation (Freire 2017/1970) reject a deficit perspective that requires faculty to "repair" student flaws and serve as the sole producers of knowledge. We reject a system where information is siloed and is the "property" of one discipline over another. A redefined model encourages educators to recognize the assets that each student brings to the classroom and builds upon their abilities to engage in real-world problem-solving. Collaborative teamwork and deliberative problem-solving build relationships and solutions that transcend disciplines. When students cocreate knowledge with others, unheard voices continue to change, and the invisible becomes visible. Personal story sharing builds relationships and engages diverse groups in civic learning and democratic engagement.

How Have We Engaged Others?

Our combined work has involved various ways to engage community college students in real-world teaching and learning, as well as to establish partnerships to advance opportunities for faculty, campus, and community. This has included Verdis' positions serving various roles with national organizations as a community college civic learning and democratic engagement specialist, and, for Patty, leaving administration to serve as COC's Faculty Director, Civic and Community Engagement Initiatives.

National Example

The impact of the COVID pandemic on community colleges has been severe. In educating 39% of the country's undergraduates in 2020, and because of a declining enrollment trend, community colleges were already stretched thin before the pandemic (AACC, 2022). While community colleges are ramping up their promotional materials with messages of safe, cost-saving, remote learning, they are also promoting the fact that they are well situated to train workers for a new and emerging economy. However, the larger and more urgent role of the community college is to address its commitment to the "civic mission" of higher education, which, unfortunately, is often ignored to support workforce training. Community colleges have proven that they are still especially well positioned to harness the need and desire to develop ways to benefit their communities and, at the same time, deepen the educational experience of their students who come from the local community. One way that community colleges have been innovative is in deliberative pedagogy.

Deliberative pedagogy is a democratic educational process and a way of thinking that encourages students to encounter and consider multiple perspectives, weigh trade-offs and tensions, and move toward action through informed judgment. It is simultaneously a way of teaching that is itself deliberative and a process for developing the skills, behaviors, and values that support deliberative practice. Perhaps most important, the work of deliberative pedagogy is about space-making: creating and holding space for authentic and productive dialogue, conversations that can ultimately be not only educational but also transformative (Shaffer et al., 2017). In response to the pandemic, some community colleges have not only embraced deliberative pedagogy but adapted it for the new virtual educational wave that the pandemic ushered in. They were able to engage students and the community advancing deliberative democracy virtually through Zoom and other means. One example includes the virtual dialogues organized by COC's Partnerships for Listening and Action by Communities and Educators (PLACE) and Engage the Vote Action Teams that examined the topic of *Defining Freedom* for Constitution Day. The Kettering Foundation, a nonprofit operating foundation rooted in the American tradition of cooperative research, which focuses its gaze on what it takes to make democracy work, is currently engaged with community colleges across the country. The report of these activities and innovations is forthcoming (Robinson, 2020b, pp. 62–97).

Patty's Campus Examples

College of the Canyons has recognized and leveraged opportunities for democratic engagement and collaborative partnerships. Our Center for Civic Engagement (CCE) has grown through taking part in networking, training, and grant opportunities combined with building regional and national collaborative partnerships. The CCE has worked with many diverse groups over the past few years, including the Kettering Foundation and ALL IN Campus Democracy Challenge. The Kettering Foundation advocates the role of dialogue and deliberation in advancing democracy. Although it provides valuable resources on its website, it is also closely aligned with the work of the National Issues Forums (NIF) which has created scores of issue guides exploring a wide variety of local, national, and global topics. These two organizations provide the perfect starting place to organize a campus dialogue. In addition, any campus promoting voter registration and education can benefit greatly by joining the ALL IN Campus Democracy Challenge. While focused on voter engagement, All In provides helpful resources to campuses working to increase voter participation, as well as encourages the development of campus vote action plans. As a participant of ALL IN, campuses also take part in Tufts University National Study of Learning, Voting, and Engagement (NSLVE) and receive an individual report detailing campus voter engagement after midterm and general elections. In addition, depending on the increase in campus engagement and "quality of vote plan," ALL IN campuses can receive nationwide recognition (Robinson, 2022).

More specifically, faculty development opportunities in project-based learning and integrative learning have occurred through multiple teams taking part in the annual Worcester Polytechnic Institute (WPI) Project-Based Learning Institute and Association of American Colleges and Universities (AAC&U) Integrative Learning and Signature Work Institute (renamed Institute on Engaged and Integrative Learning). Several grant awards by Bringing Theory to Practice (BT2P) have supported the initiative with one of its most recent being the intersegmental partnership between COC, Cerritos College, Los Angeles City College, Cal State Dominguez Hills, Cal State Los Angeles, and Cal State Northridge as part of *The Way Forward* grant. This group has created a state-wide Civic Dialogues series with California Community Colleges' Success Network (3CSN), the leading community college faculty development organization in California. Expanding on training by the Kettering Foundation, CCE has facilitated several campus community dialogues addressing topics like *The Nation We Want to Be, The Community We Want to Be, and The Citizen I Want to Be.* LEAD California has also provided support of over ten student fellows as part of its Community Engagement Student Fellows program. Voter engagement is a significant part of the Center's work and includes joining ALL IN Campus Democracy Challenge and receiving NSLVE data. This effort has also aligned the campus with the work of A Band of Voters by working closely with its founder and initiator of California Assembly Bill 963, Student Civic Engagement and Voter Empowerment Act, Joey Forsyte, to address its state-wide mandates for public institutions of higher education. The PLACE project, however, currently defines the signature work of the Center.

Culture Change at College of the Canyons

The PLACE project is part of a multiyear Mellon Foundation grant (see Scobey, 2022)[1] focusing on housing insecurity and affordability while highlighting the public humanities and pedagogical methods of dialogue, reflection, and problem-solving, as we examine this topic from the perspectives of student, faculty, staff, and community. Community partners include the Santa Clarita Valley (SCV) homeless shelter, Bridge to Home, SCV Senior Center, Bella Vida, City of Santa Clarita Homelessness Task Force—Housing Affordability Subcommittee, LoveSCV, COC's Basic Needs Center, known as The BaNC, and Los Angeles artist Deborah Aschheim. The project is especially interested in fostering personal storytelling and story sharing to address topics of community, belonging, and well-being. PLACE provides a new transdisciplinary, holistic, and student-centered model of teaching and learning that encourages civic equity, focusing on student interests, passions, and talents. Students envision project outcomes, design activities, and implement ideas, as two faculty coleads guide the PLACE Student Action Team. The PLACE project provides an example of transdisciplinary, civic-minded, action-influenced PBL that encourages design thinking and social entrepreneurism. The project's motto is *Our home. Our community. Our PLACE.* PLACE is grounded in a project-based learning pedagogy. For example, students have created two whimsical characters, "Sam and Alex," who embody the gender-neutral, all-inclusive vision of the students, as they address issues affecting housing insecurity and affordability. Sam and Alex have been portrayed in several mediums, including drawings and videos. Storylines use Sam and Alex to confront social stigma ranging from homelessness to mental health.

PLACE exemplifies a new model of integrative teaching and learning that is transdisciplinary, student centered, and designed to reflect coknowledge, cocreation, and coproduction of ideas and solutions between students, faculty, and community. As one student suggests:

> The PLACE project places an emphasis on student co-creation by allowing each student to nurture their projects and see them grow. This fosters confidence and allows others to learn through someone of a different demographic. Instead of the students simply learning, they can teach others as well. Allowing students to share their voices and participate in these projects makes it possible for them to ask questions and work on projects that can grow into something bigger. It enables the transformation of social issues and inspires growth from other students as well.
>
> *(Anonymous PLACE Student, 2022)*

The PLACE experience provides an example of "flipping" the traditional educational model from the "sage on the stage" to the "guide on the side."

Students take ownership of the problem as the instructor guides their work to problem-solve for local community solutions.

Conclusion

In order for Democracy's College to flourish, community colleges must consider avenues for change, including new and innovative ways to teach, learn, and define institutional priorities. Community colleges campuses must act with intentionality to encourage participatory democracy, dialogue, and deliberation through action research, design thinking, critical pedagogy, and asset-based community development (McKnight & Kretzmann, 1996; Stringer, 2007; Mitchell, 2008; Enos, 2015) as ways to solve today's *wicked* problems (Hanstedt, 2018). Institutional culture change will create civic equity, encourage inquiry, and strengthen association. Community colleges can position themselves to foster hope, innovation, and action (McBride & Mlyn, 2020; Stitzlein, 2020). They can also change the course of higher education by employing civic learning and democratic engagement using an integrative, holistic, and transdisciplinary model. Employing such a model will increase student success, encourage transformational experience, and foster participatory democracy through social entrepreneurism.

It is time to reexamine the current state of the civic mission of Democracy's College and assess the kinds of subjects offered, delivery styles provided, and to consider newer pedagogies that result in higher rates of student engagement, success, and completion. This means connecting campus to community in intentional and purposeful ways where students learn, research, and analyze local problems with community experts. To reclaim the civic mission of Democracy's Colleges, community colleges need to implement the core purposes of a liberal education identified by Charles Dewey (Hinchey, 2018) that stress the need to focus on the civic and combine experience and knowledge with social responsibility to ensure the well-being of society. If community colleges are ready to confront civic inequity head-on, they will assume their responsibility to prepare students with the knowledge, skills, and motivation to fulfill their roles as informed, responsible, and engaged citizens who experience purpose, pride, and passion for self, community, and nation. The well-being of the nation's future depends on the role of community colleges.

Note

1 David Scobey, Director, Bringing Theory to Practice, is the Principal Investigator of a 2022 Partnerships for Listening and Action by Communities and Educators (PLACE), a 2-year Mellon Foundation Grant project.

References

American Association of Community Colleges. (2022). *AACC 2022 Fast Facts*. American Association of Community Colleges.
Anonymous PLACE Student. (2022). *Personal reflection* [Unpublished manuscript]. PLACE Action Team Member, College of the Canyons.
Avila, M. (2018). *Transformative civic engagement through community organizing*. Stylus Publishing.
Bailey, T., Jaggars, S., & Jenkins, D. (2015). *Redesigning America's community colleges: A clearer path to student success*. Harvard University Press.
Boyer, E. (1990). *Scholarship reconsidered: Priorities of the professoriate*. The Carnegie Foundation for the Advancement of Teaching.
Boyer, E. (1996). The scholarship of engagement. *Journal of Public Service and Outreach*, 1(1), 11–21.
Boyte, H.C. (2014). *Democracy's education: Public work, citizenship, and the future of colleges and universities*. Vanderbilt University Press.
Boyte, H. C., & Kari, N. (1996). *Building America: The Democratic promise of public work*. Temple University Press.
Boyte, H., & Scarnati, B. (2014). Transforming higher education in a larger context: The civic politics of public work. In P. Levine & K. E. Soltan (Eds.), *Civic studies* (pp. 77–89). Bringing Theory to Practice Monographs.
California Community Colleges Chancellor's Office (CCCCO). (2022a). *Datamart*. https://datamart.cccco.edu/
California Community Colleges Chancellor's Office (CCCCO). (2022b). *Homepage*. www.cccco.edu/Students
California Community Colleges Chancellor's Office (CCCCO). (2022c). *Students*. www.cccco.edu/Students.
Civic Learning and Democracy Engagement Coalition (CLDE). (2022). *A CLDE briefing paper: Civic Learning and Democracy Engagement Coalition: Purpose, partnerships, and vision for students' democracy learning*. CLDE Coalition. https://static1.squarespace.com/static/62db01158612b042d7e0f5b8/t/6311666bf2b0df2fa3f2823d/1662084716508/The+CLDE+Coalition+-+July+2022+-+Goals+and+Priorities.pdf
Cronon, W. (Autumn 1998). "Only connect..." The goals of a liberal education. *The American Scholar*, 67(4), 73–80.
Ehrlich, T. (Ed.). (2000). *Civic responsibility and higher education*. Orynx Press.
Enos, S. L. (2015). *Service-learning and social entrepreneurship in higher education: A pedagogy of social change*. Palgrave Pivot.
Federally-Designated HSIs. (September 2021). *Federally-designated Hispanic serving institutions in California*. www.ucop.edu/graduate-studies/_files/list-of-ca-hsis.pdf
Finley, A. (2021). *How college contributes to workforce success: Employer views on what matters most*. Association of American Colleges and Universities.
Flores, W. V. & Rogers, K. S. (Eds.). (2019). *Democracy, civic engagement, and citizenship in higher education: Reclaiming our civic purpose*. Lexington Books.
Foundation for California Community Colleges (FCCC). (2017). *Vision for success: Strengthening the California community colleges to meet California's needs*. Foundation for California Community Colleges.

Freire, P. (2017/1970). *Pedagogy of the oppressed*. Penguin Press.
Hanstedt, P. (2018). *Creating wicked students: Designing courses for a complex world*. Stylus Publishing.
Harkavy, I. (2006). The role of universities in advancing citizenship and social justice in the 21st century. *Education, Citizenship and Social Justice, 1*(1), 5–37.
Hart Research Associates. (2018). *Fulfilling the American dream: Liberal education and the future of work selected findings from online surveys of business executives and hiring managers*. Association of American Colleges and Universities.
Hinchey, P. (2018). *Democracy and education by John Dewey: With a critical introduction by Patricia H. Hinchey*. Myers Education Press.
Jacoby, B. (2009). *Civic engagement in higher education: Concepts and practices*. John Wiley & Sons.
Larmer, J., Mergendoller, J. R., & Boss, S. (2015). *Gold standard PBL: Essential project design elements*. Buck Institute for Education, pp. 1–4.
Lawry, S. (2009). *Liberal education and civic engagement: A project of the Ford Foundation's knowledge, creativity and freedom program*. Ford Foundation.
Levine, P. (May 2009). The civic opportunity gap. *Teaching Social Responsibility, 66*(8), 20–25.
Levine, P. & Kawashima-Ginsberg, K. (2015). *Civic education and deeper learning*. Jobs for the Future.
Levinson, M. (2010). The civic empowerment gap: Defining the problem and locating solutions. In L. Sherrod, J. Torney-Purta, & C. A. Flanagan (Eds.), *Handbook of research on civic engagement* (pp. 331–361). John Wiley & Sons.
Levinson, M. (2012). *No citizen left behind*. Harvard University Press.
Mathews, D. (2020). *With the people: An introduction to an idea*. Kettering Foundation.
McBride, A. M. & Mlyn, E. (2020). *Connecting civic engagement and social innovation: Toward higher education's democratic promise*. Campus Compact.
McKnight, J.L. & Kretzmann, J.P. (1996). *Mapping community capacity (revised ed.)*. Institute for Policy Research, Northwestern University.
Mitchell, T. D. (2008). Traditional vs. critical service-learning: Engaging the literature to differentiate two models. *Michigan Journal of Community Service Learning*, Spring 2008, 50–65.
Musil, C. M. (2021). Personal conversation as part of a project in-progress by Patty Robinson and Verdis LeVar Robinson examining the civic mission of community colleges. September 10, 2021.
National Task Force on Civic Learning and Democratic Engagement. (2012). *A Crucible moment: College learning and Democracy's future*. American Colleges and Universities.
Padrón, E. (2021, June 23). Don't downplay the role of community colleges in healing a nation. *The Campus*. www.timeshighereducation.com/campus/dont-downplay-role-community-colleges-healing-nation
Provenzano, N. (2018). *The maker mentality*. Create Space Independent Publishing Platform.
Rittel, H. & Webber, M. (1973). Dilemmas in a general theory of planning. *Policy Sciences, 4*, 155–169.
Robinson, P. (2015). *A call to action: An initiative for civic engagement, self, and society*. College of the Canyons.
Robinson, P. (2022). *COC engage the vote action plan and report*. College of the Canyons.

Robinson, V. L. (2020a). Advancing institutional priorities through civic and community engagement. In V. L. Robinson & C. Hurd (Eds.), *Community colleges for democracy: Aligning civic and community engagement with institutional priorities* (pp. 1–7). Campus Compact.

Robinson, V. L. (2020b). Community college deliberative democracy and the pandemic: A conversation with community college civic engagement faculty. In D. W. M. Barker & A. Lovit (Eds.), *Higher Education Exchange 2020: Democracy divided* (pp. 62–97). Kettering Foundation.

Rogers, J. (2019). *An equitable approach to strengthening civic engagement*. The Center for Educational Equity, Teachers College, Columbia University. https://civxnow.org/wp-content/uploads/2021/09/J.-Rogers-Essay-on-Equity-in-Civic-Education_v.-2.26.19.pdf

Seemiller, C. & Grace, M. (2018). *Generation Z: A century in the making*. Routledge Press.

Shaffer, T. J., Longo, N. V., Manosevitch, I., Thomas, M. S. (2017). *Deliberative pedagogy: Teaching and learning for Democratic engagement* (Transformations in Higher Education). Michigan State Press.

Stanford d.School. (n.d.). *Get started with design thinking*. https://dschool.stanford.edu/resources/getting-started-with-design-thinking

Stembridge, A. (2020). *Culturally responsive education in the classroom: An equity framework for pedagogy*. Routledge, Taylor & Francis Group.

Stitzlein, S. (2020). *Learning how to hope: Reviving Democracy through our schools and civil society*. Oxford University Press.

Stringer, E. T. (2007). *Action research* (3rd ed.). SAGE Publications.

U.S. Department of Education. (2012). *Advancing civic learning and engagement in Democracy: A road map and call to action*. U.S. Department of Education.

Witt, A. A., Wattenbarger, J. L., Gollattscheck, J. F., & Suppiger, J.E. (1994). *America's community colleges: The first century*. Community College Press.

Wobbe, K. & Stoddard, E. A. (2019). *Project-based learning in the first year*. Stylus Publishing.

Zook, G. F. (2015). *Higher education for American democracy: A report of the president's commission on higher education* (Vols. I–VI). Facsimile Publisher. [Original work published 1947].

5

SOCIAL MEDIA AND YOUTH CLIMATE ACTIVISM

Community-Engaged Learning for the 2020s

Ellen Middaugh, Mark Felton, and Henry Fan

In September of 2019, in one of the largest youth-led movements in history, millions of protesters around the globe gathered in the streets to pressure their leaders to meet the demands of the #climatecrisis (Kaplan et al., 2019). In the past decade, an entire cohort of young climate change activists have emerged, using a combination of well-established tactics of protest, community action, fund-raising, and legal action to press for a coordinated global response to what the majority of youth believe to be *the* most pressing issue threatening our collective future (UNESCO, 2021). Alongside these efforts, social media has proven to be a critical tool wielded by activists to add urgency and moral clarity to the public conversation about climate change, using a combination of hashtags, images, memes, and sharing of personal experiences to capture the global imagination and mobilize supporters.

The importance of social media as a tool for activism is now well established (Jackson et al., 2020; Pinon, 2019). Activists use social media to frame issues, to maintain energy and engagement in between on-the-ground campaigns, to build coalitions between movements, and to maintain solidarity and bring new people into a movement (Jackson et al., 2020; Pinon, 2019). Young leaders have been an important resource for innovating uses of social media for social good, and there is much to learn from their practice.

At the same time, engaging in online activism comes with challenges and risks related to misinformation (Allcott et al., 2019), exposure to harsh disagreement or personal attacks (Middaugh et al., 2017), misrepresentation as posts are circulated out of context (Soep, 2014), and drowning in vast seas

DOI: 10.4324/9781003448525-6

of internet voices (Levine, 2008). Studies that focus on youth (adolescents and emerging adults, typically spanning ages 15–24) more broadly, rather than activists, find significant reliance on social media for news and information (Walker & Matsa, 2021) but a great deal of hesitation among youth when it comes to expressing their political voice through comments or creating original posts (Cohen et al., 2012; Middaugh et al., 2021).

The CLARION (Civic Learning and Reasoning in Online Networks) project is a collaborative within the Lurie College of Education at San José State University in which we (Mark, Ellen, Henry, and affiliated colleagues) conduct research and design educational interventions to work *with* youth to develop the capacities needed to build a better online public sphere. To understand how to best meet these challenges, we began by learning from social media and from youth themselves, asking questions about how young people use social media to learn about, discuss, and express themselves on issues that matter to them. We asked about the benefits and the challenges they face, and strategies they have developed to manage risk. We spent time examining how issues are presented, circulated, taken up, or ignored on different platforms.

After 2 years of this research, we developed our model for online civic inquiry, discourse, and action, which served as the foundation for designing a new course entitled Social Media and Social Issues to collaborate with students in developing new strategies for learning how to use social media effectively to make a difference in civic life. In this chapter, we share strategies for engaging students in online civic inquiry, discourse, and action on the issue of climate change. Our approach is hands-on, and activity based, building on students' natural curiosity and capacity for exploration, and focused on creating playful and engaging presentations of learning that are well-suited to the culture of social media.

Social Media and Social Issues: Making a Difference through Civic Engagement

On August 19, 2020, Mark and I (Ellen) logged into Zoom for the first class of a new experimental course. After a year of working together on a new collaborative line of research with Computer Science and Humanities double major undergraduate Henry Fan to understand whether and how constructive dialogue about social issues takes place on social media, we were excited to test out our ideas and to coconstruct best practices for civic inquiry, dialogue, and action on social media with the 19 undergraduates who signed up for the course. There was just one problem. We were in the middle of what has come to be known in California as "fire season." The sky was dark orange, and we were ordered to stay indoors, creating a palpable

78 Ellen Middaugh, Mark Felton, and Henry Fan

sense of dread and cutting off everyone's access to yet another public space during a spike in the pandemic. Classes were canceled that day after a brief round of introductions, and the realities of our growing climate crisis were top of mind.

The class carried forward with some minor adjustments, and we worked with students from justice studies, child and adolescent development, humanities, and social work to surface the issues that were important to them—reproductive rights, immigrant rights, mental health, LGBTQ+ issues, abortion, and mass incarceration, among others. Students learned from existing research about different models of civic engagement, such as electoral engagement, activism, volunteerism, and the difference between individual and collective action (Adler & Goggin, 2005) and research on how digital media is changing the practices of civic engagement (Soep, 2014). From there, as a class, we coconstructed activities based on the model that grew out of our research on inquiry, dialogue, and action through social media (Figure 5.1). Our model presumes that civic action should constantly be informed by civic inquiry and dialogue and that these processes often take place in rapid cycles when happening through social media.

Throughout the semester, students analyzed how issues they cared about were represented in traditional media and on social media, fact-checked

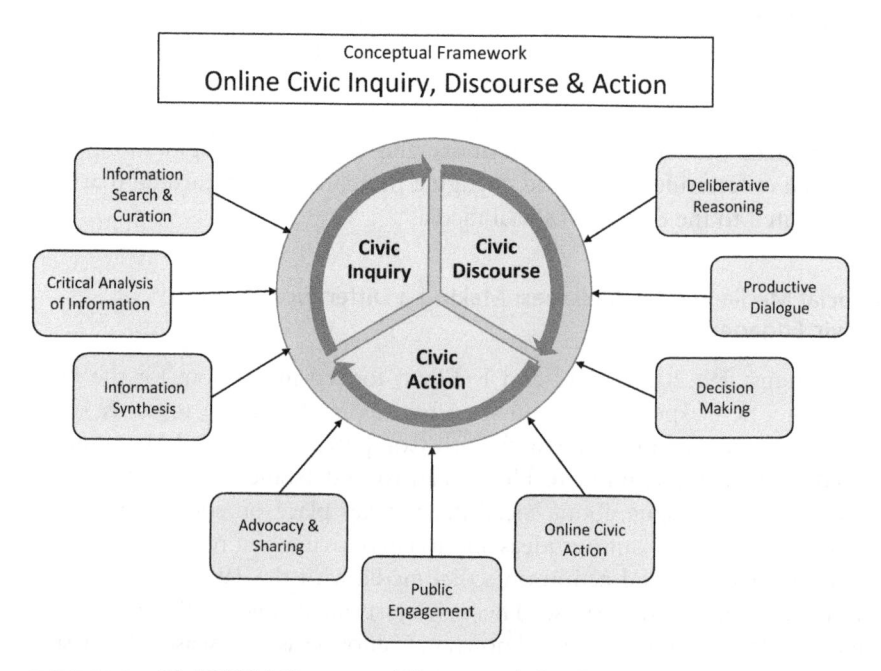

FIGURE 5.1 CLARION Conceptual Framework for Civic Engagement.

media messages on PolitiFact or Snopes, and created Instagram stories to share what they learned (Module 1: Inquiry). As a class, we discussed different purposes of political dialogue, different approaches to unblocking dialogue about contentious issues, and how to find common ground (Makau & Marty, 2013; Inclusive Teaching at UM, n.d.). Students analyzed dialogue about an issue on two different platforms (Twitter vs. Reddit) and compared the norms on the platforms. They studied examples of nonproductive dialogue, posed recommendations for unblocking dialogue, and produced Google Site pages with their analysis and recommendations (Module 2: Dialogue). Finally, we learned about the role of social media in framing issues and mobilizing movements, discussed examples of youth activists and how they used social media, and learned about best practices in crafting messages that will motivate action (Pinon, 2019). Students' final projects involved choosing their own medium and creating a knowledge product to define a problem, present evidence for the problem, and propose a solution and call to action.

Feedback throughout and at the end of the semester showed that although our students were, for the most part, active social media users and passionate about issues in their community, they had not taken an analytical approach to understanding how the internet mediates their understanding of issues and their interactions with others. For example, in spite of being aware of the problem of fake news, students were largely unaware of fact-checking sites. In analyzing online dialogue, they spoke of being surprised by the depth of dialogue happening on platforms like Reddit and Instagram and also seeing new perspectives on issues that they had not thought about. And as they were actively experiencing the pandemic, the 2020 election, racism targeted toward Asian Americans, the Black Lives Matter movement, and concerns about how the pandemic was impacting our immigrant communities, they channeled their concerns about these issues into raising awareness and calls to action.

In this chapter, we build on the lessons learned from our research and our teaching of the first iteration of this course to propose a framework and set of activities for community-engaged learning focused on using social media to address the topic of climate change.

How We Come to This Work: Positionality and Motivation

This chapter is the result of more than 3 years of work as a team. Drawing on our complementary areas of expertise in digital media in youth civic engagement and civic education (Ellen) and argumentative reasoning and deliberative dialogue (Mark), we began to think about how we could leverage our collective expertise to create learning opportunities for youth to use social media in informed, ethical, and impactful ways for civic good. Henry Fan joined our team early in the process, motivated by his experience as a computer science student with a passion for making computer science education more humanistic and relevant to how people learn. As a team, we have begun to gravitate toward centering the issue of climate change in our work. In this section, we each describe our motivation and positionality in relation to community-engaged learning in the California State University system, social media, and climate change.

Ellen: My interest in supporting youth civic engagement has grown out of my experience growing up in the South and feeling frustrated that school was not providing me with the language to name the injustices around me or the skills to address them. My academic career has focused on understanding what young people care about and how to inspire and support them to advocate for themselves and their communities. My work always starts with meeting young people where they are, which has inspired my interest in social media. Since joining the faculty at San José State University, a large urban public West Coast comprehensive university, I have been thrilled to see how community-engaged learning is embraced and how much our students are motivated to give back to the communities they come from. The strong presence of community-engaged learning at our institution and the value placed on interdisciplinary and applied work has enabled me to pursue this line of scholarship with much more ease than I experienced as a graduate student at a predominantly research-focused university.

The decision to focus on climate change in this work is a more recent development, inspired by a combination of my concern about the increasing frequency and intensity of climate-related natural disaster, but importantly, because climate change is one of the top concerns among youth globally (UNESCO, 2021) and in the United States (Harris, 2022). The most recent national poll suggests that more than 80% of teens are actively worried about climate change and believe it is an urgent issue that will impact their future. Thus, I believe it is our responsibility as citizens and educators to focus on this issue and support their efforts to understand and address it.

Henry: As a supplemental instructor and learning assistant, I work to inspire and guide students to create significant learning experiences for themselves and others, so that they may become more equipped to solve the visceral, subtle, and nuanced problems that exist in their communities. I'm motivated by teaching students how to understand and utilize technological tools and mediums, to meet them where they are, for public purpose and social change. My mission, similar to that of all educators, is to actualize human cultural capital so that students may discover and share their greatest gifts with our world.

Having worked in the fields of hospitality and technology for over a decade, I find the problems that exist in education are the most demanding yet fulfilling problems I have faced as a focus of my work. I see that peers and colleagues who engage in civic labor, as scholars, educators, and scientists, are often unheralded. My fear is that outdated policies in higher education reduce beautifully complex humans into flat replicas, clones of expertise, and connoisseurs of digital "fast-food," in order to fuel the market world. I chose to be a community-engaged learner to resist what I see as unhealthy habits cultivated by traditional learning environments. In my lifetime, it's never been more urgent for us to teach students to believe in themselves, see their social-ancestral identities, and to get along with others, through whatever discipline or expertise we have. Later in the chapter, I will share my recent inquiry, discourse, and action as a Next Generation Garden Environmental Justice Fellow through the SJSU César E. Chávez Community Action Center.

Mark: Youth civic engagement is a relatively new area of interest for me, which grew out of my prior work in argumentative dialogue in the classroom. Making the transition from elementary school to middle school was a pivotal experience in my development as a learner. Throughout elementary school, I found myself "behind" in Language Arts and often felt lost during class time, which was mostly spent completing worksheets that lacked real meaning and context. It wasn't until I arrived in middle school that I started to encounter teachers who centered their students' voices in the learning process. I was asked to explore literary themes in classroom discussions and support claims about these themes with textual evidence. Focusing on these higher-order tasks, which emerged from inquiry and dialogue, played to my strengths as a learner. I have spent much of my research career studying how to foster productive, evidence-based dialogue to facilitate collaborative problem-solving and learning in classroom settings. At SJSU, I helped prepare K–12 teachers who are interested in fostering student voice and agency in their classrooms to see the potential of argumentation to engage and animate their students as they engage in scientific, historical, and literary inquiry. The most satisfying part of this work is seeing how many of our program graduates return to the communities where they grew up to educate the next generation. These experiences have led to an interest in promoting community-engaged work more broadly. I am starting to explore the ways in which schools can become a vehicle for teaching students how to take an active role in addressing issues of concern in their community. My collaborations with Ellen and Henry focus on empowering youth to find their voice on public issues and express themselves in public forums to engage, inform, and mobilize their communities to take action. Social media is a powerful tool for civic action among youth not only because it draws on their talents as digital natives but also because it allows them to amplify their voices in ways that were beyond the reach of most citizens just a few decades ago.

Structuring a Unit Around Social Media and Climate Action

Climate change is an enormous issue, and while recent surveys suggest that more than 80% of teens aged 16–19 say that climate change is top of mind for them (Harris, 2022), it is easy to be overwhelmed by the complexity of the problem and the political realities involved in trying to make change. Indeed, the Yale Program on Climate Change Communication (Chryst et al., 2018) has conducted a yearly national survey of Americans' attitudes about climate change and finds that by 2021, 58% of Americans of all ages believed that global warming is a serious concern, and 33% were classified as "alarmed," representing the fastest growing group. However, they also note that "most do not know what they or others can do to solve the problem."

Slowing and reversing climate change will require a global effort with action on multiple fronts, and people need to find their own entry points and approaches to advocating for climate change solutions. In this chapter, we apply lessons learned from our research on inquiry, dialogue, and action through social media, our work with the SJSU Diversifying STEM Initiative (Lemkuhl-Dakhwe, 2022) and Henry's environmental justice fellowship to propose a unit on social media, and climate action that can be integrated into a range of courses at the high school and undergraduate level.

Specifically, we structure the unit as a process that begins with inspiring students to discover their personal connection to climate change and fostering hope that action is worth pursuing (Figure 5.2). From there we illustrate how students can use both social media and institutional sources for inquiry into the issue of climate change and climate action, how they can use deliberative dialogue to decide on a theory of action that includes advocating for an evidence-based solution to an appropriate audience with an appropriate message, and how they can develop knowledge products to convey a message about climate change that they can use to advocate for their chosen solution.

We begin the unit by taking seriously the importance of *inspiration* with students discovering their own connection to climate change. The past 25 years of research on youth civic engagement suggest that a combination of factors motivate lifelong commitments to civic engagement (Flanagan, 2013). Research on *critical consciousness* suggests that critical examination of root causes of issues and the ways in which existing power structures lead to unequal opportunity and harm can motivate civic engagement, particularly among minoritized youth (Diemer & Rapa, 2016). This suggests that to

STRUCTURING A UNIT AROUND SOCIAL MEDIA & CLIMATE ACTION

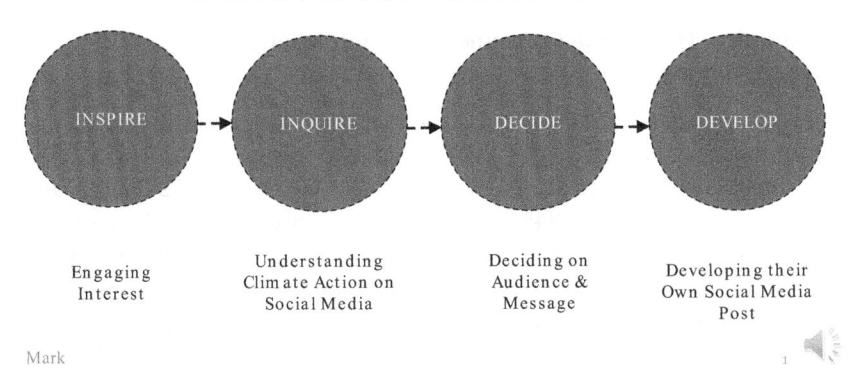

| INSPIRE | → | INQUIRE | → | DECIDE | → | DEVELOP |

| Engaging Interest | Understanding Climate Action on Social Media | Deciding on Audience & Message | Developing their Own Social Media Post |

FIGURE 5.2 Overview of Unit Structure Using Social Media for Climate Inquiry, Dialogue, and Action.

motivate students to care about and want to address climate issues, an effective approach would be to engage them in examining the evidence for climate change, its impact on human well-being as well as on wildlife (e.g., polar bears), and the evidence of the greater impact of climate crisis on communities with less political or economic power.

At the same time, engaging social critique without simultaneously providing some sense of critical hope that problems can be addressed can lead to cynicism (Bozalek et al., 2014; Freire, 1970; Shelby, 2015). This suggests that it is important to develop students' sense of *agency and efficacy* by introducing them to specific actions that can help, showing them organizations and role models who are already doing the work, and helping them develop the skills of engagement (Watts & Flanagan, 2007). Additionally, research from both youth civic engagement (Youniss, 2011) and youth organizing (Delgado & Staples, 2007) emphasize the importance of social relationships in civic engagement work. For example, when young people see that they are not the only ones who are impacted by an issue, they feel less isolated and show more motivation to engage (Middaugh & Evans, 2018). Additionally, when they see an issue has a direct impact on their community or their interests (e.g., Surfers for Climate) they can access both the motivation *and* the community to work together to address the issue.

Building on this work, we begin the learning module with exploration and inspiration that engages all three entry points described above—critical consciousness, critical hope, and collective exploration of personal relevance.

Appendix A provides three activities that instructors can do to begin this process of inspiration and exploration.

Civic Inquiry: Thoughtful Consumption of Information About Climate Change

While social media has been heavily criticized for its role in spreading misinformation (Allcott et al., 2019) and fostering polarization through echo-chambers (Taylor et al., 2018), the majority of adults (72%) and vast majority of young adults (84%) and teens (97%) use social media (Auxier & Anderson, 2021; Anderson & Jiang, 2018). Furthermore, research suggests a growing tendency among young adults and teens to rely on news and information to come to them through social media instead of visiting news sites to intentionally consume media (Fletcher & Nielsen, 2018). In a recent study our team conducted using think-aloud interviews with California youth aged 15–24, we noticed that the kinds of sources our participants gravitated toward for information about civic issues were activist and aggregator accounts in addition to or instead of institutional sources. This suggests a need to teach for the existing media ecosystem and help students critically evaluate and curate their social media feeds so that they are receiving high-quality information.

Our approach to teaching civic inquiry in this context includes first introducing students to the importance of inquiry to high-quality civic action. The best forms of civic action are guided by a desire to understand issues from multiple perspectives and the use of information to understand the root causes of issues and potential public solutions. In the case of climate change, we need scientific information about the causes and promising solutions for climate change. We also need political information to understand what is currently being done through policy, what is not, and why. Finally, we need human stories to understand how people experience climate change and why they may or may not support efforts to address it.

In the era of social media, there are a few important concepts and skills that can help students navigate the media landscape more effectively. The first concept is *curation*, which means applying strategies to collect information that is more likely to be high quality. This can include choosing to *follow* reputable sources of climate change information, such as the Intergovernmental Panel on Climate Change (IPCC), National Aeronautics and Space Administration (NASA), and news organizations with journalistic standards (i.e., *New York Times*) for reporting that is more digestible. Following these sources makes it more likely that relevant and reputable information will show up in a feed. Additionally, *bookmarking* or *saving* posts from reputable sources to go back to and read later is another form of curation, and one that helps people manage the rapid pace of information flow on social media. Having students analyze their own feeds for (a) whether information about climate change is presented; (b) what they know about the accounts they follow; and (c) comparing institutional and activist accounts can help them become more intentional curators of their own social media feeds.

A second, related concept, has to do with *algorithms* and how they shape feeds. Most, if not all, social media platforms have algorithms that respond to behavior (reading, endorsing, sharing, commenting) to prioritize posts that will appear from the accounts a user follows and to suggest posts from accounts that they do not actively follow (Noble, 2018). This can quickly reduce the amount of information you see about certain issues as well as different perspectives on an issue (Paraiser, 2015). Having students monitor and compare their feeds over time as they more intentionally engage with high-quality content about climate change (or not) and comparing their feeds to each other's feeds can help them be more conscious of the fact that their feeds are constantly being shaped.

Another aspect of online civic inquiry is the importance of *search terms* both when engaging in effortful search through Google, databases, and on social media but also when choosing hashtags to follow and populate feeds. When looking for information about civic issues, the terms people use are often highly politicized. For example, Williams et al. (2015) conducted social network analysis of social media discussions of climate change on Twitter and found that posts with the #climatechange hashtag were shared by climate activists, whereas #globalwarming and #agw (anthropogenic global warming) were used by climate activists *and* climate skeptics. Having students try out different search terms and compare the information they are getting can help them think beyond a single search term. Teaching skills of advanced search using multiple search terms, date limitations, and types of sources can also help them create more effective searches.

Finally, learning to engage in *fact-checking* as a routine practice in the absence of traditional indicators of factual accuracy is critical on social media. While most students are aware of the problems of fake news and have learned about credible sources (Robb, 2017), the reality is that when on social media, they will encounter a mix of sources and may not remember to or may struggle to apply the strategies they learn in school when sorting through feeds and making quick judgments. For example, when learning to do research in high schools, many students are given rules to follow, such as sticking to .gov, .org, or .edu sites (none of which are guarantees of high-quality information) or sticking to peer-reviewed sources or newspapers. In the latter case, these rules make sense in the context of a classroom project, but they do little to help students make sense of information coming to them through social media which, at best, will include a mix of peer-reviewed/ institutional information and clips of information repurposed by users.

Learning to apply *judgment* through strategies such as the *CRAAP test* (currency, relevance, accuracy, authority, and purpose) (Blakeslee, 2004) or *lateral validation*—looking up claims made through social media for verification through trusted sources (Hall et al., 2021)—can help students become more discerning consumers. While it is unlikely that anyone would engage in effortful validation of every post they encounter on social media, engaging in fact-checking and validation activities on a regular basis can increase awareness of credibility concerns as they scroll through media but also serve as occasional moments to intentionally surface and check assumptions. See Appendix B for an example of an activity to guide students through this process.

Civic Dialogue: Deliberation as a Tool for Developing a Theory of Action

Social media can be a powerful tool for community engagement and civic action but finding ways to communicate effectively can be challenging in our complex political environment. Certainly, political dissent and cross-cutting dialogue fuel the democratic process, but without a clear sense of one's audience and purpose, conversation can devolve into polarizing screeds and personal attacks. Guiding youth in the work of leveraging social media for civic action begins by helping them learn to distinguish discrete goals and audiences for productive political dialogue. At different times, we may use social media to connect with others and build coalitions, to explore an issue, to inform the public, to decide what action to take, or to mobilize a community. Each of these purposes may involve different audiences and different forms of dialogue. In our Climate Action module, we focus on one particular form of political discourse, *deliberative dialogue*, and illustrate how it can be used by a community to explore a variety of climate solutions and formulate a theory of action for mobilizing the public.

Unlike some forms of argumentation, which may aim at persuading others or negotiating outcomes, deliberative dialogue is about deciding what action to take (Walton, 2010). Persuasive dialogue is typically a competitive exchange in which speakers advance alternative arguments with the goal of prevailing. Because of its adversarial nature, persuasive dialogue can lead us to ignore reasonable critiques or counterevidence in the interest of advancing our agenda. In contrast, deliberative dialogue is a collaborative exchange in which speakers consider alternative views, critique those views collaboratively, and resolve arguments to arrive at a consensual decision. In our prior work (Felton, Crowell & Liu, 2015), we have found that college students are more likely to cite arguments that originated from their conversational partners and are more likely to integrate arguments with counter arguments when they have been asked to argue to reach consensus.

Not surprisingly, the ability to engage in effective deliberative dialogue takes time to develop and research suggests that the balanced, critical reasoning that characterizes deliberation is neither an automatic nor a common process in everyday conversation. More often, our *cognitive biases* lead us to reason in reverse—from conclusion to premises—so that we find ourselves selecting evidence to support our initial intuitions rather than using evidence to interrogate those intuitions. Some theoretical models, like argumentative theory (Mercier & Sperber, 2011), propose that such biases in reasoning are not flaws at all, so much as features of persuasive discourse. They suggest that argumentation has developed as a social tool for negotiating interests in groups. Seen in this light, cognitive bias is construed as a means of marshaling a persuasive argument to sway others. But Mercier and Sperber propose that the ability to persuade in argumentative reasoning is counterbalanced with the ability to be vigilant. That is, we have a countervailing set of skills that allow us to critically examine arguments when making decisions, too, which allows us to guard against persuasion when it is against our best interests. Elsewhere (Felton et al., 2009), we have argued that deliberation represents a third argumentative function, which combines the persuasive and critical functions of social reasoning into a single collaborative process whose primary aim is not simply to advance or to critique a position but to coordinate the two processes in order to optimize a collective course of action (see also, Asterhan, 2013).

Thus, in our module, we have students deliberate about which climate solutions to advocate for on social media. They research a variety of solutions aimed at mitigating climate change. However, in this case, optimizing a solution involves not only considering the strengths of a climate solution itself but also the ability to mobilize an audience to take action. Establishing empathy with an audience to understand their point of view is critical to making a persuasive appeal. For this reason, we have students research public opinion in their community to get a feel for what motivates their audience and what makes them hesitant to take action. Once they have developed this understanding of their options and their audience, they can think strategically about crafting an appeal and engage in deliberative dialogue. We have structured the deliberative dialogue as a fishbowl activity in which a group of students sitting in an inner circle deliberate about which climate action to advocate while students sitting in an outer circle observe. The job of the outer circle is to listen for evidence of productive dialogue.

Three norms stand at the heart of productive deliberative dialogue (Felton et al., 2022). The first is a commitment to *surfacing* arguments in favor of possible courses of action. This involves suspending judgment, allowing others to speak, asking questions to better understand a course of action, and coconstructing arguments in favor of taking that action. However, advocating for a course of action without considering potential pitfalls is just as bad as dismissing it. As a result, effective deliberation also requires a commitment to *critiquing* arguments for a course of action. This involves voicing concerns, identifying flaws, and critically evaluating arguments and counterarguments. Speakers must remain humble about ideas they've advocated for and listen carefully to alternative perspectives. Finally, effective deliberation requires a commitment to *coalescing* arguments to arrive at a decision. Here, speakers review proposed actions, weigh the pros and cons of each, and look for ways to leverage the strengths of a proposal or mitigate its weaknesses. Again, speakers must remain tentative about their ideas and open to adapting or changing a course of action. Oftentimes, the process of coalescing arguments involves making simple amendments or even combining options to produce a more robust solution.

Finally, we recognize that youth often possess adaptive strategies based on their prior experiences with political dialogue on social media (James & Cotnam-Kappel, 2020). In our module, we close by having students explore the affordances and constraints of different platforms for productive talk. Our aim is to tap into their implicit knowledge about whether and how to engage with different communities on different social media platforms.

Central to the CLARION model of community-engaged learning is the concept that civic action should be informed by civic inquiry and dialogue that leads to a *theory of action*. The civic action that happens in a classroom over the course of a semester can have a meaningful short-term impact on the community, but the longer-term impact is on the group of students who are learning how to engage in meaningful action individually and collectively over the course of many years, which is what is required for such complex issues as climate change. Thus, we aim to engage students in activities that help them analyze the root causes of issues, engage in deliberative dialogue about the best course of action, and choose a form of action that best aligns with what they hope to accomplish. Appendix C outlines an activity that can be used with students to develop a theory of action around climate change.

Civic Action: Finding, Reaching, and Persuading Your Audience

There are many ways to organize civic action within a community engaged learning course. In this model, we emphasized developing a *theory of action* through inquiry and dialogue prior to engaging in action. The goal is for students to leave the course with a working model of a process of gaining knowledge about an issue and choosing from a variety of potential solutions over time. This means revisiting 1) the root causes and potential solutions for climate change, 2) the different levers of change (elected officials and processes, corporate policies, social movement organizations, and the behaviors of individuals), and 3) the kinds of actions (voting, persuasive communication, protest, collective action) that can press on these levers of change productively. The previous section used deliberative dialogue to model this process of creating a theory of action. In this section, we discuss how to lead students through a process of organizing and taking their own action based on their theory of change, and how to tap the affordances of social media.

Research on the use of social media in civic engagement broadly, and climate change specifically, has identified several ways in which social media can enhance the impact of activism. *Social movement organizations* are critical to organizing the actions of individuals into more impactful long-term efforts and have evolved rapidly to use social media to maintain energy and collective identity of members in between actions and to *mobilize* people (turn out the vote, show up for a protest, raise money) for specific actions (Pinon, 2019; Earl et al., 2014). Organizations like Fridays for the Future have grown out of youth-led climate strikes and use hashtags and images like #climatestrike and #fridaysforthefuture to help create an online collective identity and a sense of joining something bigger among youth around the planet. As discussed earlier, the sense of collective action or belonging to a greater effort can be crucial to sustaining motivation to address difficult issues over a long period of time (Delgado & Staples, 2007).

When we have identified issues that we would like to be aware of and act on, following hashtags and social movement organizations on social media increases the likelihood of being recruited into civic action on that topic. Often in civic education, youth are encouraged to come up with and act on solutions, which is a valuable exercise for gaining understanding of issues and skills of engagement and leadership. However, decades of research on adult participation point to the importance of recruitment for activating civic engagement (Schlozman et al., 2012). Political parties, community associations, and social movement organizations exist to reduce the barriers to participation for everyday citizens and prevent people from having to reinvent the wheels of action.

A final affordance of social media is the way in which it can allow people who do not have access to institutional sources of mass media (newspaper, radio, magazine, TV) to reframe issues. Long before the invention of social media, youth-led organizing efforts have focused on the importance of *framing* and countering dominant narratives as part of focusing public attention on under-attended causes and solutions to a problem (Kirshner, 2015). Examples include efforts to change the narrative around school dropout to recognize school push-out and the school-to-prison pipeline. Activists have leveraged social media to introduce and popularize new framings, such as in the case of #blacklivesmatter, using the hashtag to string together messages, images, and incidents into a narrative that evolved over years and across wide geographic terrain (Jackson et al., 2020). Recently, in relation to climate change, we see hashtags like #climatecrisis being used to build urgency and #climatejustice to build bridges to other movements related to environmental racism.

Thus, in the final activity presented in Appendix D, we invite students to develop their own theory of action, engage in one of four options for action (Education, Advocacy, Material Support, or Volunteering) aimed at either informal networks, social movement organizations, corporations, or elected officials, and to consider what media they are using for their action. We explicitly do not require students to use social media within this section because social media is one of many tools for communicating with, persuading, or mobilizing others. By reflecting on and sharing their actions with others, they have the opportunity to consider the affordances of different modes of action and expression.

Conclusion

Higher education has long been recognized as an important resource for community improvement (Campus Compact, 2022). Key to the mission of the California State University (CSU) system is the goal to "prepare significant numbers of educated, responsible people to contribute to California's schools, economy, culture, and future," (The California State University, n.d.). In this chapter, we center two elements of the future that we see as being particularly urgent—the state of our democracy and the sustainability of a livable climate. We take our inspiration from the commitment and innovation of youth climate and environmental justice activists like Xiye Bastide (2021), Greta Thunberg (2022), and Mari Copeny (2022) and the SJSU undergraduate students we have interviewed and coconstructed curriculum with to envision how undergraduate education can integrate these lessons into community-engaged learning courses. Addressing the issue of climate change is going to require a massive, coordinated global effort leveraging scientific and also significant political breakthroughs and public will. Our hope is that educators and students alike will take up these ideas, experiment with them, and contribute their own insights as we build toward a more sustainable democracy and planet.

References

Adler, R. & Goggin, J. (2005). What do we mean by civic engagement? *Journal of Transformative Education*, 3(3), 236–253.

Allcott, H., Gentzkow, M., & Chuan, Y. (2019). Trends in the diffusion of misinformation on social media. *Research and Politics*, 6(2), 1–8.

Anderson, M., & Jiang, J. (2018). Teens, social media & technology 2018. *Pew Research Center*, 31(2018), 1673–1689.

Asterhan, C. S. C. (2013). Epistemic and interpersonal dimensions of peer argumentation: Conceptualization and quantitative assessment. In M. Baker, J. Andriessen & S. Jarvela (Eds.), *Affective learning together* (pp. 251–272). Routledge.

Auxier, B. & Anderson, M. (2021). Social media use in 2021. *Pew Research Center*, 1, 1–4.

Bastida, X. (2021). *Xiye Bastida*. www.xiyebeara.com/

Blakeslee, S. (2004). The CRAAP Test. *Loex Quarterly*, 31(3), pp. 6–7.

Bozalek, V., Carolissen, R., Leibowitz, B., & Boler, M. (Eds.). (2014). *Discerning critical hope in educational practices*. Routledge.

Campus Compact. (2022). *Mission and vision*. https://compact.org/who-we-are/mission-and-vision/

Chryst, B., Marlon, J., van der Linden, S., Leiserowitz, A., Maibach, E., & Roser-Renouf, C. (2018). Global warming's "Six Americas Short Survey": Audience segmentation of climate change views using a four question instrument. *Environmental Communication*, 12(8), 1109–1122.

Cohen, C. J., Kahne, J., Bowyer, B., Middaugh, E., & Rogowski, J. (2012). *Participatory politics: New media and youth political action*. http://ypp.dmlcentral.net/sites/default/files/publications/Participatory_Politics_New_Media_and_Youth_Political_Action.2012.pdf

Copeny, M. (2022). *Littlemissflint*. www.instagram.com/littlemissflint/?hl=en

Delgado, M. & Staples, L. (2007). *Youth-led community organizing: Theory and action*. Oxford University Press.

Diemer, M. A. & Rapa, L. J. (2016). Unraveling the complexity of critical consciousness, political efficacy, and political action among marginalized adolescents. *Child Development*, 87(1), 221–238.

Earl, J., Hunt, J., & Garrett, R. K. (2014). Social movements and the ICT revolution. *Handbook of Political Citizenship and Social Movements* (pp. 359–384). Google Scholar.

Felton, M., Crowell, A., Garcia-Mila, M., & Villarroel, C. (2022). Capturing deliberative argument: An analytic coding scheme for studying argumentative dialogue and its benefits for learning. *Learning, Culture and Social Interaction*, 36, 100350.

Felton, M., Crowell, A., & Liu, T. (2015). Arguing to agree: Mitigating my-side bias through consensus-seeking dialogue. *Written Communication*, 32(3), 317–331. https://doi.org/10.1177/0741088315590788

Felton, M., Garcia-Mila, M., & Gilabert, S. (2009). Deliberation versus dispute: The impact of argumentative discourse goals on learning and reasoning in the science classroom. *Informal Logic*, 29(4), 417–446.

Flanagan, C. (2013). *Teenage citizens: The political theories of the young*. Harvard University Press.

Fletcher, R. & Nielsen, R. K. (2018). Are people incidentally exposed to news on social media? A comparative analysis. *New Media & Society, 20*(7), 2450–246.

Freire, P. (1970). *Pedagogy of hope*. Continuum.

Hall, T., Well, J., & Emery, E. (2021). Fact-checking in an era of fake news: A template for a lesson on lateral reading of social media posts. *Connected Science Learning, 3*(3), 1–14.

Harris Poll. (2022). *Environmental impact survey: Exploring the impact of the environment on teens*. bit.ly/4774P1j

Inclusive Teaching at University of Michigan. (n.d.) *Responding to common dialogue blockers*. https://sites.lsa.umich.edu/inclusive-teaching/inclusive-classrooms/dialogue-blockers/

Jackson, S., Bailey, M., & Foucault-Wells, B. (2020). *#activism: Networks of race and gender justice*. MIT Press.

James, C., & Cotnam-Kappel, M. (2020). Doubtful dialogue: How youth navigate the draw (and drawbacks) of online political dialogue. *Learning, Media and Technology, 45*(2), 129–150.

Kaplan, S., Lumpkin, L., & Dennis, B. (2019, September 20). "We will make them hear us": Millions of youths around the world strike for action. *The Washington Post*. www.washingtonpost.com/climate-environment/2019/09/20/millions-youth-around-world-are-striking-friday-climate-action/

Kirshner, B. (2015). *Youth activism in an era of education inequality*. New York University Press.

Lemkuhl-Dakhwe, V. (2022). *Professional learning community for climate action*. www.sjsu.edu/stemed/UDL/index.php

Levine P. (2008). A public voice for youth: The audience problem in digital media and civic education. In: Bennett L. (Ed.), *Civic life online: Learning how digital media can engage youth* (pp. 119–138). The MIT Press.

Makau, J. & Marty, D. (2013). *Dialogue and deliberation*. Waveland Press.

Mercier, H. & Sperber, D. (2011). Why do humans reason? Arguments for an argumentative theory. *Behavioral and Brain Sciences, 34*(2), 57–74.

Middaugh, E., Bowyer, B., & Kahne, J. (2017). U suk! Participatory media and youth experiences with political discourse. *Youth & Society, 49*(7), 902–922. https://doi.org/10.1177/0044118X16655246

Middaugh, E. & Evans, C. (2018). Did you know?!… Cultivating online public voice in youth. *Theory & Research in Social Education, 46*(4), 574–602.

Middaugh, E., Felton, M., & Fan, H. (2021, April). *"People can get really harsh," Supporting youth as they engage with contemporary issues through social media*. Paper presented at the Virtual Annual Meeting of the American Education Research Association.

Noble, S. U. (2018). *Algorithms of oppression: How search engines reinforce racism*. NYU Press. https://doi.org/10.18574/9781479833641

Paraiser, E. (2015). *The filter bubble: How the new personalized web is changing what we read and how we think*. Penguin Group.

Pinon, N. (2019). *How to ensure your online activism has an offline impact*. Mashable interview with authors of #Activism.

Robb, M. B. (2017). *News and America's kids: How young people perceive and are impacted by the news*. Common Sense.

Schlozman, K. L., Verba, S., & Brady, H. E. (2012). The unheavenly chorus: Unequal political voice and the broken promise of American Democracy. In *The Unheavenly Chorus*. Princeton University Press. https://doi.org/10.1515/9781400841912

Shelby, T. (2015). Impure dissent: Hip hop and the political ethics of marginalized Black urban youth. In D. Allen & J. Light (Eds.), *From voice to influence: Understanding citizenship in a digital age*. University of Chicago Press.

Soep, L. (2014). *Participatory politics: Next generation tactics to remake public spheres*. MIT Press.

Taylor, C., Mantzaris, A., & Garibay, I. (2018). Exploring how homophily and accessibility can facilitate polarization in social networks. *Information, 9*(12), 325.

The California State University (n.d.) *The mission of the California State University*. https://compact.org/who-we-are/mission-and-vision/

Thunberg, G. (2022). *Gretathunberg*. www.instagram.com/gretathunberg/?hl=en

UNESCO. (2021). *The World in 2030: Public survey report*. https://unesdoc.unesco.org/ark:/48223/pf0000375950.locale=en

Walker, M. & Matsa, K. E. (2021, September 20). News consumption across social media in 2021. *Pew Research Center's Journalism Project*. www.pewresearch.org/journalism/2021/09/20/news-consumption-across-social-media-in-2021/

Walton, D. (2010). Types of dialogue and burdens of proof. In P. Baroni, F. Cerutti, M. Giacomin, & G. R. Simari (Eds.), *Computational models of argument: Proceedings of COMMA* (pp. 13–24). IOS Press.

Watts, R. J. & Flanagan, C. (2007). Pushing the envelope on youth civic engagement: A developmental and liberation psychology perspective. *Journal of Community Psychology, 35*, 784–788.

Williams, H. T. P., McMurray, J. R., Kurz, T., & Hugo Lambert, F. (2015). Network analysis reveals open forums and echo chambers in social media discussions of climate change. *Global Environmental Change, 32*, 126–138. https://doi.org/10.1016/j.gloenvcha.2015.03.006

Youniss, J. (2011). Civic Education: What schools can do to encourage civic identity and action. *Applied Developmental Science, 15*(2), 98–103. https://doi.org/10.1080/10888691.2011.560814

Appendix A
Exploring Climate Change

Six Americas Quiz
- Go to tinyurl.com/YaleClimateQuiz
- Take the short quiz & write down your result
- Go to https://tinyurl.com/Yale6Americas to see the 6 types
- Fill out a class poll to what views are represented in your class.

Exploring Climate Data

The International Panel on Climate Change (IPCC) has been convening scientists to come to consensus about the causes, effects and solutions to climate change. In a recent report, they shared information about what we can expect to happen to the planet and to people if the world in three scenarios: 1) Late, uncoordinated action, 2) Delayed, decisive action, and 3) Early, effective action.

Visit tinyurl.com/IPPCWorldsApart and discuss the following with your peers
- What does the report identify as a major cause of global warming?
- What are some of the negative outcomes they identify as being likely to happen in the scenario of late, uncoordinated action?
- What are some of the changes that they identify being made in the "Early, effective action" scenario that should lead to better outcomes?

Examining Social Media Messages

Whole Class
- Watch this Instagram Story Video by Xiye Bastida https://www.instagram.com/tv/B9M6p5TFegA/?hl=en
- Note for yourself, how does this video make you feel? (enter on class jamboard)

Small Groups
- Visit the class Google Site (note to instructors: this site tinyurl.com/CLARIONExamplesis an example, but you should update your examples)
- Discuss:
    - How is language being used to frame the issue?
    - What issue(s) are highlighted?
    - What emotions are being expressed?
- Report out to whole class or review other group posts online to consider similarities and differences by group

Appendix B
Fact-Checking Information about Climate Change Activity

This can be done individually or in groups

Applying Judgment to Social Media Posts about Climate Change

Find five posts about climate change on the social media feed of your choice and use the CRAAP Test and Lateral Validation to fact-check these posts.
　　CRAAP Test. Is the information in the post:

- Current? Can you tell when the information being shared was gathered?
- Relevant to the issue of climate change?
- Accurate? Can you tell how they got their information?
- Authority, what can you tell about the person or organization that is sharing this information? Do they have expertise?
- Purpose, what is the post trying to get you to think or believe?

Lateral validation:

- What claim is the post making?
- Conduct a separate search in a search engine (like Google) for that claim. What do the results suggest?

Using Fact-Checking Sites to Understand Common Misconceptions

- Go to Snopes.com and climatefeedback.org
- Go to the "About" section of each site to learn more about who is part of the team fact-checking information and what their qualifications are.
- Pick a site to use for your fact-checking and explain why you chose that site.
- Choose an example of mis/disinformation about climate change explained on the site of your choice (Snopes or Climate Feedback) and explain what the original claim was and why it is either incorrect or misleading.

Appendix C
Deliberation Dialogue on Climate Action

Purpose: The purpose of this activity is to practice deliberative dialogue and reflect on what it looks like to engage in productive dialogue about social action. You will contrast three potential climate actions and consider which might make the most successful climate action to promote on social media. Preparing for class: To prepare for this activity please complete the reading and the discussion preactivity before class.

Reading: Sundheim, D. (2020, June 11). How to have productive dialogue on challenging topics. *Forbes*.

Discussion preactivity: Visit Drawdown.org (https://drawdown.org/solutions) and read the summaries for the following climate actions:

- Bamboo production: https://drawdown.org/solutions/bamboo-production
- Bioplastics: https://drawdown.org/solutions/bioplastics
- Recycling: https://drawdown.org/solutions/recycling

Discussion question: Consider the three climate change mitigation solutions listed above.

Which solution is best suited for successfully mobilizing the public on social media? Why?

Instructions for in-class dialogue activity: This dialogue will be structured as a fishbowl activity in which a group of students is divided into two groups—an inner circle and an outer circle. The inner circle will engage in the discussion above and the outer circle will monitor the discussion, looking for examples of productive dialogue moves (suspending, listening, respecting voicing, and inquiring), and debrief the inner circle's discussion afterward.
   Activity instructions:

- Step 1 (5 min): Divide the group into an inner and outer circle. Instruct the outer circle to listen to the discussion and jot down examples of the productive dialogue moves outlined by Sundheim (2020). During the debrief, they will be asked to give examples of productive/unproductive dialogue moves.

- Step 2 (20 min): Give the inner circle 15–20 minutes to discuss the prompt ("Which solution is best suited for successfully mobilizing the public on social media? Why?")
- Step 3 (15 min): Give the outer circle 10–15 minutes to discuss examples of productive (or unproductive) dialogue moves. What did the speaker say? What made it productive or unproductive for a successful deliberation?
- Step 4 (5 min): Invite the inner circle participants to share their perspectives on the productivity of the discussion. Did they feel heard? Did they find their peers' points compelling?

Appendix D
Engaging in Action to Address Climate Change Activity

Following the Dialogue Activity, students will be asked to go back to drawdown.org and choose a solution to advocate for using one of four options:

1) Education and awareness raising. Using social media to make friends and family aware
2) Advocacy—organizing people to pressure an official (elected, corporate, etc.) to change their practices
3) Material support—fund-raising or resource gathering for a social movement organization or candidate in line with the policy
4) Volunteering with an organization that is addressing climate change.

Need some inspiration? Check out these activities that Henry Fan participated in as part of his SJSU Environmental Justice Fellowship:

- Listened and took notes to recorded or live presentations of environmental advocates to get ideas for action
- Contributed to the development of a community garden (volunteerism)
- Phone banking with peers. Using a script provided by an organizer, the group discussed the script and what it meant, identified each person's State Senator/Committee chair, and called to read the script and either engage in dialogue with the representative or leave a voicemail (Advocacy)
- Wrote a public comment as part of a campaign organized by a Social Movement Organization to Stop Line 5 (rerouting of a pipeline through waterways) (Advocacy)

Students will complete a reflection (written or oral) explaining the following:

1) What kind of action did you take? Please provide a picture or video that shows your action (for example, a social media post, a funding-raising message or petition, a letter to a candidate, a picture of your volunteer experience, etc.)
2) Why did you choose that action? How does this action address one of the root causes of climate change?
3) What do you think your action accomplished?
4) What would you want to do in the future to increase your impact on climate change?

PART 2
Building a Movement
Establishing Infrastructure for Community Engagement

PART 2

6
COALITION BUILDING FOR TRANSFORMATION AND CHANGE IN HIGHER EDUCATION

Elaine K. Ikeda

Introduction

A healthy democracy requires that its citizens are informed and engaged. One of the most important functions that colleges in the United States serve, therefore, is preparing students to be active and knowledgeable participants in our democracy. 20th-century education reformer John Dewey wrote, "Democracy has to be born anew every generation, and education is its midwife" (Dewey, 1916). Indeed, many colleges publicly declare the values of promoting "good citizenship" and "developing future leaders" in their mission statements.

Despite these lofty goals, in the 1980s, evidence emerged that college students were becoming more materialistic and individualistic—viewing college as a private gain (Astin et al., 1997; Astin, 1998). Data collected annually as part of the UCLA Cooperative Institutional Research Program's (CIRP) Freshman Survey documented a shift in how students responded to two contrasting value statements: "the importance of developing a meaningful philosophy of life" and "the importance of being very well off financially." In the late 1960s, developing a meaningful philosophy of life was the top value, being endorsed as an "essential" or "very important" goal by more than 80% of the entering freshman. Being very well-off financially, on the other hand, lagged far behind, ranking fifth or sixth on the list, with less than 45% of the freshmen endorsing it as a very important or essential goal in life. Over the next 20 years, these two values switched places, with being very well-off financially becoming the top value (at 74.1% endorsement) and developing a meaningful philosophy of life occupying sixth place at only 42.1% endorsement. These contrasting trends began in the early 1970s, continued through the decade (crossing paths in 1977), reaching their opposite extremes in the late 1980s.

In contrast, during this same period, higher education research revealed that college students who engaged in community service were more likely to develop a sense of civic and social responsibility (Astin et al., 2000). Further research conducted in the 1990s clearly demonstrated that participation in service activities during the undergraduate years has beneficial effects on students' academic development, sense of civic responsibility, and life skills (including leadership skills) (Astin et al., 1996). Consequently, the development of service-learning and community engagement centers on college campuses steadily increased over the next 40 years. These centers focused on institutionalizing community service in the academy through service-learning, community-engaged research, problem-based learning, and volunteerism. Over the past four decades, individuals and organizational stakeholders have joined together to form coalitions and build a movement to grow and deepen higher education community engagement and develop the next generation of engaged citizens.

This chapter is written for college administrators and Community-Engagement Professionals (CEPs), and it highlights the use of coalition building as a strategy to advance the growth and development of community engagement in higher education. According to Wolff (2001), coalitions can be powerful mechanisms for change. Indeed, coalition building is a well-documented community engagement strategy that has been effectively utilized for building community health and social well-being (Minkler & Wakimoto, 2021).

The first section of this chapter focuses on the important role that coalition building plays in promoting community engagement on individual campuses. A predominance of the literature on community engagement focuses on institutional change within individual colleges (Dolgon et al., 2017). The second section of this chapter illuminates a less common narrative—the importance of coalition building across campuses (statewide and nationally) to influence community engagement in higher education and ensure that the goals of developing an informed and engaged citizenry are achieved. In particular, this section of the chapter highlights the role of an outside organizer (LEAD California) and the strategies employed to develop, support, document, and grow the larger community engagement field in California and in the nation.

Building Coalitions on Individual Campuses

As the executive director of LEAD California (formerly California Campus Compact), I have been engaged for over 20 years in building coalitions to transform higher education and thereby positively impact student development. LEAD California is a state-wide membership organization of college presidents, annually supporting over half a million university and college students, administrators, faculty, staff, and community members. Our organization's resources, expertise, training, and connections offer innovative ways to build a healthy, just, and democratic society. Coalition building (coming together to achieve a goal) is a priority for our organization, and at the core of our work is a focus on advancing community engagement on the individual campus, as well as in the broader state-wide and national field.

As executive director, I frequently travel around California—the most populated state in the country—to visit our member campuses. On these campus visits, I am often asked by campus administrators to provide examples or models of how service-learning and community engagement are integrated across the curriculum at other colleges and universities. Community engagement professionals want to discuss how the practices of other institutions might translate to their own campus. I caution, however, that every institution's model of engagement is different.

The strategies and steps adopted at each institution must be determined in the context of that institution (its history, culture, values, location, community, etc.). While we can learn from the experiences of others, there is no prescriptive "one-size-fits-all" approach to community-engaged learning. Some strategies and experiences may indeed be transferable, but it is imperative that each institution embrace active and reciprocal involvement with local communities and make the model of involvement their own. Over the years, it has become clear to me that building coalitions is one of the most effective strategies for institutionalizing community engagement throughout the campus. Paying attention to campus leadership, culture and mission, professional development, and partnerships is essential to building coalitions on a campus to move community engagement forward.

Leadership Matters

There are many college presidents and provosts who support community engagement and believe in its relevance and importance in higher education. These presidents and provosts often champion community engagement and make it a priority on the campus, supporting the creation, sustenance, or growth of a center on the campus. For example, in this book, Yamamura and her colleagues provide insights and reflections from two college presidents who have publicly embraced and supported community engagement on their campuses. Unfortunately, there are countless examples of how the college's commitment diminishes when leadership turns over. According to Votruba, "The key leadership challenge is to weave public engagement so deeply into the fabric of the campus that it remains strong, even when key leaders move on" (Votruba, 2004, p. 265).

In fact, the influential role of the college president was one reason that Campus Compact was founded in 1985 as a presidential leadership organization. Indeed, a "compact" of college and university presidents' intent on promoting civic engagement was conceived by the presidents of Stanford, Georgetown, and Brown Universities. Their chosen language—a compact—signified a commitment to each other to work together to advance the public purposes of higher education on their campuses and in their communities. It also signified a commitment to honor the long-standing compact between higher education and the public good. Campus Compact thus began as a coalition of college and university presidents committed to helping students develop the values and skills of citizenship through participation in public and community service.

Coalition building on a campus is crucial in retaining support for community engagement when there is leadership transition. It is important to think about how other leaders on and off campus can influence new leadership coming to the campus. For example, in supporting California campuses in my role as Executive Director of LEAD California, I often ask:

- How is community engagement featured in presidential or provost leadership recruitment? Are there interview questions that explore examples of support for community engagement at their previous campus?
- How might community leaders that regularly partner with the institution share with the incoming administration how much they value the engagement of the college with the community?
- Are there key community engagement faculty who serve on the academic senate and will have the ear of a new provost or dean?
- Are the college's trustees and influential donors aware of the community engagement work of the college?

While a president or provost can provide the vision and leadership for developing community engagement initiatives on the campus, it is important to recognize that campus and community representatives can influence the president and campus leadership. Providing research evidence of the effectiveness and impact that service-learning and community engagement have on student development, student retention, community engagement, campus reputation, and other valued outcomes can help campus leadership recognize the important contributions that community engagement makes toward fulfilling the campus's mission and vision.

Campus Culture and Organizational Structures Matter

It is imperative to understand campus culture and the philosophical approach to community engagement on the campus. For some, community engagement is a part of a larger philosophy about the purpose of higher education. Some faculty and administrators view community engagement as a means to creating a more just and equitable democracy—part of higher education's public purpose. Others have adopted community engagement as a pedagogical strategy—a method of teaching course content. Being mindful of your institution's philosophical approach can assist you in identifying appropriate strategies to build coalitions on the campus to implement, sustain, or grow community engagement on the campus.

If you are on a campus that is just getting started in organizing a community engagement movement, it is important to consider whether a goal should be to establish a center or if the community engagement work should be dispersed across the campus. Some believe that creating a center of community engagement can send the message that one place is taking care of this work for the entire campus. It is easier to abdicate responsibility within one's department to offer resources to support the growth of community engagement because that is the work of "that center over there on campus." On the other hand, having a center on the campus can make it easier for the nonprofit agencies and organizations in the community to gain access to the resources of the campus. It is not always easy for community organizations and partners to navigate the complex infrastructure and organization of a college. Having a clearly designated "community engagement center" on the campus can make a statement to the larger public about the importance of this work. When working strategically with the Office of Development on the campus, it may even be possible to find donors who support the goals or programs of the center and, eventually, provide an endowment.

When invited to work with a college campus on the development of their community engagement work, I often begin by asking representatives at the campus to give me the "lay of the land" (campus culture and politics) on that campus. In preparing to advise and work with the campus, I often ask:

- What do members of the campus community call engagement on their campus (service-learning, community engagement, civic engagement, etc.)? Will utilizing certain words (service-learning versus community engagement) cause more resistance or acceptance on the campus?
- What is the level of administrative support for community engagement? Are there particular goals that your administration has or issues that your campus is struggling with (i.e., town-gown relationships) that community engagement can address?
- How might campus politics and culture influence the choice of strategies to employ in moving community engagement work forward on your campus?

- Are there respected, full-time tenure track faculty who are teaching service-learning or promoting community engagement? Is there a faculty director or faculty lead who is responsible for engaging their faculty peers?
- Is there a curricular requirement (or a graduation requirement) in place for service-learning, or are there any faculty incentives for implementing a community engagement component in their courses?
- Can you leverage funding and other sources of support (staffing, fundraising campaign, etc.) to move your agenda forward while supporting or contributing to a larger movement on the campus? Are there initiatives or significant events that are coming up (such as the campus' 100th anniversary) that you may be able to strategically leverage to your advantage?
- How is community engagement tied to the mission of the college or university? Do your community engagement outcomes fit in well with the campus strategic plan or reaccreditation process?
- Is there an established center on the campus for community engagement, and is it housed on the academic or student affairs side of the university or college?

This last question draws attention to the organizational structure of the campus. It is important to consider whether the community engagement work resides on the academic affairs side of the institution, or on the student affairs side (Hartley & Saltmarsh, 2016). Where the center resides on the organizational chart can send a message to the faculty or staff on the campus about the perceived focus or priorities of the community engagement center. For example, if the center is housed under the academic affairs umbrella, faculty may perceive that the center is focused on community engagement as a pedagogy, and that there will be significant support for faculty who wish to teach a service-learning course. If the center is housed under student affairs, it may send the message that the focus of the center's work is on cocurricular student development. Occasionally, there are community engagement centers that have a dual reporting structure—with the director of the center reporting to the vice president of student affairs and to the provost or vice president of academic affairs. In recent years, due to reduced budgets, I have witnessed some campuses merging their community engagement centers with the career center or their volunteer centers.

It is important to explore whether there are other colleges or universities that have created a program or implemented a strategy that you are considering. Are there colleges that your own institution considers aspirational models (in other words, your college would like to be more like a particular college or set of colleges or considered in the same class of colleges)? In this instance, modeling your community engagement program after another college's program might make your own administrators or faculty more apt to look favorably upon your proposal or recommended model.

Sometimes it is appropriate to utilize various institutionalization rubrics (Furco, 1999; Holland, 2000; Campus Compact Civic Action Plan, 2015) or the Carnegie Elective Community Engagement Classification as tools to mobilize and organize the community engagement movement on the campus. Utilizing these well-respected standards of measurement can be an effective way to create a campus-wide task force to establish a baseline (where the campus is at) and aspirational goals (where they want to be in 5 years) with measurable strategies and outcomes. If there is strong upper administration support, then creating a "presidential task force" can add legitimacy to the efforts of a campus coalition for community engagement.

If your center has been in existence for a while, could engaging in a program review (something that academic departments are familiar with) help you to identify new strategies and programs that align well with campus priorities? I witnessed a campus utilize a program review to raise the visibility of their center with the campus administration and leverage the review findings to obtain additional funding and a new, more visible location on campus for their center. As a result of this relocation, student and faculty engagement with the center increased exponentially over the following year.

Professional Development Matters

I have often heard practitioners and faculty in higher education express surprise at how generous professionals in the community engagement field are with sharing resources and advice. It is common to hear people offer to share templates or materials that they have developed, in support of someone who is attempting to reach a similar goal. Reaching out to the administrators or faculty at the other college to learn more about how they developed their community engagement program may be a helpful and time-efficient strategy to employ in the development of your own program and building your campus coalition. In addition to getting sound advice and reflective comments on their development, you may obtain some easy-to-replicate forms, program ideas, and strategies.

There are many books, journal articles, and manuscripts that have been written sharing strategies and case studies. For example, *The Michigan Journal of Service Learning* features research on service-learning, and several of the contributors to this volume have written books highlighting strategies and approaches to institutionalizing service-learning and community engagement (Yamamura & Koth, 2018; Welch & Plaxton-Moore, 2019). These are excellent guides for campuses that are trying to build or grow their community engagement programs. In the 1990s, there was a decisive shift to move from promoting student involvement in community service to effectively link service and the curriculum (Hartley, 2009). The American Association for Higher Education (AAHE) produced 21 monographs that described the use of service-learning in a range of academic disciplines. The rapid growth of faculty service-learning trainings resulted in numerous faculty development guides developed and modified by campuses across the nation.

As more and more faculty were trained in service-learning pedagogy in the 1990s, there was a strategic move to develop coalitions of "engaged departments" and "engaged campuses." Campus Compact initiated a series of Engaged Department Institutes across the country, inviting departmental teams to come to 2- to 3-day institutes. It is important to note that a major focus of these institutes was on curriculum development and introducing discipline-specific models of service-learning. However, there was also attention paid to building relationships among faculty within a department, and within a disciplinary field. Campus Compact was intent on building a critical mass of faculty engaged in service-learning on college campuses, seeing this as a way to institutionalize service-learning in higher education and move it from the margins to the mainstream. There are a number of books and resources that provide guidance on leading these types of trainings and institutes (Keskes, 2006; Kleinhesselink et al., 2015; Langseth & Plater, 2004; Welch & Plaxton-Moore, 2019) and many colleges continue to offer these faculty and departmental trainings today.

Partnerships and Relationships Matter

The building of relationships can happen both organically and strategically. Whether we are talking about building coalitions on an individual campus to further our community engagement efforts, or beyond campus borders to build coalitions that move the work forward more broadly, relationships with others can play a vital role in our progress.

Embrace mutually beneficial partnerships whether at the local campus and community level or at the larger organizational/movement level. No one can do it all and it is important to find those who have similar interests or whose goals align with yours. Leverage your efforts and funding sources to have a greater impact. Sometimes there are complementary partners who bring skills, connections, or perspectives to the table that are different from yours.

We may naturally be drawn toward others because we recognize that we are working toward a similar goal. Or we may strategically reach out to others because they have skills or talents that complement our own and put together will help us both advance toward our goals. Regardless of the motivation, the relationship with the other person or persons requires intention and attention. Nurturing new relationships takes time and energy, with the intention of getting to know the other person(s).

Being vulnerable with each other and leaning on each other for support can help to build trust over time. Confronting or enduring a common challenge can bring individuals together. Sometimes feelings of solidarity with another can lead to a relationship developing quickly while also giving us the courage to take action. It is important to operate with integrity and follow through on commitments. Seek input and feedback. Coalition work is messy and understanding the goals of all stakeholders is key to partnering most effectively. Communication is essential—communicate often and clearly.

Over the years, the important role that community partners play in educating our college students has gained more attention. Another guiding principle of service-learning and community engagement has been "reciprocity" between the campus and the community. Community members are valued coalition partners and there are many factors to consider in building effective partnerships. While all aspects of community partnerships are not necessarily in our control (for example, the campus risk management office may require certain regulations), we can do our best to create honest and respectful relationships. Here are some questions for CEPs to consider:

- How will you reach out to community partners in a specific neighborhood or within a certain radius/proximity to the campus? What role has your institution historically played in the neighborhoods that surround the campus? How will you build trust with representatives in the community? Will your institution make a public commitment to a particular neighborhood or to specific community organizations?
- What role will you play in connecting community partners with faculty on the campus or vice versa? Will you invite faculty into the community to meet with community representatives or will you invite the community onto the campus? Can you ensure that you are not viewed as a gatekeeper by the community members, limiting access to the resources of the college or university?
- What are the ways that your community engagement center can reduce the barriers for community partnerships with your college or university? Are there liability forms and other requirements that your campus requires community partners to complete? Is there a way to streamline those documents or can you create clear guidelines to facilitate easier compliance with regulations?

- Will your campus focus on long-term partnerships with fewer community organizations, or will you engage students in short-term, possibly one-off, types of service with community agencies?
- How will you ensure that the voices of community partners are heard and respected by the campus community? Will you offer compensation to community partners for their time and effort in providing educational opportunities to students? Will you invite community partners to have a seat at the advisory council table? How will you invite a conversation with community partners—one-on-one or via open forums? What community partners or community agencies are partnering with the campus and are they involved with the design of the community engagement courses?

There are countless strategies to consider in moving community engagement forward on the campus, and there are a lot of moving parts, entrenched structures, and procedures on campus. Regardless of the strategies you choose, it is important to remember that institutional transformation or reform is inherently local. As Jay and Jones (2006) state:

> While one can find great ideas at other institutions, developing the right formula for your home campus depends on a grassroots process of soliciting ideas, listening to stakeholders, mapping the terrain, piloting experiments, codifying best practices, and only then, institutionalizing what works.
>
> *(p. 95)*

In *An Engagement of Hope: A Framework and Equity-Centered Theory of Action for Community Engagement*, the authors call us to "re-center relationships in the community engagement field" (Green et al., 2021, p. 129). While we may be encouraged to think strategically about how to institutionalize community engagement at our institution, our campuses and our communities are made up of human beings. A focus on structures, systems, and transactions often does not take into account power dynamics, culture, equity, relational networks, and connection to one another. It is indeed this connection to one another that moves us from the transactional to the transformational.

Building Coalitions to Influence the State and National Community Engagement Field

The first part of this chapter focused primarily on building coalitions to further the institutionalization of community engagement on individual college campuses. Much of what is written is transferable to thinking beyond the individual campus and to a larger movement. This section of the chapter focuses on strategies that California Campus Compact (CACC)/LEAD California has utilized over the past two decades to influence the state and national community engagement field. The presence of statewide, regional, and national coalitions is important because they provide the vision, leadership, and organizing strategies that influence local and individual higher education institutions.

A few years after the founding of Campus Compact in 1985, the presidents leading the organization recognized the importance of fostering networks of geographically proximate institutions that could share ideas and resources more effectively (Hartley & Saltmarsh, 2016). Thus, in 1988, CACC was one of the first state-based offices established to provide member campuses with local, state, and regional support. CACC began with 17 members and grew over the years to have an average of 45–60 members annually. The development of 30 state-based Compact offices over the next two decades expanded Campus Compact's membership to over 1000 institutions. At the same time, leveraging federal and foundation funding through the 1990s and early 2000s resulted in the rapid expansion of service-learning in higher education across the country (Hartley & Saltmarsh, 2016) and Campus Compact was at the heart of this expansion.

I first heard of Campus Compact while I was in my doctoral program at the University of California, Los Angeles (UCLA) in the mid-1990s. I was drawn to the concept of educating students and transforming higher education institutions to create a more just and healthy democracy. I resonated with the founders of Campus Compact who were concerned about my own generation's (I was a college undergraduate in the 1980s) lack of participation in behaviors such as voting. I was fortunate to have Dr. Alexander "Sandy" Astin as my doctoral advisor at a time when he had grant funding to lead a national study on the effectiveness of service-learning (Astin et al., 2000). After I completed my doctoral degree, I ran the National Service-Learning Clearinghouse Higher Education Project at UCLA, which focused on providing resources on service-learning to the higher education national field. I traveled around the country providing "Service-Learning 101" workshops at national and regional conferences. In 2000, after overseeing the Clearinghouse Project for a year, I was selected to be the Executive Director of California Campus Compact (now LEAD California). I was excited to be leading an organization of college presidents who were committed to engaging students in community service and service-learning. I was honored and grateful to be joining an organization that I deeply respected, with colleagues across the country that I could turn to for support, advice, and collaboration.

Over the past 22 years, I have intentionally focused our work on meeting the needs of our constituents in California while building a state-wide coalition of colleges and universities and, in doing so, influencing the national field of community engagement. I feel that each of these goals was complementary, benefiting the other. By working to transform higher education culture and pedagogy, we are simultaneously achieving the broader goal of educating students to be engaged in shaping and leading our democracy.

Building Coalitions through Dialogues and Networking

One of LEAD California's strategic goals is to foster deeply reflective and inclusive dialogues that help shape the community engagement field in California and the nation. When I began serving as the executive director in the early 2000s, there was often a lone service-learning director leading the institutionalization efforts on each campus. Thus, I quickly recognized the importance of periodically bringing these people together to provide opportunities to learn and interact with colleagues.

In those early years of my tenure, I was fortunate to develop a mentoring relationship with Dr. Richard Cone (director of the University of Southern California Joint Education Project at the time), a "pioneer" in the field of service-learning (Stanton et al., 1999). He too recognized the importance of convening the directors to build a coalition in the state. For the next 5 years, he hosted gatherings at the University of Southern California once or twice a year to bring directors from Southern California together to network, share resources, and engage in reflective dialogues about effective practices. Armed with this feedback, we began to tailor our programs and events to address specific concerns and newer trends or challenges that our members were facing.

In addition to the gatherings that were held in Southern California, we regularly convened directors and others in the San Francisco Bay Area, the Central Valley, the San Diego region, and whenever possible in the northern-most parts of the state. Over the past two decades, with the growth in national associations and organizations promoting and supporting service-learning and community engagement, the number of community engagement conferences, institutes, and trainings have proliferated, and our constituents have expressed that they now have ample opportunities to connect with colleagues. However, it is still important to convene people strategically (and virtually or in-person) around various issues or challenges they are facing.

Over the years, we have designed and implemented a number of institutes and retreats that influenced the field, while also deeply impacting those who attended. We intentionally organized these gatherings to build coalitions among the participants, creating lasting networks of support and spawning collaborations on future projects. A consistent outcome of these gatherings was that attendees took the ideas back to their campuses and initiated or replicated programs that helped to advance community engagement in higher education. For example, we have implemented several statewide faculty institutes that have been replicated at individual campuses.

In 2016, we embarked on a joint research project with Minnesota Campus Compact, to capture the longer-term impacts and lessons learned from reflective retreats and intensive learning and leadership communities we hosted between 2000 and 2015. Respondents to our survey stated that their participation contributed to developing new and/or deeper relationships with colleagues. One respondent shared:

> Getting to know each other as people really created a community of trust and allowed us to creatively imagine new ways of advancing our work on our campuses and in the field at large. I felt we were cheering each other on rather than competing.
> *(Mitchell & Telles, 2016, p. 2)*

Many of our programs included participants from outside California and thus, our gatherings, institutes, retreats, and trainings had an influence on the larger national community engagement field. A more recent example of our work to engage the field and bring the latest research to bear on this ever-evolving area is our collaboration on the Dissertation Dish which was launched in April 2022 and brings together LEAD California, the International Association for Research on Service-Learning and Community Engagement (IARSLCE), and Imagining America. This webinar series highlights recent doctoral degree recipients' high-quality, new research focused on service-learning and community engagement. Coalition building requires staying apprised of the latest research and practices influencing the field.

We also developed deeply transformational cohort experiences for staff and faculty from our member institutions. In 2006 we designed and implemented a 16-month leadership development experience for emerging and seasoned professionals of color in higher education who integrated community engagement agendas, such as social justice, equity, and multiculturalism, with the interests of stakeholders in diverse communities. This was the first professional development program designed for community engagement professionals of color in the field.

During this same period, we created an interdisciplinary faculty fellows program that linked community engagement, service-learning, and political engagement. Through this 2-year program, fellows developed, implemented, and evaluated courses that used service-learning to increase students' understanding of, and skills and motivation for, political participation. This program resulted in the book *Democratic Dilemmas of Teaching Service-Learning* (Cress & Donahue, 2011)—a collection of critically framed teaching cases addressing often unspoken challenges of teaching service-learning courses. Many of the relationships that were formed between faculty in this program, continue to exist today.

These are just a few examples of how an organization such as LEAD California can, through our convenings and professional development programming, build coalitions of support to deepen the quality and breadth of community engagement in a state, region, or the nation.

Developing Resources That Support Coalitions and Grow the Field

Another strategic goal of LEAD California is to serve as a resource to our member institutions as they address critical issues facing California. With support from federal grants, we were awarded from 2002 to 2012, LEAD California was able to regularly seek out and respond to the needs articulated by our campus partners. Many of the resources we develop for our California campuses are utilized or referenced by other community engagement professionals in the national field of community engagement. For example, in the early 2000s, there were concerns about risk management and liability issues in campus service programs. Our organization wrote the first risk management resource *Serving Safely*, which was widely disseminated across the country.

We also conducted a number of research studies that not only provided evidence of the impact of high-quality service-learning but also revealed common recommended practices to guide the work of service-learning centers across the nation. Our first research study, *How Higher Education Is Integrating Diversity and Service-Learning: Findings from Four Case Studies* (Vogelgesang et al., 2003), examined how service-learning and diversity might be more closely connected from an institutional perspective. Our second research study involved community partners from a diverse mix of colleges and universities in California. As part of this study, 99 community partners participated in 15 focus groups. This was the largest study of community partner perspectives in the literature at that time and provided valuable insight on building successful community-campus partnerships.

Recently, when the global pandemic caused us to suddenly shift how we were supporting our students, faculty, and community partners and engaging with each other, LEAD California actively gathered online resources and examples of COVID-19 responses from other institutions and organizations. We held regular dialogues with our members to support them and facilitate sharing across our network. We recognized the important role that we played in creating a sense of community and support as everyone sheltered in place and dealt with human tragedies, the unsettling uncertainty of what the future would hold, and feelings of isolation. We worked with a collective of community engagement directors in California to write the essay *The Urgency and Relevance of Community Engagement*, which was an inspiration for this book, to make the case for the importance of supporting our community engagement centers during the pandemic.

As the events of summer 2020 unfolded, we recognized the need to provide a different kind of support to our campuses. We again gathered information and resources to share with the field regarding racial justice and equity. We recognized that as a network and a movement, we have a responsibility to speak up and take action. We organized an opportunity for the community engagement professionals of color in California to come together in support of one another. Additionally, we lifted up other opportunities for education and advocacy to support the Black Lives Matter movement, by connecting our members to training and conferences offered by equity-focused organizations such as the National Conference on Race and Ethnicity in Higher Education (NCORE) and Equity in the Center.

Coalition Building to Leverage Resources and Maximize Impact

LEAD California has always been a relatively small organization with a modest budget and limited staffing. Our organization consistently seeks out opportunities to build relationships and partner with other organizations and key leaders in the community engagement or related fields. This allows us to maximize the reach and impact of our organization while at the same time bringing innovative programs to our constituents.

For nearly a decade, we met monthly with other statewide volunteer service organizations, the California Department of Education, and the Governor's Office of Service and Volunteerism (later renamed California Volunteers). This enabled us to keep ourselves apprised of the issues and programs that existed in our large state. Currently, we serve on the leadership advisory council of the Californians for Civic Learning, a state-wide organization advocating for civic education in K–12 and higher education.

We frequently partner with other organizations and higher education system offices to strategically offer programming to our colleges. We have partnered with the Community College Chancellor's Office to implement an annual state-wide community college service-learning conference. We regularly meet with the director of the state-wide California State University Chancellor's Office of Community Engagement (most of the 23 California

State Universities are members in our organization) to coordinate services and resources we are providing to these campuses so that we offer complementary programs and leverage our funds and staffing effectively and efficiently.

Our affiliation with the Campus Compact organization offered us access to a network of state directors across the United States that all had a similar mission—to build coalitions and promote service-learning and community engagement in their states with their higher education members. There was a strong culture of generosity among the state directors who were eager to share program ideas and answer the question, "how did you do that?"

In the late 1990s, we formed the Western Region Continuums of Service Consortia, made up of the State Compacts of Washington, Oregon, California, and Hawaii. In later years, we added in the State Compacts of Utah, Montana, and Colorado. Together we implemented the first Western Region Continuums of Service Conference in 1998 and, each year, we held the conference in the spring in one of our western states. We intentionally involved the community engagement field (representatives from our member institutions) in designing each conference and we focused on highlighting keynote speakers and conference presenters from the western states. Attendance at these conferences ranged from 300 to 500+ participants. Over time our conferences, which brought to light innovative ideas for the advancement of the community engagement field, were replicated in other regions of the country.

Evolutions for Continuous Improvement and Impact

Throughout our history, we have regularly and rigorously reflected on the relevancy and fulfillment of our mission. Our team conducts a variety of assessments (surveys, focus groups, interviews, and visioning teams) to ensure that we are meeting the needs of our constituents at our member colleges while also designing innovative programs and leading thoughtful and reflective dialogues. We recognize that evolution is always necessary and inevitable as we strive to make sure that our transformative mission-driven efforts align with our organizational structure. These assessments have reconfirmed our mission of prioritizing the place-based nature of our work—promoting community engagement in California and addressing challenges specific to California.

During the past three decades, we have prioritized our two founding principles—educating students to engage in our democracy and inspiring higher education to fulfill its mission of contributing to the public good. In California, our place-based focus—building community connections and coalitions, addressing local concerns, and working alongside local assets—succeeds because it is relational, sustainable, and trust based.

Recently, the destructive impacts of COVID-19, combined with the long history of institutional racism that continues to profoundly affect our state's marginalized communities, have once again laid bare the staggering social and economic inequalities and injustices that continue to plague not only our state but also our country. We recognize that while institutions need to persist in educating students to develop the knowledge, skills, values, and motivations to make a difference in the civic life of our communities, they also need to address issues of systemic social, economic, and racial injustice in our society.

The societal events beginning in 2020, along with shifts in organizational priorities at Campus Compact, led us to realize that it was time to leave our national parent organization and more fully devote our time, resources, and energy to supporting our California institutions. We made this decision after extensive conversations with our membership, our board of presidents, and other leaders in the community engagement field.

Recently, after completing a vision process with our member campuses, we announced our new name: LEAD California. LEAD California begins with the verb "lead," which serves as a call to action for the organization's staff, Board, member campuses, and communities. With equity, reciprocity, and trust at our core, LEAD California improves the lives of Californians throughout the state by leveraging the knowledge, resources, and assets of higher education. As a coalition of California's leading colleges and universities from all sectors of higher education and all corners of the state, LEAD California also strategically collaborates with other organizations whenever such partnerships serve the needs of our constituency. While our priorities continue to include fostering student engagement in our democracy and leading higher education in fulfilling its public purpose, equity will be at the center of LEAD California's future work. We will continue to facilitate professional networking across institutional types in order to promote collaboration, innovation, and effective practice. We are energized and excited to begin this new chapter for our organization and we move forward with an innovative spirit and an unwavering commitment to educate students for lives of public engagement while building equitable and thriving institutions and communities.

Conclusion

Building community engagement coalitions in higher education is complex and this chapter presents only a small fraction of the factors and strategies that should be considered or that may be instrumental in achieving one's goals. Movement building takes place over time and continually builds on the work of those who came before.

Most importantly, at the very heart of coalition building is the development and caretaking of relationships. Having strong relationships with other individuals and with organizations makes all else possible. After all, our higher education institutions and our communities are made up of people and it is the people, working collectively with trust and respect, who will create the world that we all wish to live in.

As the noted author Margaret Wheatley states, "People are the solution to the problems that confront us" (Wheatley, 2002, p. 12). A collection of people (a coalition) who are able to think and reflect together, care about one another, and act courageously together can challenge and address the crises we are facing in our democracy and our world.

References

Astin, A. W. (1998). The changing American college student: Thirty-year trends, 1966–1996. *Review of Higher Education, 21*(1), 115–135.

Astin, A. W., Parrott, S. A., Korn, W. S., & Sax, L. J. (1997) *The American freshman: Thirty year trends.* Higher Education Research Institute, UCLA.

Astin, A. W., Sax, L. J., & Avalos, J. (1996) *Long-Term effects of volunteerism during the undergraduate years.* Los Angeles, Higher Education Research Institute, University of California.

Astin, A. W., Vogelgesang, L. J., Ikeda, E. K., & Yee, J. A. (2000) *How service learning affects students. Executive summary.* Higher Education Research Institute, UCLA.

Campus Compact Civic Action Plan. (2015). https://compact.org/resource-posts/creating-a-great-campus-civic-action-plan/

Cress, C. M. & Donahue, D. M. (2011) *Democratic dilemmas of teaching service-learning: Curricular strategies for success.* Stylus Publishing, LLC.

Dewey, J. (1916). Democracy and education. In J. Boydston (Ed.), *John Dewey: The middle works 1889–1924, volume 9: 1916.* Southern Illinois University Press.

Dolgon, C., Eatman, T. K., & Mitchell, T. D. (2017). Conclusion: The devil at the crossroads: Service learning and community engagement from here on out. In C. Dolgon, T. D. Mitchell, & T. K. Eatman (Eds.), *The Cambridge handbook of service learning and community engagement* (pp. 527–534). Cambridge University Press.

Furco, A. (1999). Self-assessment rubric for the institutionalization of service-learning in higher education. *Service Learning, General,* 127. https://digitalcommons.unomaha.edu/slceslgen/127

Green, P. M., Bergen, D. J., Stewart, C. P., & Nayve, C. (2021). An engagement of hope: A framework and equity-centered theory of action for community engagement. *Metropolitan Universities, 32*(2), 129–157.

Hartley, M. (2009). Reclaiming the democratic purposes of American higher education: Tracing the trajectory of the civic engagement movement. *Learning and Teaching: The International Journal of Higher Education in the Social Sciences*, 2(3) Winter, 11–30.

Hartley, M., & Saltmarsh, J. (2016). A brief history of a movement: Civic engagement and American higher education. In M. Post, E. Ward, N. Longo, & J. Saltmarsh (Eds.), *Publicly engaged scholars: Next generation engagement and the future of higher education* (pp.34–60). Stylus.

Holland, B. A. (2000). Institutional impacts and organizational issues related to service-learning. *Michigan Journal of Community Service Learning, Spec*(1), 52–60: *Strategic Directions for Service-Learning Research*, 2000. http://hdl.handle.net/2027/spo.3239521.spec.107.

Jay, G., & Jones, S. E. (2006). The grassroots approach to curriculum reform: the cultures and communities program. In S. L. Percy, N. L. Zimpher, M. J. Brukardt (Eds.), *Creating a New Kind of University: Institutionalizing community-university engagement* (pp. 92–121). Anker Publishing Company, Inc.

Kesckes, K. (2006). *Engaging departments: Moving faculty culture from private to public, individual to collective focus for the common good*. Anker Publishing Company, Inc.

Kleinhesselink, K., Schooley, S., Cashman, S., Richmond, A., Ikeda, E., McGinley, P. (Eds.). (2015). *Engaged faculty institute curriculum*. Community-Campus Partnerships for Health.

Langseth, M. & Plater, W. M. (2004). *Public work & the academy: An academic administrator's guide to civic engagement and service-learning*. Anker Publishing Company, Inc.

Minkler, M. & Wakimoto, P. (2021). *Community organizing and community building for health and social equity*, 4th edition. Rutgers University Press.

Mitchell, T. D. & Telles, A. (2016). *The value of professional communities: Learning from long-term and intensive community engagement leadership programs*. California Campus Compact.

Stanton, T. K., Giles Jr., D. E., & Cruz, N. I. (1999). *Service-learning: A movement's pioneers reflect on its origins, practice, and future*. Jossey Bass.

Vogelgesang, L. J., Drummond, M., & Gilmartin, S. K. (2003). *How higher education is integrating diversity and service learning: Findings from four case studies*. San Francisco, California Campus Compact.

Votruba, J. C. (2004). Leading the engaged institution. In A. J. Kezar, T. C. Chambers, & J. C. Burkhardt. *Higher education for the public good: Emerging voices from a national movement* (pp. 263–271). Jossey-Bass.

Welch, M. & Plaxton-Moore, S. (2019). *The craft of community-engaged teaching and learning: A guide for faculty development*. Campus Compact.

Wheatley, M. J. (2002). *Turning to one another: Simple conversations to restore hope to the future*. Berrett-Koehler Publishers, Inc.

Wolff, T. (2001). The future of community coalition building. *American Journal of Community Psychology*, 29(2): 263–268.

Yamamura, E. K. & Koth, K. (2018). *Place-based community engagement in higher education: A strategy to transform universities and communities*. Stylus Publishing.

7
AND SO GOES THE NATION
California Gets to Work

Josh Fryday, Elena Klaw, and Andrea Tully

Introduction

Many of us implementing community engagement in higher education have been involved in one way or another with AmeriCorps, a federal service program "in which members and volunteers serve directly with nonprofit organizations to tackle our nation's most pressing challenges" (AmeriCorps, n.d.). According to their website, every year, AmeriCorps enrolls "more than 250,000 individuals to serve organizations making a difference in communities across America." To contextualize the vast scope of this effort, 40,000 communities are served each year by AmeriCorps members and their Corps of Senior Volunteers.

In this chapter, we describe the emergence and implementation of the #CaliforniansForAll College Corps, a groundbreaking collaboration between AmeriCorps and California Volunteers, "the state office tasked with engaging Californians in service, volunteering and civic action to tackle our State's most pressing challenges" (California Volunteers, 2022). This initiative has received national attention in media sources such as *The New York Times* (Karlamangla, 2022) and *The Atlantic* (Fallows, 2020) in addition to local outlets. California Governor Gavin Newsom boldly asserts, "College Corps is an antidote to this crisis of isolation, a down payment on the reconstruction of our society and the preservation of our democracy" (Newsom, 2022). As proponents of national service efforts, it is our sincere hope that the model described here will be replicated, adapted, and expanded so that, as the adage suggests, "as California goes, so goes the nation" (Newsom, 2021).

DOI: 10.4324/9781003448525-9

Beyond the ease of uplifting rhetoric, the contributors to this chapter are experienced in managing the challenges involved in securing and maintaining functional partnerships between a myriad of government and university offices to ensure students' success in serving local communities. Given the enormous complexity of this endeavor, we believe that the story of the California College Corps is worth telling, both in terms of its emergent mission and in terms of the distinct experiences of its diverse stakeholders, including the State government, university community engagement professionals, and student fellows. In this chapter, we provide three perspectives regarding the development and implementation of this ambitious program. Josh Fryday, the program's architect, first describes his vision for building the #CaliforniansForAll College Corps from his unique perch within the Office of the Governor as California's Chief Service Officer. In the next section, Elena Klaw and Andrea Tully discuss implementing the initiative at a large urban public university. The chapter concludes with the experiences and words of Fellows themselves.

Key Stakeholders in Realizing the College Corps: Implementing a Vision for California's Future

View from the State: How California Volunteers Created the #CaliforniansForAll College Corps by Josh Fryday, California Chief Service Officer, Office of the Governor

I grew up outside of San Francisco where earthquakes are a normal part of life. Nothing was normal about this one. I was stationed in Yokosuka, Japan in March 2011, when a 9.0-magnitude earthquake struck causing a subsequent tsunami and nuclear disaster. I had three hours to grab my seabag and fly to the USS Blue Ridge, the Flagship overseeing what would become the largest humanitarian aid and disaster relief effort in our military's history. There was barely enough time to hug my wife before she evacuated. She was three months pregnant with our first son and the Fukushima nuclear power plant had just started to melt down. I didn't know when I'd see her again or how the crisis would end.

During "Operation Tomodachi," we deployed 24 warships within days and over the course of the mission, with more than 15,000 sailors and marines, we delivered over 280 tons of relief supplied to an ally in need, and thousands of people who had lost everything. I'm tempted to just say "Go NAVY" but there is a more global lesson to this.

In my experience, service creates the opportunity for people to connect, build trust, tackle daunting problems, and accomplish great things together. When serving in the armed forces, political differences do not matter. What matters is working together around a common purpose to accomplish a shared mission.

Our world is facing serious challenges—a climate crisis, historic inequality, crippling student debt, and political division, to name a few. As concerns over the fragility of our democracy grow, we feel the urgency of a generational challenge to build the civic infrastructure necessary to meet the moment of today's existential threats. In California, we are working hard to meet this urgency and institutions of higher education are at the center of our work.

In the coming years, California Volunteers, Office of the Governor will be supporting, mobilizing, and deploying across multiple programs a force of young people in California nearly twice the size of the Peace Corps—the gold standard for national service programs in our country. These service members will take on climate change, tutor and mentor in low-income schools, support food banks, and tackle a variety of other community needs.

On the campaign trail, then Lieutenant Governor Gavin Newsom and I rolled out a policy proposal plan called "Uniting Californians in Service" to revitalize our civic fabric and reinvigorate the California spirit of service. Governor Newsom has a deep passion and bold vision for bringing people together and investing in service to foster a culture of compassion and connection.

One of these proposals was to appoint a cabinet-level position to expand and strengthen service, volunteerism, and civic engagement throughout the state, which is my current role as California Chief Service Officer leading California Volunteers, Office of the Governor.

Service and College

When I was mayor of my hometown, the great city of Novato in Northern California, the city partnered with Dominican University, the local private college, to create a program we called Re-imagining Citizenship. It was a relatively simple concept: students who graduated from a Novato high school and committed to serve two summers with the City of Novato and were admitted to Dominican University were given a scholarship to essentially allow them to graduate debt free for their service. This framework also included service-learning academic courses to ensure students could apply new skills acquired through community service to any sector or future career.

In my first year as Chief Service Officer with state investments from an extremely passionate Governor, California Volunteers partnered with AmeriCorps to expand this program model to eight universities. At 2 University of California (UC) campuses, 3 California State University (CSU) campuses, and 3 private colleges, 250 students served their community and received help paying for college. We called this first-in-the-nation pilot initiative the Civic Action Fellowship.

Participating students from the eight universities spent their academic year tutoring and mentoring K–12 students, supporting food banks, and taking climate action. For example, through 2 years of the Civic Action Fellowship at San José State University (SJSU), more than 80 Fellows mentored over 150 local third- through sixth-graders. During their service, SJSU Civic Action Fellows helped alleviate educational and technological proficiency gaps for lower-income students through tutoring and mentoring while earning money to pay for their own education. Due to the success of the pilot program, California Volunteers developed a plan to scale and establish a college service program across the state.

In 2022, California Volunteers created the #CaliforniansForAll College Corps (College Corps) to engage over 3,200 students a year in critical community work throughout the state. We launched the program on nearly 50 campuses, representing all systems of higher education in the state—UCs, CSUs, community colleges, and private universities. College Corps Fellows commit to serving 450 hours throughout the academic year and receive $10,000 toward their education. Like a California GI Bill, we are saying to a whole generation of Californians, "If you are willing to serve your community, we are willing to help you pay for college." It's a win-win-win for students, the community, and all of society.

Win for Students

College Corps has many benefits for the Fellows. First, we are helping students graduate with less debt. The $10,000 financial support for each Fellow is significant. In the first College Corps cohort, 68% are Pell Grant eligible. The $10,000 is the average amount a Pell Grant recipient or low-income student must come up with by either taking out loans (going into debt) or working.

When I was a Pell Grant student, I washed golf carts to help pay for school. Others work at restaurants, cafes, or at other basic jobs. At a roundtable of CSU San Bernardino College Corps Fellows in the Inland Empire, I asked what the impact of the program had been on the students. A Fellow named Rocco raised his hand and explained, "If it weren't for College Corps, I would be working at Jack-in-The-Box now. Instead, I get to do something very meaningful to me and give back to the community I grew up in."

With College Corps, students are able to build professional skills, networks, and social capital often only available to those who already have access. College Corps students no longer have to decide between pursuing their passion or a paycheck. They are able to simultaneously launch their career and uplift their community.

College Corps also aims to help students graduate on time. Fellows are required to work 450 hours over the academic year, limiting the work to roughly 15 hours a week so that they can focus on their academic work. The additional support provided by the program and connections created to the campus, community, and their cohort will improve graduation success.

Finally, students will finish the program with a better understanding and appreciation of the value they have to society. They will experience the pride of helping others and knowing their community values their contributions.

I was emotionally moved by Djuan, a focused and passionate College Corps Fellow with a history of financial and food insecurity. He told me he decided to do College Corps because he wanted to be a model for his kids. Djuan is not just a model for his kids, he is a model for our state, and thousands of his colleagues will be seen as models in their communities across California.

Win for Communities

College Corps is a win for communities who benefit from the meaningful work of the Fellows. In the beginning of the COVID-19 pandemic before California took the nation's first steps to shelter in place, we saw a drastic increase in need at food banks throughout the state. At the same time, food banks experienced a dramatic drop in the volunteers (mostly seniors) they rely upon to operate and distribute food. I oversaw the Food & Supplies Taskforce Workgroup for the state and the Governor immediately deployed the California National Guard, Conservation Corps and AmeriCorps members to support food banks facing a dire situation. The California National Guard performed critical work supporting food banks until their mission ended in the Spring of 2022.

Unfortunately, the increase in food insecurity has not gone down and food banks like the Find Food Bank serving the Coachella Valley, which is one of the poorest regions of California, continue to feed 150,000 individuals each month. In the areas the California National Guard previously supported, 40 College Corps Fellows now provide critical support to the Find Food Bank.

In addition to working in food insecurity, Fellows are focused on taking climate action and tutoring. College Corps Fellows are placed with local nonprofit organizations to complete their service, which also helps build the capacity of organizations to address local priorities.

Almost half of the Fellows are serving as tutors in low-income schools across the state. Tutors are especially needed now to support the one-on-one attention so desperately needed by students trying to make up for pandemic-related learning losses. President Biden called on states and communities to expand the number of tutors and mentors in our nation's schools to 250,000. California is answering the call.

Our hope is to also create the future pipeline of teachers our state needs. Mihn, a foster youth who attended the University of California, Merced, shared at a College Corps recruiting event that after spending a semester in the Civic Action Fellowship tutoring young people in low-income schools, she decided to dedicate her career to teaching. We imagine tens of thousands of young people just like her serving while in college and being inspired to spend their lives helping others.

Finally, College Corps is helping communities by creating access for those historically excluded from opportunities. During the Great Depression, President Franklin Delano Roosevelt famously launched a work relief program called the Civilian Conservation Corps (CCC) to employ mostly White young men in environmental projects throughout the country. While the CCC program helped shape the parks, tree canopies, and greener environments we enjoy today, it had a darker side—women were not allowed to join, and non-White participants were made to live and work in separate camps. While much work has gone into improving access to and participation in these types of programs, national service programs today still exclude specific populations of people like DREAMers because of federal funding.

As a result of State investment from Governor Newsom and the Legislature, we are proud to make College Corps the first state service program to allow AB 540 CA Dream Act students to participate. Often excluded from opportunities, there are now DREAMers from around the state able to receive funding for the first time as full-time students while experiencing the impact of giving back to their community.

Win for Society

College Corps is also a win for society when we graduate a generation of Californians and future leaders equipped with the tools and experience to work with people from different perspectives and backgrounds to solve problems together. We share the story of Augustus, a Fellow who grew up in a conservative household and whose vision about poverty and the people struggling to make ends meet changed when challenged by the real-life experience of serving a semester at a food bank.

California is also creating a generation connected to each other. College Corps Fellows work within a regional hub of students from schools in surrounding areas. They participate together in learning workshops; speaker seminars; and beginning, mid-year and end-of-year events. They are building a network of peers across the region and state to support them through their service, college career, and throughout their lives.

I know how strong the bond forged through service can be—how meaningful it is to meet a fellow veteran and within moments have an instant connection and common identity. Even if we are not the same age. Even if they look and think differently than me. Even if they are in another political party. Every year, thousands of College Corps Fellows will forever be connected by this special bond, a bond rooted in a common experience of service. California will be made stronger by the strength of these social bonds.

Where We Need to Go

College Corps is already helping students find their passions, start their careers, and become thoughtful, civically engaged leaders. Our hope for the future is simple: expand these kinds of service opportunities in every corner of the state and country. We know why it is so important. Increasing opportunities for people to serve builds trust by connecting people around a common mission, addresses community needs, and provides a shared sense of purpose, value, and connection in a world where we too often find ourselves isolated.

We can start by aggressively engaging all of civic society—elected officials, including mayors and school board members, universities, corporations, philanthropy, faith-based institutions, and anyone who will listen to build the civic infrastructure we so desperately need to unite this country and tackle the challenges we must solve. There can absolutely be a College Corps in every state and there should be a College Corps in every state. Let's get to work!

View from a University: Creating a Service Fellowship during a Pandemic by Elena Klaw and Andrea Tully, San José State University

So what does it mean to "get to work" in implementing California's vision for engaging college students in a service fellowship to address community problems? At San José State University, a large urban comprehensive commuter-focused institution, the Center for Community Learning & Leadership (CCLL), added to an already maximized workload by responding to a solicited call for proposals from California Volunteers. Housed within the Division of Academic Affairs, the Center had recently celebrated its 20th anniversary, with a party held in the campus bowling alley in which attendees received a copy of Putnam's classic book, "*Bowling Alone*," a cri de coeur for community engagement. At the time, CCLL was comprised of only 1.5 permanent staff members, a half-time faculty director and two AmeriCorps Volunteers in Service to America (VISTA). Despite a minimal staffing structure, the mission of CCLL was and remains large. As stated on its website, "CCLL is the primary office that supports curricular service-learning and community engagement experiences at SJSU" (Center for Community Learning & Leadership, 2022). Simply put, CCLL provides resources and guidance to faculty, students, and community organizations who engage in intentional partnerships that enhance students' education and contribute to the public good. By supporting service-learning and community engagement as a transformative pedagogy, CCLL aims to develop civic leaders that have the necessary skills and attitudes to remedy disparity.

When California Volunteers solicited a proposal in 2019 for SJSU to engage college students in addressing local disparities through a funded Civic Action Fellowship, the Center was able to build upon existing service-learning efforts to develop an effective and convincing program model. With the explicit goal of expanding the SJSU Cyber Spartans program, a successful SJSU service-learning effort that generated significant increases in computer programming self-efficacy in children attending subsidized after-school programs (Salubre et al., 2020), CCLL arranged meetings with longstanding trusted community partners to determine their interest in working with the Center to implement a service fellowship. Once partnerships were established and a funding award was received in 2020, CCLL was able to offer 44 SJSU students a monthly living allowance and an end-of-program education award for providing a minimum of 675 hours of service per academic year with an objective of reducing disparities in access and exposure to computer programming. The program model involved having all Fellows learn to provide developmentally appropriate instruction in the Scratch computer programming language and to engage youth attending local subsidized after-school programs in coding activities.

On a campus comprised of 37% of students self-identified as Asian, 28% as Hispanic/Latinx, and less than 14% as White (Academic Affairs, 2022), the Center sought to ensure that the diversity of our Fellowship reflected that of the campus. Thus, students were recruited across majors and the opportunity was promoted to the University's academic and cultural student success centers, the Career Center, to service-learning faculty, and clubs and organizations within the Divisions of Academic and Student Affairs. The composition of the cohort represented the ethnic diversity of the University, and Fellows were enrolled from all nine disciplinary SJSU colleges.

Unbeknownst to the implementation team, initial plans for the Fellowship would soon be radically altered by the COVID-19 pandemic. Just as the program readied to launch in 2020, shelter in place mandates shuttered most schools and agencies throughout the County. Already under contract with our funders, with agreements secured from our partners and our Fellows, the SJSU Fellowship staff observed in horror as educational disparities widened as a result of the shutdowns (Dorn et al., 2021; Greenfield, 2022). Simultaneously, both members of the university community and community partners confronted the dramatic isolation and uncertainty facing all stakeholders in education and community development (Dorn et al., 2021).

While managing increased individual caretaking responsibilities, CCLL deliberated as to how to best fulfill the Center's responsibility to serve the students attending the University, many of whom faced stressors related to poverty, themselves, as well as to our urban community, particularly school-aged children who needed opportunities for learning enrichment and mentoring even more than they had before. In line with the Center's commitment to data-based approaches, focus groups and interviews were conducted to explore the barriers and opportunities for faculty and nonprofit community partners regarding community-engaged learning efforts during the shutdowns, and to chart a path forward based on the findings. This investigation led to the conclusion that partnerships with higher education were needed by community agencies more than ever, and that local youth would appreciate receiving instruction and encouragement from college students, as planned, during this unusual period of completely virtual schooling.

With no clear direction or guidance from the University itself, or from the Chancellor of the California State University "who oversees 23 campuses, 477,000 students and 56,000 faculty and staff" (CSU Leadership, 2022), and no timeline for a return to in-person learning (the 2 weeks of closures that were initially anticipated became nearly 2 years), CCLL developed new program models to implement virtual transformative community-engaged learning experiences. In solidarity with educators across the globe, the Center for Community Learning & Leadership shifted to remote electronic modalities of instruction, aiming to provide the quality of community-engaged learning that we had envisioned prior to the COVID-19 pandemic while relying on technologies that many of us had never used. Thus, the Center cautiously but fullheartedly pivoted our funded Civic Action Fellowship to a remote model containing both synchronous and asynchronous components. The newly designed Fellowship program involved 43 college students providing weekly computer programming lessons through Zoom, along with individual kits that contained educational games made by the Fellows specifically for elementary school students enrolled in local subsidized after-school programs.

Meeting the specific, conflicting, and sometimes nonsensical requirements of multiple unwieldy bureaucracies, including those of the University, the Chancellor's Office of the California State University (CSU) system, California Volunteers, and the federal AmeriCorps program, in addition to implementing and managing a new model of service delivery, added levels of complexity that often threatened to undo all efforts at providing meaningful enrichment to local youth and community-engaged learning for college students. For example, managing the multiple funding streams and state and federal policies involved in the grant award proved daunting and documents often had to be corrected, rerouted, and resubmitted multiple times before contracts could be executed. Despite these hurdles, CCLL maintains that the success of the 2020–2022 Civic Action Fellowship provides an exemplar of innovation and persistence in community-engaged learning. In 2023, the Center continues to assert that civic development and community engagement is a necessary response for higher education to the demands posed by cataclysmic ruptures to our social contracts, our democracy, and our educational systems.

View from the Student Fellows: Benefits and Challenges of Participating in a Service Fellowship

In total, 31 of 43 SJSU Civic Action Fellows agreed to participate in interviews at the conclusion of their service term in 2021, a unique year in which due to pandemic-related shutdowns, all service was provided through remote modalities. All interviews were conducted by student research assistants and were recorded and transcribed verbatim. To identify themes and subthemes within the Fellows' interview transcripts, a Grounded Theory approach was used for coding and analyzing qualitative data (Strauss & Corbin, 1990).

The findings from the interviews were encouraging, demonstrating that as a result of their participation, almost 100% of the 43 Civic Action Fellows who were interviewed reported growth in three primary areas, *professional development* (31/31), *community and campus engagement* (31/31), and *awareness of self and others* (29/31). The theme of *professional development* included the development of core skills (77%, 24/31), specific technical skills (65%, 20/31), and new career interests (48%, 15/31). Core skills, competencies that are generalizable across fields of specialization, were developed in the areas of collaboration, time management, flexibility, and leadership. Technical skills included learning the computer programming language, Scratch, and learning to provide instruction through Zoom.

In terms of *engagement*, all Fellows interviewed reported multiple ways in which they became more involved and connected. Fellows reported that they built relationships with both the youth they mentored (81%, 25/31) and their peers in the Fellowship program (65%, 20/31). They felt more connected to the community they served (53%, 16/31) and for some, to their academic experience (32%, 10/31).

Further, the Fellows indicated that they gained *awareness* about themselves and others. Specifically, they noted gaining insight into their own strengths (77%, 24/31) and their areas of growth as well as learning about others' experiences and viewpoints (74%, 23/31). The results of this study, conducted just as the Civic Action Fellows completed a year of service, mirror the research team's findings regarding the transformative effects of service-learning on alumni (Tully et al., 2019). Prototypical quotes selected from the Fellows' transcripts illustrate the common themes that emerged. The findings of this research have inspired the CCLL team to continue developing, refining, and expanding this program model in its new iteration, the #CaliforniansForAll College Corps at SJSU.

Prototypical Quotes

"I definitely have the opportunity to reflect on my privilege this year and I think being part of the Fellowship helped with that. I think I just gained ... a better sense, more awareness of both my racial and financial privilege."

"Building connections with my student. That was hands down the best part."

"The rewarding stuff was meeting friends ... seeing the different perspectives and different types of thinking."

"I definitely gained empathy, patience, and I've definitely gained working in a team and being a team member ... and, overall, I think just confidence, knowing that I can impact the future for us."

"I'm staying involved with the community and being a volunteer. ... I want to continue doing stuff ... because it makes me feel good, and I really enjoyed the experience overall."

"It also gave me the chance to interact with other people and get that social interaction from people outside of my house. It made the pandemic a little bit more bearable and not make me feel isolated and alone."

Challenges and Limitations

Although interviewees identified challenges related to participating in the Fellowship including balancing competing priorities and managing shifting expectations and complex team dynamics, results suggest that participation in a year-long virtual service fellowship enabled college students at an urban public institution to hone professional skills, increase engagement, and expand their awareness and understanding of themselves and others. The research builds upon the substantial body of evidence revealing that community-engaged learning is significantly correlated with increased academic engagement, professional skills, leadership development, and civic involvement (Celio et al., 2011; Engberg et al., 2018; Mitchell & Rost-Banik, 2019; Ramnani et al., 2016; Tinto, 1993; Tully et al., 2018). Longitudinal research is needed to more fully elucidate the connections between community-engaged learning and career development.

For Fellows serving during the COVID-19 pandemic, community engagement was particularly important as an antidote to the isolation, despair, and powerlessness experienced during the difficult years of quarantines, lockdowns, and societal ruptures. In recognition of the integral role of higher education in addressing the ever-changing challenges of the current era, CCLL remains committed to continuing to develop flexible, accessible, and engaging formats for community learning.

Conclusion

At this time, State offices, nonprofit community organizations, and institutions of higher education remain strained by overly complicated bureaucratic procedures that are slow to adapt to the changed landscape of education, as well as by a continued federal assault on democracy, safety, and bodily freedom. Yet, the contributors to this chapter believe that the California College Corps, a state-wide movement that builds on decades of programs offered by AmeriCorps and California Volunteers, offers a blueprint for forwarding democracy by providing a (substantially increased from prior programs) living allowance and education award to more than 3,200 college student Fellows across the State. Notably, recipients are college students with varied academic majors, 80% are students of color, 65% are first-generation college attendees, and 81% are experiencing financial need. Research findings from the initial iteration of this program, known as the Civic Action Fellowship, mirror the exact motivations expressed by the incoming cohort of statewide College Corps Fellows, including developing personal and professional skills and networks, making an impact on their community, and increasing their sense of belonging (WestEd, 2023). Encouragingly, findings on the state-wide cohort of College Corps Fellows (WestEd, 2023) reveal that nearly two-thirds of current Fellows are interested in careers involving public service and approximately 39% reported a reduced burden from student loans as a result of the College Corps Program.

At the state-wide level and on the ground at SJSU, we remain convinced that, now, more than ever, community-engaged learning approaches that are grounded in both social justice and scientific data play a vital and transformative role in empowering future college graduates as change agents who will effectively address the persistent social problems that plague our communities, our nation, and our planet. Although college student service is not a panacea for systemic inequalities, such efforts point the way toward a more socially just future. Armed with promising data about effective approaches, and powerful partnerships that provide universities with state and federal funding to partner with local communities, let's "get to work" indeed!

References

Academic Affairs. (2022, December 1). *Quick facts*. San José State University www.sjsu.edu/iesa/ir/dashboards/quick-facts.php

AmeriCorps. (n.d.). https://americorps.gov/

California State University. (2022). *Leadership*. www.calstate.edu/csu-system/about-the-csu/leadership/

California Volunteers. (2022). *College Corps*. www.californiavolunteers.ca.gov/

Celio, C. I., Durlak, J., & Dymnicki, A. (2011). A meta-analysis of the impact of service-learning on students. *Journal of Experiential Education*, 34(2), 164–181.

Center for Community Learning & Leadership. (2022). *Mission*. San Jose State University. www.sjsu.edu/ccll/about/mission.php

Dorn, E., Hancock, B., Sarakatsannis, J., & Viruleg, E. (2021, July 27). *Covid-19 and education: The lingering effects of unfinished learning*. McKinsey & Company. www.mckinsey.com/industries/education/our-insights/covid-19-and-education-the-lingering-effects-of-unfinished-learning

Engberg, M. E., Carrera, L. F., & Mika, L. P. (2018). Utilizing domestic off-campus experiences to influence social justice awareness and career development. *Journal of Higher Education Outreach*, 22(1), 63–86.

Fallows, J. (2020, April 7). A new way for Californians to serve. *The Atlantic*. www.theatlantic.com/ideas/archive/2020/04/service-in-the-time-of-pandemic-californias-approach/622104/

Greenfield, M. (2022, January 10). *Children's health during the COVID-19 pandemic: What have we learned?* McKinsey & Company. www.mckinsey.com/industries/healthcare-systems-and-services/our-insights/childrens-health-during-the-covid-19-pandemic-what-have-we-learned

Karlamangla, S. (2022, December 20). California begins service program for college students. *New York Times*. www.californiavolunteers.ca.gov/nytimes-california-begins-service-program-for-college-students/

Mitchell, T. D., & Rost-Banik, C. (2019). How sustained service-learning experiences inform career pathways. *Michigan Journal of Community Service Learning*, 25(1), 18–29.

Newsom, G. @GavinNewsom (2021, July 18). As California goes, so goes the nation [Tweet] Twitter. https://twitter.com/GavinNewsom/status/1420399102211227650

Newsom, G. (2022, November 12). *In the news*. California Volunteers. www.californiavolunteers.ca.gov/college-corps-could-be-the-model-for-higher-education-america-desperately-needs/

Ramnani, A., Ramos, J., Lopez, A. A., & Klaw, E. (2016). Application: A social psychology experiment on learning by social immersion. In S. Randal (Ed.), *Social psychology: How other people influence our thoughts and actions (2 volumes)* (pp. 409). Greenwood.

Salubre, K., Tully, A., Ghavami, N., & Klaw, E. (2020, April). *Cyberspartans: Assessing youth self-efficacy and engagement in STEM*. Paper presented at the Western Psychological Association Conference, San Francisco, CA.

Strauss, A., & Corbin, J. M. (1990). *Basics of qualitative research: Grounded theory procedures and techniques.* Sage Publications, Inc.

Tinto, V. (1993). *Leaving college: Rethinking the causes and cures of student attrition* (2nd edition). University of Chicago Press.

Tully, A., Klaw, E., & Da Silva, N. (2018). *The effects of service-learning on undergraduates* [Unpublished manuscript].

Tully, A., Klaw, E., Maciel, M., & Young, B. (2019, March). *What about alumni?* Presentation conducted at the Western Region Continuums of Service Conference, San Diego, CA.

WestEd. (2023, January 27). *College corps evaluation early findings & reflections.* College Corps Convention. Report presented by WestEd, UC Merced.

8

A PRESIDENTIAL PERSPECTIVE

Place-Based Community Engagement in Faith-Based Higher Education

Erica K. Yamamura, Kent Koth, and Chris Nayve

Introduction

Colleges and universities that have a connection to organized religion and are mission focused, better known as faith-based institutions, are a unique institutional type. Compared to public institutions, faith-based colleges and universities often draw upon their religious inspiration to pursue their mission and purpose. Community engagement is a central element of most faith-based higher education institutions. While there is abundant research on leadership (Martin et al., 2005), especially presidential leadership in higher education, less is known about presidential leadership of community engagement at faith-based institutions, despite the call for leaders at faith-based institutions over the past decade to strategically address the growing concerns of students, faculty, and community members. In addition, the recent COVID-19 pandemic and national racial crisis endemic have shifted higher education into crisis mode. This chapter explores the interconnection between faith-based institutions and community engagement, particularly during these heightened times of crisis. Drawing upon in-depth interviews, we examine the values, priorities, and strategic actions of two college presidents of faith-based institutions (Catholic and Jesuit Catholic), one current and one emeritus, who served as leaders of their campus during the first 2 years of the COVID-19 pandemic.

Presidential Leadership Is Evolving

College presidents are serving shorter tenures while becoming more diverse, especially by race and gender. The 2017 American Council on Education study of presidential leadership notes that the average tenure of a college president is six and one-half years (ACE, 2017). According to the ACE study, 30% of college presidents are women and 17% of college presidents are Black, Indigenous, and People of Color (BIPOC) (ACE, 2017). The cadre of presidents serving faith-based institutions is also becoming increasingly diverse (Winters, 2019).

In addition, college presidents are facing new and enduring challenges in higher education. While some parents are questioning the value of college and their return on investment, Zaloom's (2019) research shows that the cost of a college education continues to rise and many more families are struggling to pay for their children to attend. In addition, Grawe (2018) projects that a demographic shift in college-age students leading to an "enrollment" cliff, resulting in a 15% decrease in traditional college-aged students. In his more recent book, Grawe (2020) posits that in addition to an enduring enrollment cliff, more college students will be choosing options outside of the Northeast and Midwest, two areas replete with faith-based institutions. Taken together, this research suggests an enduring economic crisis in higher education will start soon. For many tuition-dependent institutions without a substantial endowment, presidential leadership will require increased innovation and strategic use of finite resources, including their leadership of community engagement on their campuses.

Placed-Based Community Engagement

For several decades, hundreds of colleges and universities have engaged in local or global community engagement through service-learning courses, community-based research, or direct volunteer service (Astin et al., 2000). Drawing upon these tools of engagement, faith-based institutions have utilized community engagement to animate their institutions' missions and religious traditions while providing service to the community. Historically, research on community engagement has focused on student learning and outcomes (Post et al., 2016; Welch, 2016) which may not be too surprising since most colleges and universities are initially motivated to pursue the work for the benefit of their students.

Yet many scholars have questioned the power dynamics, racism, classism, and student-exclusive focus of these traditional forms of community engagement (Green et al., 2021; Mitchell, 2008; Mitchell & Latta, 2020; Santiago-Ortiz, 2018; Stoecker, 2016). In addition, more recent research addresses the benefits and impact of community engagement beyond students including impact on other campus stakeholders, such as faculty, staff, alumni, and donors (Yamamura & Koth, 2019), and the community, including community members and community organizations (Lau et al., 2021).

Place-based community engagement (PBCE) is a newer and evolving type of community engagement that begins to respond to the critiques of more traditional forms of community engagement. Yamamura and Koth (2018) define PBCE as "a long-term university-wide commitment to partner with local residents, organizations, and other leaders to focus equally on campus and community impact within a clearly defined geographic area" (Yamamura & Koth, 2018, p.18).

PBCE takes a more critical approach to community engagement that centers the community more equitably and focuses the engagement opportunities beyond just students (Yamamura & Koth, 2018). Given the challenging economic times facing higher education during this period of crisis, PBCE provides universities with a collective impact strategy to have maximum impact with their finite resources.

PBCE is quite compatible with faith-based institutions. For example, four of the five institutions highlighted in Yamamura and Koth's (2018) book on PBCE were faith based (Catholic) and over half of the universities that are members of the Place-Based Justice Network (a national network focusing on place-based strategies) are faith-based institutions. In their book, Yamamura and Koth (2018) noted the importance of presidential support to advance PBCE. More recently, in an article focused on leading PBCE initiatives, Koth and Yamamura identified three leadership competency areas for community engagement professionals: 1) managing geographies of place and space, 2) focusing equally on community and university impact, and 3) leading with multicultural competency and inclusion (Yamamura & Koth, 2019).

Building upon the emergent research on PBCE, this chapter explores presidential leadership of faith-based institutions that have pursued a place-based strategy. Our research questions are:

- What does presidential leadership look like in highly community-engaged faith-based institutions?
- In particular, in times of crisis, how do presidents support community engagement?

Presidential support is typically important to advance a campus initiative, yet there is very little literature on presidential leadership in community engagement, especially place-based community engagement. Understanding presidential perspectives is even more important, given the role that community engagement could play in helping institutions navigate times of crisis (such as the COVID-19 pandemic).

Methodology

Data Collection

For this study, we utilized convenience sampling (Creswell, 2014) to identify two seasoned college presidents. In particular, we sought to identify presidents at faith-based institutions who championed and strategically integrated community engagement on their campus and nationally. We also wanted to identify experienced presidents (those who had served as president at their college for at least 5 years) who had established their leadership teams and set their strategic plans. The first two presidents we identified agreed to participate in our study (Catholic and Jesuit Catholic).

One of the two presidents we interviewed is President Emeritus Father Steve Sundborg S.J., who served as the President of Seattle University from 1997 to 2021. Founded in 1891, Seattle University is a Jesuit Catholic university located on 50-acres in central Seattle. The university enrolls over 7,400 students in undergraduate and graduate programs within six distinct colleges and schools. Drawing upon its mission of "educating the whole person, to professional formation, and to empowering leaders for a just and humane world," Seattle University has a long history of service to society and advocating for social justice. About 44% of undergraduate students are from Washington state, 9.3% are international students, and 46.6% of all students are from ethnically diverse backgrounds, including Black, Indigenous, and People of Color. Very few Seattle University students are from the neighborhoods near campus which creates an imperative for the University to provide students with the context and history of the very diverse and significantly important neighborhoods of central Seattle.

The other president is President James T. Harris III, who became the University of San Diego's (USD's) fourth president on August 3, 2015. Founded in 1949, USD is a Catholic university located on 180 acres in the San Diego County community of Linda Vista, California and located in one of the world's great diverse urban centers. USD enrolls more than 9,000 students from 85 countries and 50 states within 7 colleges and schools. 58% of the undergraduate students come from California and 43% come from ethnically diverse backgrounds. San Diego's proximity to the United States-Mexico border, where communities and cultures converge, provides students and faculty members with unique opportunities to learn, to put theory into action and to find new ways to lead purposeful lives within a context that celebrates contemporary Catholic values grounded in the liberal arts tradition. As part of a 5-year strategic planning project, the Horizon Project, USD is currently exploring becoming a Hispanic-Serving Institution by 2026.

Relationships and trust are important to having open and honest interviews. For this reason, the coauthors of this chapter who serve as the lead campus community engagement administrators on their particular campus interviewed their respective president. Each of these administrators has served in their role with their respective president for more than 5 years. For Seattle University, the faculty coauthor also joined the interview. Through in-depth semistructured interviews with each president, we explored three distinct areas: 1) general leadership and values; 2) challenges, change, and crises; and (3) community engagement. Interviews were recorded and transcribed verbatim.

Positionality

As coauthors, we have developed a strong colleagueship over the last decade growing and deepening our understanding of and work in community engagement. We will each share our positionality in this research. Kent Koth: In my role as the founding Executive Director of the Seattle University Center for Community Engagement, I lead Seattle University's efforts to connect our campus and community to pursue our university missions of "empowering leaders for a just and humane world." Frequently in my work, I draw upon my curiosity about understanding other ways of knowing to build partnerships. In addition, I am the son of a Methodist minister and I hold a graduate degree from Pacific School of Religion in Berkeley. These identities led to a close working relationship with President Emeritus Sundborg and made it quite natural for me to approach Father Sundborg for this study.

Chris Nayve: In my official role as the Associate Vice President for Community Engagement and as someone who has worked at USD for over 20 years leading our institution's community engagement mission and strategy, I recognize that my influence within my campus and in the field of community engagement has grown over time. My first communication with President Harris was in June 2015, shortly after it was announced that he would be the next president of USD. He had a reputation as a national leader in community engagement, so I sent him a welcome email a few months prior to his start. I was pleasantly surprised by his prompt and enthusiastic response as well as his interest in meeting once he was situated in San Diego. True to his word, President Harris and I met in early August of 2015 on his third day on campus, and in the summer California heat we walked through USD's neighborhood of Linda Vista. We shared our histories and experiences, including feeling unseen and invisible in our youth as formative to seeking vocations in public service and education. He reflected on being housing insecure as a young man and the feeling of being marginalized when he was a janitor. I shared my experiences as a youth feeling misguided and unappreciative of my Filipino culture. As we shared experiences of feeling unseen and seemingly cast away, I could not help but feel that President Harris was a kindred spirit. It was clear that both of our early experiences were formative in framing public service and equity-focused community partnerships as core values that would shape much of our leadership experiences in higher education (and converge at USD that would include incorporating an anchor and placed-based mission in our strategic plan).

Erica Yamamura: Prior to becoming a faculty member, I coordinated community partnerships for 4 years at the UCLA Center for Community Engagement building a bridge between the university and underserved K–12 schools in the Los Angeles area. I have spent the last sixteen years as a faculty member training educational leaders in K–12, higher education, and nonprofit organizations. At Seattle University, I have partnered extensively with Kent and the Sundborg Center for Community Engagement at Seattle University, specifically with PBCE. Kent and I have also connected with Chris over the years collaborating on conference panels and other spaces that focus on community engagement—and this is our first formal writing project together. I've had the opportunity to interview and engage with Fr. Sundborg as a faculty member and in my community engagement work for over 10 years. I've had the opportunity to connect with President Harris at conferences and to learn more about his journey and work from Chris.

Data Analysis

The data was open coded. Thereafter the data was further analyzed for themes in the following categories: values, priorities, and strategic actions. Lastly, we examined the role of social identities (race, class, gender, and religion). Once themes were generated, we engaged in member checking with the interviewees.

Sample: Seattle University and University of San Diego Presidents

As noted previously, the President Emeritus of Seattle University and the current President of the University of San Diego served as participants in our study. President Emeritus Stephen Sundborg S.J. served as the 21st President of Seattle University for 24 years until he retired in 2021. Originally from the territory of Alaska, President Emeritus Sundborg is a Catholic priest and has been a member of the Society of Jesus (the Jesuits) for over 60 years. During his tenure as President of Seattle University, Father Sundborg facilitated a dramatic expansion of academic programs that increased Seattle University's reputation for empowering leaders for a just and humane world. He also founded the Seattle University Center for Community Engagement in 2004 and advocated for the creation of the university's PBCE effort, the Seattle University Youth Initiative. Seattle University is a Carnegie Classified Community Engaged University.

President James T. Harris III became the fourth president of the University of San Diego on August 3, 2015. USD is the youngest, independent institution on the U.S. News & World Report list of top 100 universities in the United States and one of the small number of universities in the world designated as an Ashoka U Changemaker Campus and a Carnegie Classified Community Engaged University with a commitment to PBCE and a strong anchor institution mission. Under his leadership, Dr. Harris integrated community engagement and anchor institution practices as key strategic pillars in USD's strategic plan. Dr. Harris is a staunch supporter of community engagement and has enhanced engagement efforts at the Mulvaney Center for Community, Awareness, and Social Action. President Harris was a first-generation college student who previously served for 13 years as the president of Widener University, a private, independent institution educating more than 6,300 students on four campuses in two states—Pennsylvania and Delaware. Prior to his appointment at Widener, he was the president of Defiance College in Defiance, Ohio, where he established the McMaster School for the Advancement of Humanity and developed a service-learning program that was ranked among the top 25 in the country.

Findings

Three key themes emerged from our interviews: 1) community engagement as a way to actualize mission, 2) the importance of presidential leadership, and 3) the link between community engagement and diversity, equity, and inclusion. All three of these themes are interconnected with crisis leadership, especially with COVID-19 and racial justice.

"Mission as a Verb": Community Engagement as a Vehicle to Actualize Mission

Each president saw community engagement as important to their institutional mission, academic enterprise, community impact, and ability to attract external funding, albeit at times in qualitatively distinct ways.

Community Engagement as Valuable Mission Work

Both presidents saw community engagement as mission work. For example, Sundborg shared:

> We say we are dedicated to the "education of the whole person" [part of Seattle's University mission]. Well, that's the whole thing where you

got your education and your community. And I think that's great, great value. It's almost like a differentiator.

(S. Sundborg, personal communication, October 28, 2021)

Harris noted that earlier in his career, during his first presidency, community engagement enhanced his institution's reputation. He shared:

> Service-learning then kind of became part of the lexicon, and we adopted–our faculty took the lead of really embedding service-learning into the curriculum (J.T. Harris III, personal communication, October 25, 2021). And we had stated in our strategic plan that year that we wanted to be one of the top service-learning schools in the country and no one ranked service-learning schools at all at that point. By the time I left eight years later, US News and World Report had the top 25 service-learning schools and here's [the College] in the same category as Stanford, you know, Brown. And we've never had that kind of national recognition.

Sundborg echoed Harris' observation as he noted:

> You know, it becomes a significant part of your reputation too … if you're a university deeply involved in community engagement, that becomes known and that's part of your reputation and that drives you.

In addition, both presidents highlighted the need for this prioritization to be embedded in the university's strategic actions. Harris shared, "I think one of the most important things that we've done has been embedding the work of anchor institutions into our strategic plan, and using the language, reinforcing the great work of our faculty." Also noteworthy is that both presidents continued to focus on community engagement even during times of crises such as the COVID-19 pandemic and ongoing crisis of racism in the United States.

Putting the Mission into the Academic Enterprise

Both presidents identified community engagement as a mission-centered pedagogical method for faculty to apply theory to practice in their teaching. In particular, the presidents named a number of transformational learning benefits. President Harris, who had served as a faculty member earlier in his career, shared:

> So, it was in those very early days of teaching that [community engagement] kind of was ingrained in me that I saw the impact it had on

my students. They got the material better, they performed better in class. They were more conversant. So, I saw the impact.

Mentoring and experiential learning are also integral aspects of this transformative learning. He continued:

> I think it was that early commitment demonstrated to me that if you put a concerted effort together with students and then we had faculty that we assigned as basically the mentors of these students. Eventually, they would travel with them internationally, they travel with them locally and it became such a powerful experience.

Sundborg also highlighted the power of connecting community engagement with an academic course in order for students to understand and negotiate bias and discrimination in their lives. He shared:

> I learned from our community engagement how many very good students really want to do good within the community. They need to have more than that. They need to have real examination and maybe reconstruction almost around their principles or their views because of hidden biases and discriminations they may have. And there's probably no purpose of the university more so than in community engagement and in the Seattle University Youth Initiative that students were really challenged in needing to do that.

With Seattle University's campus-wide PBCE strategy, this work also encompassed diversity, equity, and inclusion as the recent racial endemic crisis amplified the pandemic of racism in the United States. Sundborg observed that "calls for vulnerability and deep learning" enhanced students' transformational educational experience, including their understanding of race and racism.

University Impact on Community

While both presidents saw student learning as a priority, they also emphasized the importance of pursuing positive community impact within the external communities their respective campuses served. For example, Harris noted:

> I felt it was important that we did physical service, that we actually were building homes, that we were, you know, serving food. So, I was all in and deeply involved and very hands-on.

In this example, the physical service complemented the academic learning and allowed students to engage in a different way.

Funding Incubator and Donor Engagement Opportunity

Both presidents highlighted the importance of funding community engagement, including during times of crisis. Sundborg shared, "If community engagement is going to be successful, it has to be funded. And if it's going to be funded, presidential leadership is called for prioritizing." He further added, "You know, it doesn't take a lot [of money] to start. But it takes something by way of financial resources to get going. And then it can build on itself and then it can become pretty significant." For Seattle University, this was initially primarily private donor funding. Sundborg summarized, "we would not be where we are in community engagement without that very, very strong financial support that we received." This was also the case at USD, where mission-driven giving and university investment increased when community engagement was strategically centered.

Once community engagement attains some initial success in demonstrating impact on campus and community and attracts external resources, additional funders emerge and the work can grow exponentially. As Seattle University raised funds and its work became better known in the Seattle region, additional individuals, corporations, and foundations became interested in supporting the university's community engagement efforts. The university subsequently expanded its fund development infrastructure to support donor identification, cultivation, and stewardship. Harris shared how, earlier in his career, community engagement catalyzed funding that transformed his institution. He noted:

> The board [of trustees] gave me a pass in some ways with [community engagement] in that [the College] really wasn't committed to before. And they liked it because it had a good Christian element to it and I was a good example of it. In a deeper conversation with our biggest donor, I said, "If you could do anything with your resources right now, what would you do?" and he paused. And literally, this little tear came to his eyes. "If we could have anything. If we could do anything to help eliminate human suffering, that would be our goal." ... He and I got into these deep conversations about how his philanthropy might change. And I honestly, at the time, didn't know that the money was going to come to us. I thought he was thinking about sending it maybe to a [major foundation]. And it came back to us as a college and what we were doing with service and how much he respected that and that kind of lived with his life because he was the man committed to service.

When Harris started as President at a previous institution, the college had an endowment of $4 million. The board chair made a $6 million gift. Harris shared, "So we are talking about transformational giving, transformational way of thinking about it. And what it did was it sponsored students to do international [community engagement] research and travel."

Leadership

Harris and Sundborg provided keen insight into their personal leadership practices as well as how they chose to lead in times of crisis. These are both important to understand presidential leadership more fully. Both of these factors also contribute to how presidents at faith-based institutions weave community engagement into their vision and overall work.

Personal Leadership

It should not be a surprise that both Sundborg and Harris drew upon their faith during their presidential tenure. However, there were noted differences due to their identities as a priest (Sundborg) and nonpriest (Harris). As a priest, Sundborg shared:

> I was really grounded in my faith throughout my entire time of being president at Seattle University. I took at least an hour each single day of my life as president to pray, to reflect on the day, to discern, to try to keep my feet grounded in terms of my faith, in terms of everything I do and the kind of person I am and how I relate to people.

Harris, on the other hand, reflected on his path and the role of his faith. He explained:

> And I think that the draw to a faith-based institution was something that [started] early in my career. I served at a Catholic high school and a Catholic college, and in my current role as the president of a Catholic university, I was called for this work. I always, in the back of my mind, as much as my work was satisfying in my previous institutions, I always had this sense that I would like to do the same work in an environment that supported the faith journey of the people who are part of that community. And I know that my faith journey has been instrumental—it's life-affirming. My faith really helps inform my work and sustains me during difficult times.

In addition to their path of faith, each president was also on their own diversity, equity, and inclusion journey. In particular, both had to commit to do their own personal developmental work with race and racism. Sundborg named the vulnerability needed to do this work personally. He said:

> I think that helped in terms of crises...like good intentions are not enough. Being a good person is not enough. It calls for a real kind of vulnerable willingness to see limitations in yourself and how you deal with this.

For Harris, his reflection and work on his own Whiteness were evident. He moved beyond recognizing just individual White privilege or even White fragility to move toward a systems understanding and the need for action, naming White immunity (Cabrera, 2017). Harris shared his perspective on understanding his White identity as he observed:

> It's "White immunity" instead of White privilege. It's White immunity. I am immune as a White man to what the experience would be, compared to someone who identifies as Filipino, or you think about a Black man going into a store and being followed. I have been followed because I had a beard and long hair at one point in my life, but I would never associate that with my appearance or my race. I would associate that with just, you know, not trusting of anybody. But if you're a Black man in America, a woman or a person of color, there are just things that I, as a White man, will never experience. So, I am immune to those experiences that I'm not going to be treated that way because of my race–that's different than saying I was privileged because of my race. And I don't think they're a whole lot different, honestly, between you and me. But I think it allows– by saying White immunity–I think it allows some people to step into the space and be more understanding than White privilege because you're immediately defensive if you said, "You have White privilege."

Building upon the need for self-awareness and vulnerability, another key lesson the presidents shared was to know your limit as a leader. Sundborg observed that he has learned an important lesson that he did not need to be the "front person" all the time. He explained:

> I have a very strong sense of authority, responsibility, and therefore (in times of) crisis I have to be out there and engage it. That's a mistake in the sense of count to ten and get some advice before you step out there and say what you really think about the situation. Maybe someone else needs to be involved. Maybe someone from the academic setting of the university needs to be involved. Don't go presuming because you're the president, that you're the one that has to be the front person in the

crisis. There are times when you need to be. And its certain kinds of parts of the crises that you need to be. But my mistake was too often putting myself forward as the front person. And therefore, there's no backup when you're there. You're it.

Harris framed the need for self-awareness in a different way. He shared how his institutional approach as president differs from a personal one that another nonpresidential leader on the campus could take. He shared:

> For example, there is such a commitment by many of our students to honoring Indigenous ways and Indigenous Peoples. I'm very supportive of our land acknowledgment statements and so forth. On the other hand, you think about the population—we only have 20 Indigenous students enrolled in the USD out of the population of 9,300. So, what's that appropriate role and balance? I think as a White, older man—now I'm over 60 and very privileged in my roles over the years and having access to education and so forth, it's been difficult sometimes for me to try to step right into some of this work because I try to do it at an institutional level, not a personal level.

For Harris and Sundborg, their faith, their exploration of diversity, equity, and inclusion, and their self-awareness, enabled them to navigate in times of crisis and also contributed to their ability to fully understand the complexities of PBCE, including critiques focusing on race and power differentials.

Leading in Times of Crisis

Harris and Sundborg both highlighted how they drew upon community engagement in times of crisis such as the COVID-19 pandemic. They also reflected on the importance of responding to the crisis while continuing to hold a long-term vision. Harris shared an example of continuing to think about community engagement amidst crisis:

> When we had to make decisions during, for example, the pandemic, one of the pieces we always kept at the forefront was what we're going to do for local communities. It's one thing to say we're going to get vaccinated or we're going to get COVID tested on our campus. But what do we do about the community that's right outside our door? And so that's why we sought to be a county site and work with the county.

Similarly, Seattle University also held multiple COVID-19 vaccine clinics on campus for the benefit of the campus and the broader community. Reflecting on his approach to the pandemic and other crisis situations Sundborg shared, "I guess another thing is I learned that you have to be present to the crisis and the people of the crises, be there with those situations." Reflecting on times of crisis, particularly the period of the COVID-19 pandemic, both presidents shared the importance of being present to the crisis while continuing to pursue the long-term strategies and daily work of the university. Sundborg elaborated:

> Keep your perspective. There's a lot that you need to be about, and your university needs to be about when you're in crises. So don't let it be the only thing that you're engaged in. You need to continue to speak about your mission. You need to continue to support students, faculty, research, and education. You need to develop your strategic plan. You need to raise the money in your campaigns. You need to work with your board of trustees. You need to reach out to your city and your institutions.

Harris added that, especially in a time of crisis, you must also know the direction you are heading. He shared:

> During times of turmoil, you better have your act together about where you're heading. And so many schools don't. They don't have a strategic plan in time that they adhere to. They might have something that's up on a shelf. They try to talk about values, but ours was already embedded and we embedded it into the strategic plan. So, we started making decisions. Those decisions were around these important issues. So, for example, when the pandemic first hit, you might recall that we had a number of issues with students who didn't have access to food because our cafeteria wasn't always open like it was before. We had some really nice donations. We focused on our plan to be a food bank and getting resources to students and dealing with the issue of homelessness among students.

While offering thoughtful reflections and lessons learned, both presidents shared that leading during a crisis is especially difficult. Harris shared, "I've been a president for 28 years–and there's been no more difficult period than just before the pandemic and during. And I'd say January through May of this year (2021) was the most difficult of my entire career."

Diversity, Equity, and Inclusion and Community Engagement

For many years, pursuing diversity, equity, and inclusion has been a major focus in higher education, especially with student, faculty, and staff recruitment and retention. During this time, many predominantly White higher education institutions have served communities of color. Driven by their service or justice mission, faith-based universities have focused their community engagement efforts on disenfranchised communities of color. With these histories in mind, both presidents provided deep insight into how they see diversity, equity, and inclusion linked with community engagement reshaping the future of faith-based higher education.

Diversity, Equity, and Inclusion Is More Prominent and Intentional

Both presidents highlighted how they addressed diversity, equity, and inclusion in their leadership. Sundborg noted how community engagement work has evolved with the focus of diversity, equity, and inclusion work moving from the margins to the center. He shared that when Seattle University launched its place-based Youth Initiative in 2010, the planning group looked at diversity, equity, and inclusion as an important consideration. But now the depth of understanding what's involved in connecting diversity, equity, and inclusion is much clearer. Sundborg summarized, "it's a grounded principle now rather than one that was simply a guide."

President Harris also highlighted the central importance of diversity, equity, and inclusion. First, he named how his own personal identities intersect in this work. He shared:

> As a White male leader, it's using my experiences at the institutional level and to try to influence federal and state policy to be engaged in national issues. So that will have an impact on the University of San Diego and our local community. I fail as much as I succeed.

He continued to provide an example from a strategic standpoint. He noted:

> I'll be bold in creating a vision for the future that includes diversity, equity, inclusion, and anchor work. In the actual strategy, it has to be there. If we're talking about place-based work and all the different elements of that, you better have a place for that in your strategic plan and in your vision for the future and hold yourself accountable for that work.

Diversity, Equity, and Inclusion as the Future of Community Engagement at Faith-Based Institutions

Sundborg and Harris both observed that the shifts in the demographics and backgrounds of presidents of faith-based institutions will make community engagement even more important to how these institutions animate their faith traditions, especially for Catholic and Jesuit institutions. Sundborg noted the significant shift from presidents of Catholic and Jesuit institutions being formal religious leaders (such as priests) to being lay leaders. As an example, he shared more about the present context of Jesuit higher education in the United States:

> There were five presidential changes in the last year, and four of those five went from a Jesuit president to a lay president. And there's seven changes this year from presidencies, and probably five or six of those will go from Jesuits. Right now, there's only seven of the twenty-seven presidents of Jesuit universities that are [priests], and they'll probably end up being about five by the time they get to the end of this coming year.

Drawing upon this example, Sundborg observes that because of the shift toward lay presidents, community engagement will grow in importance. He shared:

> And so, this is Jesuit in a new way ... I think that our society will increasingly secularize. That's just kind of the environment within which our faith-based universities will operate. Faith-based universities ... will less be able to count on the majority kinds of population of students or faculty that is supportive of its faith purposes. And so, that is going to be a challenge where there needs to be more focus on what's the appropriate ways to bring forward faith-based community engagement.

Furthermore, Sundborg observes that the approach to community engagement at faith-based institutions will continue to evolve. He stated:

> So, it'll probably be less explicitly we're engaged in community because of our faith purposes of the university. It'll probably be more engaged in our community because of our deep value of humanity, justice and fairness, and ethics, and so forth. But there's going to need to be more consideration around–what will be the new grounding in this kind of a culture for community engagement where I think you could sort of expect in the past that faith-based institutions could rely on their faith's sort of foundation for this. It will be less and less that it can, and they'll need to rely on something different from that, which is okay.

Harris added to this perspective observing that the shifts in the gender and race of presidents serving faith-based institutions will also influence the future of community engagement at these institutions. He shared:

> So, you think about the elements of our Catholic faith in the institution... mission and ministry or mission integration. Now the ministry

component–the [Community Engagement] Center–you start thinking of the Changemaker Hub. In those cases, we happen to have all men, but there are other elements of this university that are led by women. But it's all lay-led. It's people of color. It's people from distinct backgrounds. And it's not all Catholic. And I think that's the future of the Church. And we have to find that, I mean particularly ... you would have people who would identify as Catholic, but I really believe strongly that it's a more inclusive Church ... And so that to me feels like that's the future of Catholic higher education or faith-based higher education.

Harris and Sundborg provided numerous insights to highlight faith-based community engagement leadership, including in times of crisis. Such insights have the potential to inform the future of community engagement in higher education.

Implications

Our current study highlights how presidential leadership of community engagement at faith-based institutions is at the heart of the institutional mission. Yet presidential leadership focusing on community engagement is still evolving, especially with how to fund the work and the interconnection between community engagement and diversity, equity, and inclusion. In times of crisis, our findings illustrate that college presidents can draw upon community engagement to continue to live out the mission of their faith-based institutions. Our research has several clear and significant implications for presidents, community engagement professionals, and the field of community engagement: 1) the importance of community engagement to the institutional service mission, 2) the changing demographics and varied backgrounds and experiences of college presidents with the rise of more diverse and less religious presidents, and 3) the rising significance and intentionality of diversity, equity, and inclusion work in community engagement.

Our findings suggest that the presidential commitment to community engagement to animate the mission may become more important as faith-based institutions secularize. For faith-based institutions, the mission to engage with communities may strengthen, but with less explicit connection to the institutions' faith-based tradition. Community engagement work in this sense may become more about social justice than an explicitly religious call to action. As our findings highlight, community engagement continues to be a priority for college presidents during times of crisis, although how campuses do community engagement work may continue to shift.

In addition to shifts created by secularization, our review of the research literature and findings illustrate that there is growing diversification of the college presidency, with more women and people of color. Yet at the same time presidential tenures are shorter in duration (ACE, 2017). Moreover, as college campuses diversify their student population, some faith-based institutions like USD seek to become a minority-serving institution (Asian American, Native American and Pacific Islander Serving-Institution and/or Hispanic-Serving Institution, in particular). For community engagement work at faith-based institutions, diversification may lead to the strengthening of relationships with communities of color or engaging communities in new and innovative ways. A looming challenge is that with a shorter presidency, community engagement initiatives may not benefit from sustained (and perhaps experienced) presidential leadership with this type of work. In addition, community engagement professionals may have to spend more time on transition activities (e.g., on-boarding a new president, reengaging communities with new leadership, shifting in new directions).

Our findings also highlight the growing salience of diversity, equity, and inclusion work within community engagement. For college presidents, this may mean an exploration of their own identity and examining their power and privilege, and the ways in which the institution (or religious order) can be more inclusive. For the community engagement field, this may lend itself to putting the theory of critical service-learning into action (Green et al., 2021; Mitchell, 2008; Mitchell & Latta, 2020; Santiago-Ortiz, 2018; Stoecker, 2016). In addition, there may be a residual impact in the diversification of community engagement leaders and professionals, especially campus-level directors and vice presidents. Further research in this area is needed. For institutions that have various outreach and engagement approaches that include community engagement, anchor practices, social innovation, and PBCE, this diversity, equity, and inclusion focus is a throughline that strengthens partnerships and impact with and for the communities we serve. Arguably, faith-based institutions are well positioned to critically examine and integrate a mission of community engagement in the

> context of the institutional tensions, historical legacies of inequity and racial injustice, and the communities' multiple voices because faith-based institutions strive to operate in relationship with communities through a virtuous hope that seeks to realize a more just and equitable world [and] not from a savior approach, but rather, one in which we acknowledge our own inherent gifts and challenges, as well as those of the communities with whom we engage.
> *(Green et al., 2021)*

Limitations

While we sought out diverse college presidents, our sample was less diverse than anticipated (no women or people of color). Aside from race, there were elements of diversity: One president who is a priest and one who is not, two different faith-based Catholic institutional types were represented (Jesuit and Roman Catholic), and two different models of PBCE (naturally emerging and intentionally pursued).

Conclusion

This chapter has explored the perspectives of two presidents of faith-based universities who are deeply committed to community engagement at private Catholic institutions. What's clear from this exploration is that community engagement can provide a compelling way for faith-based institutions to attain resources; educate their students; expand their commitment to diversity, equity, and inclusion; and navigate in times of crises. Yet, what is even clearer is that, across different types of campuses, highly reflective, innovative, mission-focused presidential leadership is essential. In connecting presidential leadership with community engagement, faith-based institutions will continue to evolve and thrive in times of calm and in periods of crisis.

References

ACE. (2017, June 20). *American College President Study (ACPS)*. Research & Insights. www.acenet.edu/Research-Insights/Pages/American-College-President-Study.aspx

Astin, A. W., Vogelgesang, L. J., Ikeda, E. K., & Yee, J. A. (2000). *How service-learning affects students*. University of California–Los Angeles, Higher Education Research Institute.

Cabrera, N. L. (2017). White immunity: Working through some of the pedagogical pitfalls of "privilege." *Journal Committed to Social Change on Race and Ethnicity*, 3(1), 78–90.

Creswell, J. W. (2014). *Research design: Qualitative, quantitative, and mixed methods approaches* (4th ed.). Sage.

Grawe, N. (2018). *Demographics and the demand for higher education*. Johns Hopkins University Press.

Grawe, N. (2020). *Agile: How institutions successfully navigate demographic changes*. Johns Hopkins University Press.

Green, P. M., Bergen, D. J., Stewart, C. P., & Nayve, C. (2021). An engagement of hope: A framework and equity-centered theory of action for community engagement. *Metropolitan Universities*, 33(1), 129–157. https://doi.org/10.18060/25527

Lau, K. H., Chan, M. Y. L., Yeung, C. L. S., & Snell, R. S. (2021). An exploratory study of the community impacts of service-learning. *Metropolitan Universities, 32*(2), 106–128.

Martin, J., Samels, J. E., & Associates. (2005). *Presidential transition in higher education: Managing leadership change.* Johns Hopkins Press.

Mitchell, T. D. (2008). Traditional vs. critical service-learning: Engaging the literature to differentiate two models. *Michigan Journal of Community Service Learning, 14*(2), 50–65.

Mitchell, T. D., & Latta, M. (2020). From critical community service to critical service learning and the futures we must (still) imagine. *Journal of Community Engagement in Higher Education, 12*(1), 3–6.

Post, M., Ward, E., Longo, N. V., & Saltmarsh, J. (Eds.). (2016). *Next generation engagement and the future of higher education: Publicly engaged scholars.* Stylus.

Santiago-Ortiz, J. D. (2018). From critical to decolonizing service-learning: Limits and possibilities to social justice–based approaches to community service learning. *Michigan Journal of Community Service Learning, 25*(1), 43–54.

Stoecker, R. (2016). *Liberating service learning and the rest of higher education civic engagement.* Temple University Press.

Welch, M. (2016). *Engaging higher education: Purpose, platforms and programs for community engagement.* Stylus.

Winters, E. (2019). Meet the women leaders who are transforming Jesuit higher education. *The Jesuit Review.* www.americamagazine.org/faith/2019/05/14/meet-women-leaders-who-are-transforming-jesuit-higher-education

Yamamura, E. K., & Koth, K. (2018). *Place-based community engagement in higher education: A strategy to transform universities and communities.* Stylus Publications.

Yamamura, E. K., & Koth, K. (2019). Leadership practices for place-based community engagement initiatives. *Journal of Higher Education Outreach and Engagement, 23*(1), 181–196.

Zaloom, C. (2019). *Indebted: How families make college work at any cost.* Princeton University Press.

PART 3

Reconceptualizing Roles

Faculty, Staff, and Partnerships in Community Engagement

PART 2

9
COMMUNITY ENGAGEMENT PROFESSIONALS AND TRANSFORMATIONAL EDUCATION

Andrea Tully, Pilar Pacheco, Andrea Tafolla, Bryant Fairley, and Daniel Fidalgo Tomé

Introduction

"In order to address the complex issues of the 21st century, we need strong, purposeful, and dynamic community engagement professionals (CEP) in the field of higher education community engagement" (Ikeda et al., 2015). Soon after this exhortation at the Continuums of Service Conference in 2015, Dostilio and McReynolds wrote, "very little attention has been paid to community engagement professionals (CEPs)–in terms of how we enrich and shape engagement practices or how we become change agents within higher education" (2015, p. 113). Nearly a decade later, amidst a growing body of literature related to CEPs, including Dostilio's competency model and an accompanying guidebook, both statements remain true. CEPs, "professional staff whose primary job is to support and administer community–campus engagement" (Dostilio, 2017, p. 1), play a unique and essential role in forwarding the public purpose of higher education, especially during this particularly perilous moment of devastation wrought by the COVID-19 pandemic, climate change, national division, and a recession.

"Currently, the field seems to know more about the infrastructures (e.g. centers, offices, and spaces) responsible for managing community engagement than we do about the individuals working within these spaces" (Dostilio, 2017, p. 14). Thus, this chapter addresses a gap in the extant literature by providing first-person perspectives of four CEPs who describe their path to the field, how they develop and implement practices and pedagogies in higher education that align with their personal and institutional priorities,

DOI: 10.4324/9781003448525-12

and confront challenges in their work. The reflections from contributors, presented first, represent varying stages of CEP careers and different institutional contexts. The subsequent analysis identifies common themes in the CEPs' experiences with the goal of helping to "prepare the next generation of CEPs for the new level of expectation, purpose, and vision" (Dostilio, 2017, p. 22).

Contributors to this chapter include Pilar Pacheco, who is a longtime CE Director, Andrea Tafolla, who is a new professional in the field, Bryant Fairley, an experienced Associate Director who recently took the helm of a Center, and Daniel Fidalgo Tomé, who holds a Doctorate of Education and opted to leave a Community Engagement Director role for a position that enables more direct interaction with students and his local community. They represent not only diversity of experience, but diversity in socioeconomic and ethnic backgrounds as well. Their experiences provide context for the competencies and commitments that were established by Dostilio (2017) and are illustrative of different work profiles referenced in the competency guidebook (Dostilio & Welch, 2019). The first-person experiences illustrate Dostilio's assertion that "whereas technical knowledge can be learned didactically, ethical commitments are refined through practice and depend on professional socialization" (Dostilio, 2017, p. 9).

Case Examples

Pilar Pacheco, Director of the Center for Community Engagement, California State University Channel Islands

Our human connectedness is through storytelling. Storytelling builds empathy. Empathy is the work of the heart. Empathy creates a shared understanding of our lived experiences. And so, I share my story here with you so that you may know me, see me, and perhaps see yourselves in me, my work, and my journey.

I want to change the world, said my fourth-grade self. And I wanted to join the Peace Corps to fulfill my wide-eyed innocent dream and heartfelt passion. I did not. But my passion from an early start to work in service with others and with the community has remained and, whether I knew it or not, guided me to the place, my work, and the person I am today.

I am a native of Santa Barbara, California, and a proud graduate of the California State University (CSU) system, where I earned my bachelor's in child development and a master's in educational psychology at CSU Northridge. And now, I work at CSU Channel Islands (CSUCI) as the Director for the Center for Community Engagement (CCE), where I have spent much of my professional career as an Administrator/Educator committed to enhancing the educational and career opportunities for students in our community. I worked in preschool education while finishing my undergraduate degree (with many starts and stops along the way). While nearing the end of my bachelor's program, a professor asked me where I had applied to graduate school. That question changed the trajectory of my academic and professional career. I had not thought about graduate school, the process was mysterious and invisible, and I did not know anyone who had gone. Yet this professor believed I could continue my education. She (along with others) saw something in me that I did not see in myself. She helped me apply and when I graduated, hired me as a Research Assistant at UCLA working on an early literacy project, where I provided support to a senior researcher in a national educational research and development center. This experience introduced me to the professional world of higher education and allowed me to hone skills as I expanded my networks closer to home in Ventura County.

In 2004, I arrived at CSUCI and the Center for Excellence in Early Childhood Education (CfE) as a Research Associate. The CfE was the evaluation arm of the First 5 funded programs for Ventura County. First 5 was created in November 1998 to improve the lives of children ages 1–5; it was funded by a California tobacco tax. The Center provided technical assistance, training, and evaluation support to over 80 nonprofit programs funded by First 5 Ventura County. When the CfE dissolved, I was encouraged to apply for the advertised Service-Learning Coordinator position. I knew my professional experience proved to be a great training ground for program design and development, program evaluation, community partnership building, resource and capacity development, and workshop facilitation. These were skills that I took into the next phase of my professional career—as Director of the Center for Community Engagement (CCE).

As a Director, there are many nuances and complexities to my position. Throughout the day I navigate between the roles of Convener, Leader, Capacity Builder, Catalyst, Facilitator, Collaborator, Coordinator, and Resource Sponsor. What has most interested me personally and professionally is deepening my understanding of who I am in relation to my leadership role and positionality on campus. For me, leadership is a privilege; it is a selfless and spiritual act of service, humbling and egoless. It is creating a space that amplifies the smarts and capabilities of those around me—be it staff or students or colleagues but especially those I work with directly so that I cultivate a pipeline of future leaders for our campus. I see mentoring as a vital piece of my work. Being a leader is not about having all the answers all the time but bringing others together collectively to find the best answers for the team, the department, and the program. When there is a win, it is because of the team. When things go wrong, it is on me.

Critical to my growth and role as a leader is self-interrogation of my positionality and commitment to not reproducing systemic inequalities within the Center. How comfortable am I speaking about constructs of power/privilege, biases, and oppression? My own? Am I reproducing these systems within the service-learning program, our partnerships, and/or student programming? Or within the Center's structure? Have I created an equitable environment—where the team shows up, feels they are contributing, visible, and connected to the rest of the group? How willing am I to share my story, vulnerabilities, or self-growth? In my drive to better understand myself, I have sought out many avenues and mentors that continue to contribute to my personal and professional growth including discussions with colleagues examining power relations and attending workshops that allow me to challenge assumptions. To do this work, I must continue to become critically conscious.

Literature has mentored me. There are books I consistently reread, apply, rethink, and reuse. The first is *Pedagogy of the Oppressed* by Paulo Freire (1970), which was a book recommended to me by a community partner when I first began working in the field of service-learning. I consider this book a must-read for professionals working in the community. The journal article, *Traditional vs. Critical Service-Learning: Engaging the Literature to Differentiate Two Models*, by Dr. Tania Mitchell (2008), complements Freire's work. Dr. Mitchell's article focuses on critical service learning—which is characterized by a social change orientation, working to redistribute power, and developing authentic and equitable community relationships (p. 52). And lastly, "*Self-Assessment Rubric for the Institutionalization of Service-Learning*" developed by Dr. Andrew Furco (1999) has served as a pragmatic approach to inquiry and assessment of institutional transformation of service-learning on our campus. The Assessment has guided the work and infrastructure building and strengthening of the CCE.

I find great creativity and freedom in brainstorming, developing, and implementing ideas that translate into programming for students, the community, and faculty. There have been a few large initiatives that have allowed me to provide a leadership role which I am especially proud of. The following projects illustrate and reflect the various programmatic ways the CCE supports its stakeholders through educational experiences and community collaborations.

In 2010, CSUCI hosted the "Bittersweet Harvest, The Bracero Program 1942–1964," a traveling bilingual exhibition organized by the Smithsonian's National Museum of American History. The Bracero Program was initiated in 1942, during World War II, as a temporary war measure to address the labor needs in both the agriculture and railroad industries. The program brought millions of Mexican guest workers to the United States and spanned over 28 states, including Arizona, Arkansas, California, New Mexico, and Texas. The exhibition was intriguing to CSUCI for many reasons—Ventura County is a community with a strong agricultural history, and over 5,000 braceros came and worked here because of the Bracero Program. Many ex-braceros and their families still reside in this county and their grandchildren attend CSUCI. It was extremely important to the university to show its commitment to serving the community by honoring the contributions of former Braceros and their families. The CCE, in collaboration with many faculty, students, and community partners, connected the exhibition to opportunities that allowed students to: learn how to collect and document oral histories, act as exhibit docents, create a local Ventura County Bracero exhibit, use their Spanish skills to transcribe and translate and fundraise to establish a scholarship for descendants of Braceros to attend CSUCI. The Bracero Oral History Project created an "esprit de corps" between the campus and the community, utilized community knowledge, and contributed to student learning. It allowed students to reconnect with their families' histories. For some it was a piece of found history and for others, it was a piece of history they had never heard. Today, students continue to learn about this piece of local history by collecting and documenting oral histories of former Braceros as a part of the Chicano/a Studies Community Based Research course.

In 2019, the CCE launched the Community Engagement and Social Justice Faculty Fellows Program. The Fellows Program is a yearlong development opportunity that weaves together components of critical service-learning and pushes faculty's thinking about social justice to create or refine a course that allows students to engage with community issues through a social justice framework (i.e., examining systems of power, privilege, and oppression, questioning biases and assumptions, and working to dismantle the tools that perpetuate social and economic oppression and entrenched racial hierarchies) (Mitchell, 2008). The program is a vehicle to advance a critical practice and a paradigm shift in teaching service-learning to develop students as agents of change (Mitchell, 2008) and to engage students in critical consciousness (Freire, 1970) while actively processing issues of equity and justice in the community.

The offering of the CESJ Fellows Program is timely as it aligns with the movement toward a social justice orientation in service-learning/community engagement as a response to the COVID-19 pandemic and the generational social and racial injustices of Black, Indigenous, People of Color (BIPOC) communities. This critical agenda is evidenced by recent special issues dedicated to critical service-learning and centering social justice in the scholarship of community engagement by the *Journal of Community*

Engagement and Higher Education, *The Michigan Journal of Community Service*, Campus Compact, and National Center for Institutional Diversity at the University of Michigan.

I was asked to present key takeaways from my writings. And as I reflect on my own writing, musings, and journey, the contemplative practice asks me (as it does students) to think, connect and critically analyze experiences and examine and challenge personal values, beliefs, and opinions. To self-interrogate. Encouraging storytelling and listening to one's story builds empathy and compassion. When someone hears another's story, they gain new perspectives, better understand the world around them, and expand their approach to problem-solving.

Being given a space to tell my story allowed me to reconnect to how and why I came to be here. I did not arrive here on my own. I had many mentors, experiences, community members, and educators along the way who contributed to my journey and continue to lift me, hold me, and enable me to grow as both a professional and as a person.

Earlier I shared that as a child in the fourth grade my dream was to join the Peace Corps. And while I did not apply to the Peace Corps, I know that the Center and the programs we administer have the opportunity to transform lives and communities. Just as one question asked by a former professor transformed mine, I see that I have been paying that forward for the past 17 years.

Andrea Tafolla, Community Engagement Coordinator of the Community Engagement Center, University of California, Merced

I was born and raised in a tiny farming town close to Merced called Delhi in the California central valley. When I was in college and learning to embrace my roots, I would explain it as a small town where there are more almond trees and cows than people.

From a very young age, I knew that I wanted to help people, but I didn't know in what capacity. My parents immigrated from Mexico when my mom was about 10 and my dad was 17. My dad worked in the fields, picking fruit in Washington, Oregon, and all the way down California. He always tells us stories of how immigration officials would arrive and raid the fields for undocumented workers the day before they would get their paycheck. When I think about my parents and how they gave up everything, including their language, culture, and the life that they knew, to come to a place completely new to them in hopes that there would be a better life, I'm very grateful and proud.

Growing up I was the translator for my grandparents and parents and in their eyes, I was a master at technology. I was translating documents for them when I was 9 years old. I felt a lot of responsibility on my shoulders and at the same time I felt really good that I was giving back to my parents who had sacrificed everything to give their children a better life.

When I was in middle school, I started tutoring at my former elementary school because I wanted to receive a community service cord at graduation. I kept tutoring after I met the requirement because I liked the way it made me feel. I was helping students understand and complete assignments they might not have if people like me weren't there to help. In addition, I was also supporting my former elementary teachers who had made a big impact in my life.

In high school, I cofounded a community service club. Our mascot was the Hawks, so we called our club the Helping Hawks. We served at homeless shelters and did cleanups in areas that were overlooked in our town. Since we only had three local grocery stores and one gas station, our town did not generate a lot of revenue. There were no sidewalks, lots of potholes, graffiti, and overgrown weeds. When I played sports in high school and our competitors came to Delhi to play against us, they would always make fun of us and say it smelled like cow poop and that we were all gangsters. Part of Helping Hawks' mission was to try to close the gaps that County officials weren't addressing, so we painted over the graffiti and cleaned up weeds.

At the time, I didn't really have words to explain that helping others made me feel very full and I was making an impact. Now, I realize that community service is a way to expand emotional intelligence and make everyone feel like we belong to a community. That's the beginning of how I arrived at this work.

The summer after junior year of high school I was getting ready to apply to college and a good friend of mine mentioned that I should apply to the weeklong Chicano Latino Youth Leadership Conference, held at California State University, Sacramento (Sac State). I had just gone through a romantic breakup and wanted to do something to take my mind off it. I applied on a whim. The conference focused on leadership and empowerment. It was a perfect fit for a heartbroken 16-year-old who was interested in political science, government, economics, and history. Together as Latino identified students, we learned about how the systems of government operate and how to advocate for ourselves and others. I remember walking into the California State Capitol and being amazed to witness where laws are made. As a young girl coming from a small town, I fell in love with Sac State once I saw the greenery of the campus and the location just a few minutes away from downtown and California's capitol. My parents were very proud of me for graduating high school with honors and academic scholarships. They supported the idea of education but did not want me to go far away from home to receive that education. Being a first-generation Latina college student, it was hard for me to be away from my family. It was a plus that Sac State was only an hour and a half away from home, close enough to visit, but far enough that I could build my own identity. My parents did the best that they could with what they knew at the time, but they told me they didn't have the money for me to study away from home, so it was up to me to make it work.

As an undergraduate student at Sac State, I worked as a cashier at a grocery store on the weekends. I was looking for a weekday job and saw an opportunity as a student assistant in Public Affairs and Advocacy at Sac State. The job description mentioned building relationships with community organizations, governmental officials, and stakeholders. I was a freshman and thought the job sounded along the lines of my major, political science. I thought that getting this job would show my parents that I could find a job in my field of study and that going away from home to college was worth it. I stayed in that position for 3 years.

When I walked into the office the first day, I knew I was where I was meant to be because for the first time, I saw University staff with melanin just like me. Even better, they were my supervisors and now mentors! Seeing individuals with similar backgrounds to mine serving students in higher education and bringing their perspectives to the table was a moment that showed me that destiny is in our hands. The guidance and skills provided to me as a student assistant helped me grow as a young professional. Supervisors took the time to return my emails and suggest how to reword communications. Through them, I learned that many students face a constant battle when it comes to balancing family, college, and job expectations and honoring one's own values and identity. By sharing their personal experiences and their best practices they validated my struggles. For example, as a first-generation college student, I felt as if I could not fail because everyone in my family was watching. So I persevered.

Since Sac State is a Hispanic-Serving Institution with great diversity among students and employees I gained empathy and came to value inclusion. In 2013–2015 I interned at a small immigration nonprofit in Sacramento. The field of immigration called me, not just because of my family background but also because of how it is connected to human and civil rights. As an intern, I conducted intakes by meeting with individuals and listening to their stories, which often represented real-life nightmares. I was always in awe of how resilient and brave my clients were to seek a new opportunity in an unknown land with a language that was unknown to them. Most clients were seeking asylum, their Violence Against Women Act, or their Victims of Criminal Activity Visas. This internship led me to become Office Administrator for the Office of Immigration Legal Services for Sacramento Food Bank and Family Services. In that role, I oversaw volunteers and planned workshops and ensured we met benchmarks for funding by submitting 100 citizenship applications. I quickly realized that

I was very good at putting events together such as workshops for Deferred Action for Childhood Arrivals renewals. I realized that I enjoyed doing the outreach portion of it; I would call radio stations to give them information, go to churches to make announcements, and let people know what was happening. I realized that I was good at it too—being bilingual allowed me to have conversations with community members and I really enjoyed it. I worked for the Food Bank for 3 years before I decided I wanted to move back home. My parents had a few health issues and it felt like the right time.

When I moved back home, I discovered my current position at the University of California, Merced, while doing an online job search. I thought it was too big of a role for me, but I applied anyway. I remember thinking after I finished my cover letter, "Wow, this really has my whole heart in it." The Community Engagement Coordinator role in the Office of Leadership, Service, and Career in the Division of Student Affairs allows me to expand upon everything I have always valued. I help manage service projects that our Center divides into three different areas: signature events, short-term projects, and semester-long projects. Short-term projects are how we pique students' interest in service. Projects include a park cleanup or helping at a vaccine clinic. For the most part, these opportunities do not require training. Semester-long projects often require training, like tutoring, mentoring, and civic action. Our signature events include our community service jamboree during which we invite community members to talk to students on campus about their organization and how students can intern or volunteer. I have a part in all three areas, and I oversee five student staff members. I also oversee transportation to and from service for our students (that probably keeps me up at night the most!).

In comparison to many of my colleagues in higher education, I am new to this field, so I always look for mentors within my institution and others. Now in my third year in this field, I have realized the great benefits that Centers like mine provide to college institutions. Community engagement provides students with a sense of belonging and responsibility for their community. I think we're making more emotionally intelligent citizens of the world. We are opening new doors to students and behind each door, there are opportunities and life lessons. Community engagement is an opportunity to provide students with experience to add to their resume while also connecting them to supervisors who can provide references for them. It is the opportunity to evaluate their life as a whole and their career path. We do this by inviting them to be a part of experiences where they come across people who may be different from them but share the same neighborhood, grocery stores, roads, and public transportation that they use. We are teaching students to explore their values. Are those values up to date? Are they consistent with their new experiences? Do they reflect who a student wants to be in the world?

However, as much as Centers like mine bring many benefits to our students and our communities, we often face challenges. One of the biggest challenges is working alongside community members and organizations while trying to change their view that the UC is only here to drive up home prices and gentrify parts of the City. It's our responsibility as CEPs to lead our institutions and communities to truly believe we're on the same team. In fact, local residents often say that UC Merced should have its own zip code because it's that far away from the City of Merced itself. When they are on our campus, students are a full hour bus ride from "South Merced," home to most people of color and those with a lower socioeconomic standing. Community members do not believe that the UC is theirs when they come to campus, they have to drive up the hill, navigate parking, and build up the courage to interact with faces that they do not recognize.

In addition, policies and procedures held by the University can sometimes be seen as an additional barrier that further separates the community and the university. In 2021, we were supposed to have a big Martin Luther King Jr. (MLK) Day of Service event with community partners that we started working on the year prior. Right before the event, our Center was reminded that we had to follow the university's COVID-19 policies which meant we could not participate in or promote indoor events. I think this example demonstrates the way the requirements of the institution and the needs of the community sometimes conflict. Moments like these make me feel like the character Luisa in the movie *Encanto*, who is struggling to balance on a rope while riding a bike with one wheel. The bureaucracies and policies put in place by the institution don't always allow us to reach our goals with community members.

Despite the challenges we face, I remain a firm believer in the merits of community engagement. I continue to believe that higher education provides tools for students to find their identities and evaluate their values. I will continue contributing to this field with the expertise I bring to the table as a local resident of our beautiful city, my experience as a first-generation Latina who looks like our students at UC Merced, and now as a current Master's student in Higher Education and Leadership. I think that as long as we listen intently to our students, communities, and the challenges we are living through, we will speak with intention through our community-engaged actions. This gives me hope.

Bryant Fairley, Lead Coordinator of the Center for Community Engagement and Innovation Incubator, California State Polytechnic University, Pomona

The "Top Gun" dream lasted a little longer for me than I think it did for most other folks. I thought that my career was going to be in the military. Every male in my family fought in a major war, going all the way back to the Civil War. My family has our great, great, great grandfather's, JW Fairley's Civil War enlistment papers for the Union Army. My father served in the United States Marine Corps and served two tours in Vietnam. Military service always reminded me that service above self is one of our most valuable contributions. Then I had a growth spurt. I grew taller than Tom Cruise rather quickly and realized that being a pilot wasn't going to be a career path for me. I quickly moved on to my next ultimate dream job, which was being Mayor of Los Angeles (LA), like Mayor Tom Bradley, LA's first Black mayor.

When I arrived at California State University (CSU) Fullerton as a first-time freshman, I immediately immersed myself in cocurricular activities such as volunteering for the Special Olympics, being a New Student Orientation leader, and running Track & Field. Service and engagement transformed who I was going to be and what I was going to do. My junior year, I got an internship working for the neighboring city. My very first assignment was for the mayor of a small middle-class city with 30,000 people. The assignment, which broke me to my core, was to respond to a letter written to the Mayor from a mom who lost their child to a drunk driver. I was under the impression that in a small city, the Mayor would personally respond to a letter like that. Despite my disenchantment, I accepted a job the City offered me and I went from serving as a management intern to thinking about a career in management, but I thought there had to be more I could do to make a more direct impact in the lives of others.

When I graduated from CSU Fullerton, I was approached by the Boy Scouts about a community organizer role which I accepted. I represented a very low-income immigrant community east of Pasadena. I worked with disadvantaged young people helping to connect them with youth programs that focused on character development and provided values-based leadership training. I had numerous powerful experiences as one of a few Black people working in a primarily Hispanic and Asian community. I was an outsider serving an urban blighted community, rife with language barriers and the desire to fit into the dominant culture. One of my most haunting experiences was when one of my Scouts was shot and killed in a drive-by.

When the Supreme Court issued a landmark decision that held that the constitutional right to freedom of association allowed the Boy Scouts of America to exclude an LGBTQ person from membership in spite of state laws requiring equal treatment, I experienced major conflict with my personal values, and I recognized I needed to get out. After moving back to Southern California to be closer to my family and working for the local United Way, I was recruited to work at California State University San Bernardino (CSUSB).

I had no higher education experience and I knew very little about CSUSB despite the fact that the University has been around since the mid-60s. I soon learned that it is a commuter campus built into the foothills of the San Bernardino mountains, in a scenic location and removed from downtown San Bernardino and many of the challenges of homelessness and crime often associated with the city. The campus serves primarily Hispanic and Pell-eligible female students and I was charged with developing service-learning internships for Pell-eligible students with industry partners to build early career success and STEM retention. It was a struggle to recruit employers to take a chance on CSUSB students because many major employers didn't recruit students outside Los Angeles and Orange County. The local nonprofit and public service sectors were desperate for support and a pipeline of talented students; however, they often felt marginalized by the University's efforts to get students recruited into Fortune 500 companies. My nonprofit background helped me to quickly find success in my role; I was a matchmaker with an ability to create nontraditional connections.

I was at CSUSB for a total of 12 years. I started as a grant-funded employee on a Title V Developing Hispanic-Serving Institutions Department of Education federal grant. The Associate Director position was created based on our success with Title V. I launched programs at CSUSB that are now woven into the fabric of the campus. The President's Office and Associated Students, Inc. (ASI) annually provide stipends for academic internships that support students to seek career-relevant experience prior to graduation. I attended conferences at which I learned about new programs and brought them back to CSUSB. After attending a conference focused on democracy, civic and voter engagement, and how to get students more involved in democratic processes, I learned that many East Coast universities had campus food pantries that were addressing food insecurity within their own student populations. At these campuses, about 40% of students qualified for financial aid and were Pell Grant eligible. At CSUSB, over 60% of students were Pell eligible. I utilized my nonprofit background to construct CSUSB's campus food pantry in partnership with a community-based food bank. I encouraged ASI to make an annual financial contribution to the community partner so that, in return, the partner drops food items off to the University on a regular basis. The pantry also utilizes donations from faculty, staff, and student organizations to supplement the donations.

A Break Away session at the IMPACT Conference inspired me to launch a pilot to offset the cost of Alternative Spring Break Programs so more students would have the opportunity to participate in a structured service study away program. I collaborated with ASI and our Outdoor Recreation program. We started small by arranging transportation to volunteer service projects in our local mountains and then we expanded to include trips within the state of California, out of state, and abroad. I participated in a service-learning study abroad trip to Peru, where the students helped build an addition at a public preschool and helped test water quality in the Amazon.

While in Cusco, I got severe high-altitude sickness. I spent 4 days in a Cusco hospital, in and out of a hyperbaric chamber that increased the amount of oxygen in my blood to relieve my symptoms. Between marathon sessions of Spanish soap operas and Copa América soccer on TV, I got an email about an open Director of Community Engagement position at California State Polytechnic University, Pomona. Although I am embarrassed to be the first person from CSUSB that had to be medically evacuated from another country, if I was not hospital bound, it is unlikely that I would have seen this employment opportunity in time to apply for the position.

The City of Pomona is a special place to me because I grew up in a city next door. A few years prior to the job opening at Cal Poly Pomona, I convinced my wife and family to move to a historic district in Pomona. We love it because, as a Black and Brown family, we feel like we should be giving back to the community that's similar to ours. Cal Poly Pomona is whiter, wealthier, and more male than CSUSB by a long shot. I am blown away by how everything that I've always wanted to do at work came easy. For example, I had advocated for a downtown center in San Bernardino for 10 years, while at Cal Poly Pomona, we were able to fund and design a plan to build a new downtown center within 3 years.

The level of support for community engagement is a whole different ball game at Cal Poly Pomona. The Center for Community Engagement is housed under the Associate Vice President (AVP) for Academic Innovation. Under her leadership, the Center for Community Engagement has the freedom to create and innovate, plus the flexibility to try new approaches. My initial focus was to highlight the power of the CCE for impact, locally, regionally, and globally. We incorporated the United Nations Sustainable Development Goals (SDGs) (United Nations General Assembly, 2015) into our mission and vision for faculty, student, and partner engagement. We utilize them to guide how we fund faculty projects and to design high-quality service projects that address critical issues such as poverty, quality education, and equal opportunities for all.

I was able to not only introduce a new approach with programming, but I was also able to restructure the CCE with a faculty associate to assist faculty with developing new community-engaged learning opportunities. During the pandemic, we were able to quickly shift to a virtual volunteer fair and design new experiences for service-learning students to support parents and families sheltering in place, by hosting creative lesson plans on the CCE's interactive website. We also shifted our in-person tutoring service-learning placements with Pomona Unified School District to a virtual platform.

Our AVP saw that in a global crisis, I was able to successfully manage our team, not only to sustain our efforts but also to design impactful programs that extend our reach. I have benefited from mentorship, leadership, and wisdom of others and I invested in my own success. I am willing to take advantage of opportunities that exist. One of the big things that I tell our students is that when opportunity presents itself, take the leap.

It's been 35 years since Top Gun was first released and the long-awaited sequel came out during the summer of 2022. I feel as if my career journey has come full circle. Service above self remains an integral part of my life, and although I did not serve in the military, I am proud that throughout my career I have served others in a meaningful way. There is still much to do, and I plan to run for Mayor when the timing is right.

Daniel Fidalgo Tomé, Ed.D., Program Coordinator of the Division of Diversity, Inclusion & Civic Engagement, Rutgers, The State University of New Jersey–Camden

I identify as a White, cis-gender male who grew up with immigrant parents from Portugal and spoke Portuguese at home and English at school. My mother passed away at a young age, so my father and older sister raised me along with the rest of my cousins, aunts, and uncles. My father completed high school before going into the Portuguese military and my mother completed sixth grade before going to work with her family. They immigrated to New Jersey in the United States in November 1975, months after the Carnation Revolution which resulted in Portugal's transition to democracy. I was the first in my family to pursue higher education. Being a first-generation American and student laid a foundation that I have carried with me throughout my career. My bilingualism and the knowledge that my parents immigrated for better opportunities for themselves and their children instilled in me a deep sense of gratitude for those who support me.

My first understanding of service came from watching Captain Planet and the Planeteers as a child. It's an animated cartoon focused on an environmentalist superhero with assistance from five teenagers who took on greed, corruption, and pollution. In the show, I saw organizing, helping others, and working toward a common purpose, saving the planet from ourselves.

The show and the fact that I lived in a community with water and air contaminated from a decades-long lack of water treatment and sewer system improvements motivated me to be very involved in high school. During the summer, I participated in Upward Bound, a Federal program that "serves high school students from low-income families; and high school students from families in which neither parent holds a bachelor's degree" (Upward Bound Program, 2023). I took college and SAT prep courses while building relationships with staff and faculty on campus. This experience is why

I attended Cook College–Rutgers University and studied Environmental Policy.

During my undergraduate education at Cook College, I was involved with numerous environmental, leadership, and diversity-focused organizations which laid the foundation for my interest in social justice education. The dedicated staff in student affairs who advised many of the organizations I was a part of played an integral role in my student and character development. Their mentorship was evident in the support I received when my father was diagnosed with lung cancer in my junior year. The student life staff listened to me when I needed space to process what I was going through, allowed me to cry in their offices, and offered me hugs when my father passed away.

After my father's death and when I graduated, I chose to stay in New Jersey to be close to family. I worked with a Food Stamp Nutritional Education Program and was a 4-H youth leader facilitating a kids' cooking club and running character development workshops with teens. These opportunities enabled me to hone public speaking and group facilitation skills. When I was ready to move further from my family, I enrolled in the Social Justice Education Masters program at the University of Massachusetts (UMass)–Amherst. My undergraduate experience combined with growing up in an urban immigrant community plagued with environmental justice issues influenced me to focus my studies on environmental racism and justice. This work connected me to the UMass Amherst Office of Community Service-Learning with whom I worked as a graduate student to develop a one-credit course enabling students to examine their social identities before serving within their community.

After graduate school, I moved back to New Jersey and worked with New York Public Interest Research Group (NYPIRG) as a campus organizer, then City College of New York's CityServ program, through which I built connections with community partners for cocurricular service opportunities and facilitated leadership development workshops and social justice dialogues. After 3 years, I was exhausted from the commute to New York City and I took a position in the Office of Service-Learning (OSL) at a public university in New Jersey. There, I focused on working with faculty members on curricular community-engaged pedagogy.

With only one other part-time staff member and an office that was the size of a closet, my supervisor, the Director of the Grants Office, helped me maneuver University systems and develop necessary relationships to make big moves. Drawing on my experience as a community organizer, I grew my office to a team of four full-time staff members, rotating faculty fellows, student leadership opportunities, AmeriCorps positions, and an activist-in-residency position. By 2018, one out of every eight students at the University was participating in a service-learning course. In addition to curricular service, days of service grew to over 1,000 volunteers and our office drove multiple projects and programs outside of the classrooms to support its efforts. Our program grew so quickly over 8 years that the OSL became a part of the culture of the institution. While shepherding the rapid growth of the OSL, I was also involved in policy-making in higher education nationally through the American College Personnel Association (ACPA), American Democracy Project (ADP), and American Association of State Colleges & Universities (AASCU). During the eight and half years I worked at Stockton, I learned a lot about myself and how much I could take on. For example, I advocated tirelessly for support and resources for students, faculty members, and community partners to serve or participate in conferences. Often I felt like I was pushing a rock up a mountain when asking for the bare necessities for successful service-learning experiences. The frustration challenged my personal and professional identity. I thought enrolling in a doctoral program would enliven me, but it only added to my stress. The pressure I put on myself to run an office, manage up, and think ahead while writing my dissertation broke me. I was tired. I was annoyed. I got shingles. I left the position to lead a service-learning program at an online university, an ideal role for me that coincided with a global pandemic that led all education to pivot to online modalities.

In a full circle move, I am now the Program Coordinator of Engaged Civic Learning in the Office of Civic Engagement at Rutgers, Camden, in almost the same position I had a decade earlier. Transitioning out of a managerial role and to a staff member position enables me to address community issues at their root causes. I've spent time thinking about some of the larger systems at play throughout my career. Now I find myself being a support to many folks doing community-engaged research and teaching service-learning courses. I continue to question the brokenness within systems of higher education, service-learning, and community engagement. I think of the famous quote by Audre Lorde, "the master's tools will never dismantle the master's house."

The work that matters to me the most is mentorship, relationship building, and communication among colleagues, students, faculty, and community partners. We must challenge senseless bureaucratic processes together. We must address root causes of our systematic problems. I want to work less on arguing internally with risk management and general counsel and facilitate far fewer conversations about receiving the next national award for community engagement! Awards, honor rolls, and classifications do not support faculty members, for example, who are frustrated that their community-engaged scholarship isn't considered "real" scholarship. The mounting pressure that staff, faculty, and students feel to meet multiple competing and often contradictory demands needs to be addressed instead of adding more to our plates without requisite infrastructure. As educators, we must use our precious time, effort, and resources to engage students, our future civic leaders, in addressing the needs of the community and society at large. I have learned my own limits; I will no longer chase a career-related dream if I am not able to concurrently pursue happiness.

Analysis: Five Ways in Which CEPs Promote Transformational Education

Taken together, the first-person experiences shared by CEPs demonstrate that "our work, knowledge, and attributes are distinct from other academic professionals and distinct from other actors' within community-campus engagement (e.g. faculty, community collaborators, or institutional executive leadership)" (Dostilio, 2017, p. 28). Common themes derived from the first-person experiences elucidate the ways in which CEPs establish and advance practices and pedagogies at HEIs that align with their values and priorities as well as those of the academy. The findings underscore the pivotal role of CEPs in realizing the public purpose of higher education.

1. The work of CEPs draws upon a fundamental value of social responsibility that was cultivated at a young age and then informed their career decisions (Porfeli & Lee, 2012). Pacheco wanted to join the Peace Corps; Fairley considered the military; Tafolla translated for her family members and created a community service club; and Tomé felt compelled to be a steward for the earth. Their primary motivation for work that benefits society makes CEPs ideal agents for enacting the public purpose of higher education and leads them to confront systemic issues that perpetuate inequality. For the contributors, their early understanding of the value of service enabled them to see themselves as connected to the broader human community and to recognize varied stakeholders as equals with distinct needs and perspectives.
2. Building on their own experiences receiving transformational mentoring within higher education, CEPs play a powerful role as mentors to students, faculty, and junior staff. Although "mentoring relationships are embedded in the educational process in higher education" (Lunsford et al., 2017, p. 316), the mentoring that mattered most to the CEPs occurred outside of formal mentorship programs (Chao et al., 1992). Research indicates that mentoring positively influences "capacity for socially responsible leadership" as well as "self-confidence in professional skills and abilities" (Lunsford et al., 2017, p. 318). In the case of the contributors, receiving mentoring was pivotal to their career trajectories

even though their mentors held positions outside of the community engagement profession. The identified mentors include a faculty member whose confidence in Pacheco inspired her to pursue graduate school, staff members who provided emotional support for Tomé, administrators who recognized the ability to pivot in the face of a crisis for Fairley and supervisors that were from the same ethnic background and reworded communications for Tafolla. Thus, higher education professionals within and outside of the field of CE play an essential role in cultivating community engagement professionals who push HEIs toward social change.

3. Building upon their identities as agents of social change, the CEPs developed expertise in empowering others to work toward social justice. In their work facilitating relationships between communities and institutions of higher education, CEPs model unique career pathways. For example, Pacheco created the Community Engagement and Social Justice Faculty Fellows Program to demonstrate how to address systemic issues of inequity and injustice in courses, Tafolla acknowledges town-gown issues related to the rural location of her University by overseeing transportation to and from areas with high need, Fairley created CSUSB's first food pantry staffed by students for students to address food insecurity for those with financial need, and Tomé hosted social justice dialogues. In light of the exponential increase in CEP positions within higher education over the last several decades (Dostilio, 2017), a wide range of opportunities exist for CEPs to creatively and collaboratively address systemic inequities.

4. CEPs recognize and articulate instances in which institutional rhetoric does not match the resources and structures required to implement reciprocal community engagement efforts. This contradiction creates conflict between the personal and professional identities CEPs hold dear. In fact, CEPs often feel stymied in trying to fulfill their commitments to community partners while upholding university mandates. For example, Pacheco indicated her commitment to not reproducing systemic inequalities through her work, Tafolla shared that COVID-19 policies set by the University prohibited participation in events that were planned collaboratively with the community, Fairley referenced the level of support at his current campus compared to his last, and Tomé worked to the point of exhaustion for minimal resources. Although CEPs do not benefit from the reward structures that secure positions and prestige for tenure line faculty and high-level administrators, they advocate for students, faculty, and community partners to achieve the recognition, opportunities, and administrative resources needed to achieve collaborative projects and objectives. As Tomé asserts, CEPs are

not fooled or placated by designations, awards, or classifications that bring no direct benefit to members of the campus or community who actually do the work of community engagement.
5. CEPs serve as models of reflexive practice. They identify and articulate the importance of self-inquiry and of a continued commitment to learning as described by the pioneers of the field (Stanton et al., 1999, p. 191). Pacheco offered the questions she utilizes to self-interrogate and examine power, Tafolla described the importance of listening attentively to all constituents and speaking with purpose, Fairley shared how his personal values informed his career choices, and Tomé realized that a staff position, instead of a managerial role, enables him to work more effectively on systemic issues. In their roles as bridge builders, CEPs demonstrate a willingness to listen, to remain open to differing perspectives, and to receive feedback. In fulfilling responsibilities to the University as well as their commitments to community partners, they demonstrate creativity, flexibility, and fidelity to personal values. In representing the university to the community and vice versa, they model integrity and our fundamental responsibility to serve.

Conclusion

In conclusion, CEPs play a unique and essential role in forwarding the mission of community engagement in higher education. They "embody an engagement of hope ... the fundamental calling to serve one another and to be in relationship with each other" (Green et al., 2021). Conscious of their roles as mentors and bridge builders addressing the diverse needs of different constituencies within the university, they model integrity, vision, and a reflective practice that lights the path for students and faculty to harness the tools of their institution to effectively realize social change.

References

Chao, G. T., Walz, P., & Gardner, P. D. (1992). Formal and informal mentorships: A comparison on mentoring functions and contrast with nonmentored counterparts. *Personnel Psychology*, 45(3), 619–636.

Dostilio, L. D. (Ed.). (2017). *The community engagement professional in higher education: A competency model for an emerging field*. Campus Compact & Stylus Publishing, LLC.

Dostilio, L. D., & McReynolds, M. (2015). Community engagement professionals in the circle of service-learning and the greater civic enterprise. *Michigan Journal of Community Service Learning*, 22(1), 113–117.

Dostilio, L. D., & Welch, M. (2019). *The community engagement professional's guidebook: A companion to the community engagement professional in higher education*. Campus Compact & Stylus Publishing, LLC.

Freire, P. (1970). *Pedagogy of the oppressed* (MB Ramos, Trans.). Continuum, 2007.

Furco, A. (1999). *Self-assessment rubric for the institutionalization of service-learning in higher education*. Service-Learning Research & Development Center, University of California, Berkeley.

Green, P. M., Bergen, D. J., Stewart, C. P., & Nayve, C. (2021). An engagement of hope: A framework and equity-centered theory of action for community engagement. *Metropolitan Universities*, *32*(2), 129–157. https://doi.org/10.18060/25527

Ikeda, E., Wells, A., Cone, R., Stovall, T. & Lopez, I. (2015, April 8–10). *Utilizing inquiry to build your engagement career*. Presented at 18th Annual Continuums of Service Conference (COS), Long Beach, California.

Lunsford, L. G., Crisp, G., Dolan, E. L., & Wuetherick, B. (2017). Mentoring in higher education. In D. A. Clutterbuck, F. K. Kochan, L. Lunsford, N. Dominguez, & J. Haddock-Millar (Eds.), *The SAGE handbook of mentoring* (pp. 316–334). SAGE Publications Ltd. https://doi.org/10.4135/9781526402011

Mitchell, T. (2008). Traditional vs. critical service-learning: Engaging the literature to differentiate two models. *Michigan Journal of Community Service Learning*, *14*(2), 50–65.

Porfeli, E. J., & Lee, B. (2012). Career development during childhood and adolescence. *New Directions for Youth Development*, 2012, 11–22. https://doi.org/10.1002/yd.20011

Stanton, T. K., Giles Jr, D. E., & Cruz, N. I. (1999). *Service-learning: A movement's pioneers reflect on its origins, practice, and future*. Jossey-Bass Inc.

United Nations General Assembly (2015, October 21). *Transforming our world: the 2030 Agenda for Sustainable Development*. United Nations A/RES/70/1.

Upward Bound Program. 2023. United States Department of Education. bit.ly/43H2Q0B

10

THE TENSIONS AND REWARDS OF COMMUNITY ENGAGEMENT FOR FACULTY MEMBERS

Elena Klaw, Anh-Thu Ngo, Angie Mejia, Marie Sandy, and Jon A. Levisohn

Background

Community-engaged learning (CEL) is not a revolutionary, new innovative pedagogy. In fact, the idea of connecting academic knowledge to community action draws from a broad range of movements spanning from the extension efforts of land grant universities in the 1860s to workforce initiatives of the New Deal to Civil Rights activism (Pollack, 1996; Saltmarsh & Hartley, 2016; Stanton et al., 1999; Yamamura & Koth, 2018). Historically, American higher education has been rooted in a mission to promote the common good and to prepare students to participate ethically and effectively in a democratic society (Guarasci & Eatman, 2022; Longo et al., 2016; Welch & Plaxton-Moore, 2019). According to Stanton, the earliest descriptions of service-learning as "the accomplishment of tasks that meet genuine human needs in combination with conscious educational growth" can be found in publications that date back to the 1960s (Stanton et al., 1999, p. 2). Founders of the service-learning movement, describing themselves as "mavericks" for pushing against the dictates and structures of academic departments and disciplines, wrote in 1999 about "the breathtaking growth" of the field, noting, "A new generation of practitioners has expanded the number and variety of service-learning courses and programs across all sectors of postsecondary education" (Stanton et al., 1999, p. xv). Seven years later, Saltmarsh and Hartley (2016, p. 15) echoed this assertion stating that "since the early 2000s, engaged scholars have been part of a generational shift in higher education, inheriting a legacy and rich history." Now commonly termed "community engaged learning," in recognition of the reciprocal

DOI: 10.4324/9781003448525-13

collaboration (Keith, 2015; Welch & Plaxton-Moore, 2019; Yamamura & Koth, 2018) required between higher education and community partners to "develop and apply knowledge to address societal needs" (Weerts & Sandmann, 2010, p. 632), this approach has been recognized as a high impact practice in higher education (Kuh, 2008, p. 34), increasing students' academic engagement and thereby potentially increasing retention.

As greater numbers of faculty spanning disciplinary boundaries have employed community-engaged approaches in their courses (Angotti et al., 2012; Ward & Miller, 2016; Weerts & Sandmann, 2010), generations of college students have been able to apply academic learning to community service and social action, thereby increasing their academic motivation, gaining professional and interpersonal skills, and expanding their awareness and understanding of the world around them (Astin et al., 2000; Ramnani et al., 2016; Yorio & Ye, 2012). Moreover, community-engaged faculty have continued to affirm "a larger public, democratic purpose" of higher education (Guarasci & Eatman, 2022; Hollander & Hartley, 2000; Saltmarsh & Hartley, 2016), by including the practice of civic engagement within their curriculum.

More recently, the field has embraced the importance of a "critical service-learning" approach defined by Tania Mitchell as a "social change orientation, working to redistribute power, and developing authentic relationships" as an essential step forward for this practice and pedagogy (Mitchell, 2008, p. 50). This paradigm underscores the important role that faculty members play as course instructors in integrating community-based experiences with "thoughtful introduction, analysis, and discussion of issues important to understanding social justice" (Mitchell, 2008, p. 50). Around the same time as Mitchell's influential call for the field to deepen the examination of systemic inequity as an essential part of the pedagogy, the Carnegie Foundation offered the Carnegie Elective Classifications as an opportunity for institutions of higher education to gain national recognition for "extraordinary commitments to their public purpose" (2022). The Carnegie Classification for Community Engagement (CE), which is based on a "self-study model similar to an accreditation process," allows campuses that receive classification to "claim an institutional identity associated with high standards of community engagement" (Saltmarsh & Johnson, 2020). Since the extensive self-assessment process involved in the Classification does not result in the provision of any resources, funding, staffing, or faculty incentives for community engagement, it is unclear, however, as to whether or how it serves to enhance, expand, or institutionalize such efforts. It is worth noting that as of February 2020, only 359 US colleges and universities hold this designation (Association of Public & Land-Grant Universities, 2020).

Faculty community engagement persists across disciplines and institutions in large part due to the value framework of its practitioners, who maintain a shared belief in cultivating civic engagement as central to the "democratic purposes of the academy" (Eatman, 2016, p. xiii). Post and colleagues (2016), for example, assert that publicly engaged scholars view collaborative teaching and research as a necessary reciprocal system of sharing knowledge to benefit the common good (see also Guarasci & Eatman, 2022; Saltmarsh, 2017). Thus, they argue, unlike traditional scholars, community-engaged faculty value products that have a wider reach than that of specialized academic journals (Post et al., 2016). For example, drawing on the work of Boyer (1990), the University of Colorado Boulder Office for Outreach and Engagement supports a continuum of engaged scholarship, noting that "community-engaged scholars seek active partnerships between the university and the community as a way to generate and apply mutually beneficial and socially useful knowledge and practices" (2022). Descriptive literature illustrates that community-engaged faculty members view the integration of community action into their coursework as integral to developing the skills and attitudes that students need to participate effectively in democratic society (Yamamura & Koth, 2018; Welch, 2016). Indeed, decades of research support the practice, suggesting that as a result of participating in community-engaged learning, students gain increased awareness of diversity, critical thinking skills, academic engagement, civic involvement, and professional development (Celio et al., 2011; Engberg et al., 2018; Mitchell & Rost-Banik, 2019; Ramnani et al., 2016).

Although community engagement has been recognized as a high-impact practice in higher education, associated with academic engagement and retention, particularly for underrepresented students (Bringle et al., 2010; Yeh, 2010), institutional resources have generally not kept pace with the breadth, depth, and objectives of the field (Keith, 2015; Longo et al., 2016; Yamamura & Koth, 2018), and faculty practitioners continue to describe experiencing peril when adopting this practice (Ward & Miller, 2016; Welch, 2016). In fact, similar to the field's founders, "next generation" (Saltmarsh & Hartley, 2016; Ward & Miller, 2016) faculty members report that the practice of community engagement can be challenging, isolating, and potentially risky to their career path, particularly if they do not have the privileges and security associated with tenure (Stanton et al., 1999; Ward & Miller, 2016; Welch & Plaxton-Moore, 2019). It is therefore worth exploring how and why current faculty members develop and implement a successful academic career focused on community engagement.

Additionally, in order to understand, support, and institutionalize community engagement in higher education, it is important to explore the current tensions involved for faculty members who take up this work

(Saltmarsh, 2017). For example, while community-engaged faculty members center the principle of cultivating mutually beneficial relationships with partners (Keith, 2015), as course instructors, we need to prioritize students' learning, critical thinking, academic engagement, and development as potential professionals in our field. Our pedagogical effectiveness, an integral component of our job performance, is measured by evaluations that are completed by our students and colleagues, not by our partners in the community. In developing courses, serving on committees, conducting scholarship, and providing academic mentoring, we, just like the movement's founders (Stanton et al., 1999), are, to some extent, bound by the existing bureaucracies, traditions, and administrative structures of our institutions (Welch & Plaxton-Moore, 2019), structures and processes that are generally not aligned with the flexibility, reciprocity, timelines, and "flat and nimble networks" (Keith, 2015, p. 3) needed for successful community engagement (Welch & Plaxton-Moore, 2019). Although we seek to span boundaries (Weerts & Sandmann, 2010), as faculty members hired by a specific institution, we have each been charged with contributing scholarship to a distinct discipline, specialty, and department, along with developing students' literacy, mastery, and competence within a defined field.

Further, engendering civic engagement as a priority for higher education has been threatened by the ascendance of a capitalist neoliberal ideology that conceptualizes higher education as a "knowledge factory" (Aronowitz, 2001) and "reduces the purpose of public institutions to their role within the market" (Orphan & O'Meara, 2016). We thus face greater pressures than ever to monetize the value of our academic pursuits and to document (and quantify) the development of very specific vocational skills and learning outcomes in our students (Keith, 2015). In fact, as a result of the neoliberal view of students as consumers, we may be advised to steer our courses away from controversial topics and assignments involving painful self-reflection related to the examination of power and privilege (Angotti et al., 2012; Bose, 2012; Oluo, 2020). Despite these pressures, community-engaged scholars maintain that reflection accompanying action remains essential to the purpose of higher education itself (Beck et al., 2016; Oluo, 2020; Yamamura & Koth, 2018), particularly during these fractious times (Guarasci & Eatman, 2022). Indeed, as Eatman (2016) argues, "the health of our society in many ways hinges on the cultivation of empowered, focused, caring and determined thought leaders" (p. xiii).

Similar to the experiences of the field's founders more than fifty years ago, as renegades within higher education, the community engagement efforts of current faculty are often poorly understood and lack critical support (Easter, 2021; Welch & Plaxton-Moore, 2019). As we seek retention, promotion, or tenure, we still need to justify how the tenets of social justice and equity fit within the goals, plans, and rhetoric espoused by our institutions, departments, and disciplines (Welch & Plaxton-Moore, 2019). As we carve out our distinct career pathways in the professoriate, we are challenged to document the value of our accomplishments and frequently discover that community-engaged teaching and scholarship are not as easily recognized by academic committees as compared to other forms of scholarly innovation (Welch & Plaxton-Moore, 2019). When applying for positions, promotion, tenure, or funding, we may need to elucidate our epistemologies as well as the etiological and professional trajectories that have led us to pursue the issues, projects, pedagogies, and partnerships that define our work (Beck et al., 2016; Green et al., 2018; Saltmarsh et al., 2009).

This chapter explores why and how "next generation" (Butin & Pianko, 2012; Hartley & Saltmarsh, 2016; Saltmarsh, 2017) faculty members navigate developing and implementing community-engaged approaches and achieve support for these efforts as they build a career within the professoriate. Building upon our understanding of the history of faculty community engagement, the next section provides case examples of faculty members who are on this path. Considering these examples all together, we explore common themes identified from the case examples that elucidate the barriers and facilitators to community engagement for current faculty, delineating the ways in which faculty members have successfully achieved their career goals using community-engaged pedagogy and practice as a cornerstone.

In keeping with the goals set out for this book project, the authors of this chapter represent vastly different types of institutions, as well as different faculty statuses and disciplines. It is our hope that you will draw lessons from our particular career trajectories and experiences that enable you, in your own role and position, to transform the culture of the institution in which you work (Saltmarsh & Johnson, 2020; Stanton et al., 1999; Welch & Plaxton-Moore, 2019) so that you can develop, support, implement, sustain, and institutionalize transformational community engagement within the academic enterprise (Saltmarsh, 2017).

Cases of Traversing the Path of Community Engagement: From Lecturer to Full Professor

Service in Education and Beyond by Anh-Thu Ngo, PhD, Lecturer, UC San Diego

Tracing the significance of education and public service in my professional life, recently I realized that the influence is inseparable from my family history. I am a refugee, first-generation college graduate, and granddaughter of a former political prisoner. My paternal grandfather—whose community engagement began with grassroots leadership around bringing public works to new neighborhoods—was an elected city official in South Vietnam during the American War. He served six years in a forced labor camp after the Communist takeover. His imprisonment qualified the family for a United Nations High Commissioner for Refugees facilitated resettlement program to the United States. My grandparents and their brood of ten (along with spouses and children) landed in New Jersey, where the next generation's education would be the only key to America's door of opportunity.

My grandfather, past working age, busied himself as a president of the Tri-state area's Vietnamese senior citizen association. While I thought of my extended family as a unit unto itself, cut off from deep ties to a Vietnamese American community, undoubtedly, my grandfather's civic work shaped my extracurricular activities as a public school attendee. I joined service organizations, ran student groups, was class president, and participated in government- and policy-simulation camps. This hodgepodge exploration earned me admission to Princeton University.

As a freshman, I took a required writing seminar and chose one themed around "Social Action & Artistic Expression." The class seeded in me an inclination toward service-learning—a model I adopted as my academic modus operandi. The writing seminar was part of a curricular program that arguably best exemplifies the informal motto, "Princeton in the nation's service and the service of all nations." My concentration in anthropology aligned well with the imperatives of community-based learning, and I took three semesters of these classes. Anthropology's cornerstone method of immersive fieldwork centers on community-engaged research and simultaneously allows for disciplinary promiscuity among diverse fields like critical theory and history. That these ivory tower preoccupations could translate to praxis around the public interest was energizing enough to lead me to a PhD program in Social Anthropology.

Before that, I worked at education nonprofits in New York City through a Princeton Project '55 Public Interest Program Fellowship. Now part of AlumniCorps, it was the first alumni group whose members organized to promote civic engagement in the public interest. Ralph Nader (class of '55) championed the idea, and its flagship program remains a vibrant opportunity for recent graduates to work with nonprofit organizations while being a mechanism for these institutions to recruit early career talent. The program includes professional development, with mentorship matches and educational seminars. I helped organize New York seminars and continued in graduate school at Harvard University, where I liaised with that campus's public service organization. After coursework, I received a Fulbright grant for field research in Vietnam and went on to pursue teaching at several public universities upon graduation.

My current role as Lecturer with UC San Diego's Global Teams in Engineering Service (TIES) has been a fortuitous convergence of interests, connecting back to a six-week Engineers Without Borders irrigation project in rural Ethiopia that I joined after college. I teach Design for Development, the foundation course for a two-class series that makes up Global TIES, a humanitarian engineering and social innovation program supporting multidisciplinary undergraduate teams to design technical solutions for a problem experienced by a nonprofit or its constituent community. Students in Global TIES gain experience in sustainable human-centered design while partner entities receive pro bono work from STEM curriculum development and media campaigns to tactile maps and solar lanterns.

Global TIES is now one of two initiatives under the UCSD Jacobs School of Engineering's Center for Global Sustainable Development—directed by Mandy Bratton, PhD—which "encourages students, faculty, staff, and alumni to pursue innovation for the global good that especially benefits those at the bottom of the wealth pyramid." The Center is a founding member of the UCSD Changemaker Institute, a university-wide initiative started in 2020 to connect campus members with outside communities to undertake collaborative projects that further goals toward a just, sustainable, and inclusive world. Dr. Bratton played a key role in earning UCSD an Ashoka U Changemaker Campus designation (one of just 45 worldwide). Under her leadership, Global TIES was also featured as a model program at the Clinton Global Initiative University.

Even with this record, sustaining the program is not without hurdles. In outreach efforts to community organizations, I encounter hindrances, despite offers for fresh perspective and technical know-how. Resource scarcity means that even giving attention to gain in-kind labor can be a stretch for some. Securing community partnerships, then, depends on my professional and personal networks both, and often, these ties are experiments-in-progress for each party. And while we are conceptually ambitious, our scope of work is limited by the perennial issue of nominal budgets. Further, the administrative obstacles for Global TIES include an unwieldy bureaucracy that impedes course scheduling workarounds and incentivizing credit units that would spur enrollment.

For students who do recognize the rewards of this program, my last lecture focuses on careers in community-engaged roles. I am encouraging but also frank about the challenges that await those considering this professional path, raising issues around financial resources and continuing effectiveness. UCSD has a large immigrant and first-generation college student population, many of whom are saddled with debt and familial obligations that could be paid off more easily through competitive corporate engineering and design roles. Occasionally, I get an appreciative email, where students cite the course as an example of applied project experience that has cinched them a job or internship. In these moments, I am heartened. Regardless of their professional pursuits, I hope that students retain an ethos of responsible service long after the class, one that informs their choices as civically minded citizens.

What's Wrong with Passion? A Woman of Color Reads Her Student Rating of Teaching Surveys by Angie Mejia, PhD, Assistant Professor, University of Minnesota Rochester

> I wish she was nice.
> *(Student Comment on Student Ratings of Teaching [SRT])*

I'll never forget my first year as an assistant professor and civic engagement scholar at a small Midwestern university campus. I was teaching *Community Collaborative*, an upper-division community-engaged learning course that connects students with groups working towards the health of local communities. Although the numerical ratings of teaching effectiveness that students provided were generally high (at or above the mean ratings of my department and college), qualitative descriptors such as "too intense," "too enthusiastic," and "too much" were used by a minority of students evaluating my course. As a Woman of Color (WOC) who identifies as the descendant of Central American, Afro-Latinx, and Mexican-American familial unions and disunions, SRT allow some of my students to further mark me as someone who does not fit in their world. As a community-engaged scholar, however, I assure myself and others (mostly the BIPOC students) that there is nothing wrong with the intensity (whether real or imagined by White students) that I demonstrate in the classroom and everything wrong with the perceived "niceness" of the Midwest Whiteness underlying the comments above.

> Dr. Mejia might have gotten too passionate about the lecture material.
> *(Student Comment on SRT)*

SRT surveys allow some White students to vent their frustrations about someone like me. Someone who made them think about oppression and Whiteness. And someone like me, according to the qualitative comments in some of these SRTs, is "too intense," "too enthusiastic," and "too much." Under (Mid)western eyes, Women of Color read as "too much" might also be perceived as not "nice." By "nice," I mean a trait, behavior, or way of being attributed to (some) Minnesotans. Below, I use Yuko Taniguchi's (see Mejia & Taniguchi, 2021) experience as a Japanese 1.5 generation woman to expand on this concept of Minnesota Nice™.

> [It's] the unwritten code of Minnesota .... [T]he commitment to appear nice and polite by avoiding confrontation .... The passive-aggressive behaviors often confused me as I missed the cues for what people in Minnesota were truly expressing. I eventually learned that such behaviors were a path for unexpressed thoughts to come out and surface ....
> *(Taniguchi, 2021)*

Various scholars have documented how WOC experience being read by students and others that embody racially privileged identities. But teaching in a Midwest university, and being the person teaching a major requirement, was, for me, another level altogether. Coded words such as "passionate" and "intense" infer tired tropes and caricatures of racialized womanhood that position us to experience what Barbara Harris Combs (2016) calls the bodies out of place (BOP) phenomena. Here, the body out of place is the professor of color who happens to be at a Predominantly White Institution (PWI). Those managing the affective reality of being a body out of place need to decode the specific manner of Whiteness operating in each place and space and both learn and navigate the unique climate of Whiteness. For me, having lived on both coasts, having to decode White cultural affect meant having to understand the complexities underlying "Midwest Nice" and, in my experience, "Minnesota Nice." And for me and another WOC teaching community-engaged research around these parts, we have learned that in the land of "nice" and "you betcha," being intense, passionate, exuberant, and the like will result in being made to feel more out of place. But we also know that there is nothing wrong with intensity and passion, in and out of classroom spaces, and everything wrong with a lack of these forms of emotive performances in the places we teach, research, and advocate.

I did not begin my community-engaged academic journey in the land of "nice"—I just ended here. The work of crossing boundaries between classroom and community began in 2005. During my last year as a Master's student, I was hired by a county health department in Oregon to guide Mexican immigrant mothers to use Photovoice. This action research method places cameras in the hands of socially marginalized groups as a way to create change. The pictures-as-data in Photovoice allows community members to initiate conversations with local policymakers. However, power asymmetries among the mothers and county leaders meant that the formers' contributions were footnoted on glossy reports. To counter this institutional invisibilization, I asked the mothers to join me in coauthoring an article sharing how they changed the project to be a more Latina-centered experience (Mejia et al., 2013). This was my way to help us embody a role independent of the tokenization we experienced by the county health department leaders. Since then, I began residing in this in-betweenness of academia and community to examine the intricacies of ethnicity, power, and privilege as they play out in community health interventions.

I am currently tenure track as an assistant professor in an interdisciplinary department called the Center for Learning Innovation (CLI) and I have an appointment as a Civic Engagement scholar. According to its website, CLI "promotes a learner-centered, technology-enhanced, concept-driven and community-integrated learning environment." My position was created in response to a specific need. Thus, I teach almost all CEL classes for the campus and I guide all community-engaged learning (CEL) curricula by supporting faculty in developing community-engaged (CE) syllabi and connecting them to community partners. I received a .2 release for all my work in curriculum development and faculty support regarding CEL, including building partnerships, linking faculty to partners, and serving on advisory communities and community boards. CEL is part of the mission of the university to "inspire transformation in higher education through innovations that empower our graduates to solve the grand health challenges of the 21st century" (University of Minnesota Rochester, 2022) and every student at the university has to take a CE class to graduate.

The University website lists "community" as one of the institution's grounding values. Community is described as the value of "collective work and a culture of trust that promotes collaboration, problem-solving and partnerships while creating belonging, accountability and courageous action." Despite this, there are huge gaps between the institution's mission statements and what I have actually experienced in terms of support for my work.

> I wish this course focused more on ... engaging with our community ... rather than ... what is wrong with society ...
>
> *(Student Comment on SRT)*

As a sociologist, I use outliers to highlight the range of social phenomena under inquiry. Surprisingly, my SRT scores are consistently high. However, I must be aware that some (for example, tenure and promotion committee members) will remember you (and others) by the narrative of outliers. We do the same with data! When I bring concerns to tenured colleagues, they tell me that SRTs "is not the only metric" for tenure. But they won't go beyond "nicely" assuring me, nor address certain colleagues' racist, sexist, and homophobic treatment of other faculty members. And the outliers do not want to reflect on how inequities impact the Somali community; they simply want to finger-paint with Somali kids at the tutoring center. And senior leadership at the University does not wish to hear about our institution's role in exacerbating inequities; they want pictures of students with smeared paint on their cheeks.

The loud outliers dotting the SRTs of WOC academics who engage in community-based work are also confirming what other scholars are telling us about some of the more privileged students in our service-learning classrooms: Not only are they not ready, in some cases, but they are also actively unwilling, no matter the amount of pedagogical skill, magic, or talent we summon to deliver and make the content understandable to them, to see the effects of white supremacist thinking on the communities that they serve, which are often different than theirs. As the above quote reflects, outliers in my class want to learn about the community in the "nicest" way possible. And as we are seeing at the moment, "Minnesota nice" has its limits. It is no longer helping some rationalize away acts of racial cruelty fueled by a culture of white supremacy.

Even in my position as a civic engagement scholar, as a tenure track faculty Queer Woman of Color, there have been a lot of barriers in integrating community engagement into my own scholarly agenda. Despite its espoused rhetoric, the University does not support community partnerships, so faculty allocate unpaid labor toward supporting partners with needs such as grant writing. This unpaid labor is provided disproportionality by nontenured faculty, and tenure track BIPOC faculty.

At our institution, there is a lack of understanding of how community engagement works and how the University should support it. Our campus is less than 15 years old, so a common refrain is, "We are very new. We're trying. We're aspiring." Having University administrators, such as the president, serve on local boards would speak volumes about the genuine commitment of the University to building community infrastructure. Second, more faculty release time is needed to recognize the enormous labor cost of developing, building, and maintaining reciprocal and respectful relationships. The scholarship of engagement, for example, requires quality community connections and a long-term commitment to community partners that goes beyond traditional one-semester service-learning courses with limited direct service activities. Third, faculty who provide knowledge and social capital to local community agencies should be reimbursed for their time. Finally, since community partners are always stretched for resources, the university should also allocate resources to reimburse nonprofit partners' time when they serve on University committees, serve as coeducators/facilitators, supervise our students, or come to our campus for community engagement events.

In terms of research, the scholarship that I do always speaks truth to power and it will always bring up uncomfortable conversations about the power relationships between the University and the community. I discuss diversity regimes (bringing color capital to the university via Diversity, Equity, and Inclusion (DEI) efforts while stymying attempts to transform the university status quo), neoliberalism, and the Uberification of the university. At committee levels, and from senior faculty, I face criticism that my research and action agenda are not inclusive of perspectives that we don't see as marginalized, such as those of conservative White students. I am often excluded from higher level decision making even when decisions and policies relate to my positionality as a woman of color sociologist who is focused on community based participatory research (CBPR) research, and on understanding the academy itself.

Community-engaged scholars of color must learn the particular affective contours of the White noise and nonsense operating in time, place, and space. It is not an issue of avoiding the (White) what or that (White) who, but a need to understand one's position as a body out of place, an experience of academic racialization that is shaped by the uniqueness of that White noise and nonsense. To mitigate these barriers for future faculty, mentorship structures are needed to provide an institutional path for faculty who are activists, to help us navigate challenges, and to shield us from barriers. Committees and institutional structures still protect racist perspectives and ignore, silence, or mute those of us who are trying to push the university to confront and repair white supremacy. Community-engaged faculty face the pressures of producing peer-reviewed research while at the same time experiencing criticism and exclusion from scholarly venues and committees because we are often representing marginalized perspectives through our work. Experiencing "nods of silence" and being tokenized leads BIPOC women to leave or quietly quit tenure track jobs. Mentorship and genuine inclusion is required to both diversify the academy and institutionalize community engagement.

In my work, I find ways to enable community partners to serve as Principal Investigators (PIs) on grants and to get paid for their work. I serve on the boards of community agencies to share my knowledge and expertise. I engage with partners beyond my job functions and goals because I genuinely care about the community and want to learn. For example, I knew very little about the Somali community here and was willing to show up and make the effort to do things that are "not going to count toward my academic" career. For those of us who engage with communities from within the academy, it is often the community members we work alongside that know how to deal with the nonsense of academia and drown out the noise. They are the ones who nourish us and hold us … and can help us thrive in "nice" places.

Pathways to Community-based Scholarship by Marie Sandy, PhD, Associate Professor, University of Wisconsin–Milwaukee

Shortly after I moved from Washington, DC, to attend a PhD program in education in Southern California, I grew to be an admirer of and friends with Father Patricio Guillen and Rosa Martha Zarate, who led the nonprofit Librería del Pueblo (Bookstore of the People) in San Bernardino, California. One December, they invited me to attend the posada sin frontera festival they were having, and I immediately said yes. I had no idea what a posada was. I did know we would be supporting the organization and immigrants in the region, and I trusted that this was an event I should share. So I did, and Kebokile Dengu-Zvobgo of Pitzer College came along with me. As we marched down streets of the city of San Bernardino holding candles and struggling to read the song sheets to sing with members of the calpulli[1] of Libreria del Pueblo and other community members, I began to realize that we were physically reenacting the journey of Mary and Joseph in search of shelter at an inn in Bethlehem. According to Father Patricio Guillen (personal communication, March 18, 2003), the word "posada" refers to both the journey and the process of creating that space, that home or dwelling place that does not yet exist. That posada night, he called us all to act for justice, highlighting the parallels between modern-day immigrants in southern California and the treatment of undocumented people today, and the need for us all to do the work of homebuilding together. When there is no space, we make that space.

The posada gave me language to better understand my own experience in the world. Retelling this story also provided an opening for my grandmother and parents to share more about our family's immigrant posadas from southern and eastern Europe to the coal mining region of northeastern Pennsylvania. There were hard parts of the stories they shared, some I had heard before, and some I had not. Twenty years later, I live in a neighborhood in the upper Midwest where we reenact las posadas every December, but I think back to that first one, and how my understanding of the many layered meanings of what we were doing grew clearer through walking that posada with them.

My path of becoming a community-engaged scholar has been about becoming more open to experiences of community and solidarity by traversing and dwelling in academic and neighborhood settings. It has often involved creating new spaces to dwell in to do the work of engaged scholarship in the academy, an institution that is not always ready for it. I don't always know what I'm doing, but that often becomes clearer as I walk that path and take the lead from community partners I trust and love. I hope my efforts can clear spaces for others to do community-based work.

Shortly after attending my first posada, I went on to write a dissertation on a community-based research and outreach project at Pitzer College in Ontario, California, with support from a Housing and Urban Development (HUD)/Community Outreach Partnership grant. Immediately after graduating, I did consulting work on community-based research topics, worked with California Campus Compact, and taught as an adjunct lecturer. A couple of years after graduating with my PhD, I was fortunate to find a tenure track faculty position in a city I had never been to before the job interview. All of a sudden, everything was new again.

The public research-intensive institution at which I now work seemed to be a good fit for CEL, because it combines both an access and a research mission, with an intentional focus on serving the local urban community. The vision of the university explicitly includes "community and global engagement, and collaborative partnerships," which is helpful to justify the kind of work I seek to do. The Milwaukee Idea,[2] designed to encourage lasting community-university partnerships, is part of the DNA of this institution. When I began a tenure-track position in a city in which I had never lived before, I took it slow to allow authentic partnership relationships to develop. During my first year in Milwaukee, I visited several organizations with missions that aligned with my interests and set up informal meetings with program directors and executive directors prior to integrating any service-learning components in my coursework. Gradually, I participated in community-based research partnerships that developed over time. The university's office of community engagement also helped provide introductions. And twenty odd years later, I am still working with some of the original groups and individuals I worked with while in graduate school in Southern California.

Research productivity was the emphasis of this predominantly white-serving institution, but I knew I needed to prioritize relationships for place-based scholarship to take root. That took patience—I felt like my advocates and champions in my department were biting their nails that first year or two while my published scholarship began to flourish. I highlighted community-engaged scholarship in my tenure file, even though I knew that some who reviewed my file were mainly interested in things like journal impact factors, and I suggested external reviewers I felt were committed to this paradigm. Service-learning and community-based work is at the heart of my pedagogy and scholarship. Sometimes I focus more on the teaching side, such as how to do service-learning in online environments and supporting community-engaged graduate students; sometimes I focus more on community-based research such as working with community health workers. The infrastructure in place through the campus-wide service-learning office has been very helpful with supporting community-engaged scholars by connecting this group regularly, holding special events, and providing annual recognition of exceptional work.

However, in terms of getting recognition and support for CEL, It has been a bit of a mixed bag. CEL is still not an explicit part of the tenure and promotion process here. I needed to demonstrate the ability to perform using traditional measures of faculty success. I included evidence of CEL in my tenure narrative and CV and suggested external reviewers that were familiar with and supportive of CEL and public-engaged scholarship. Publications and successful grants are still the coin of the realm at any research-intensive institution. Annual merit reports typically reward the most points to traditional scholarly publications, with evidence of excellence in teaching scoring the next highest number of points. The emphasis on service described in the mission and vision of the university is not necessarily translated into policies that reward faculty. It is up to existing faculty, administrators, and staff to work to change that.

I learned over time that some departments on campus were more engaged than others. I ultimately requested a change in my tenure home to ensure community-based research and teaching would be supported and recognized. As the current chair of a department, I often ask, "What assets does the university have that can be of use to the local community at this time?" As always, in this work, it is good to have friends and travel companions.

Tikkun Olam in Theory and Practice by Jon A. Levisohn, PhD, Associate Professor, Brandeis University

What does service-learning or community engagement have to do with academic Jewish studies? What role should it play in my own teaching at a private, elite, distinctively Jewish institution (Brandeis University)? What does it mean to engage with the community as a Jewish studies scholar? I began to think about these questions about fifteen years ago, as service and service-learning programs blossomed in the Jewish community through an infusion of philanthropic dollars and attention (BTW Informing Change, 2008). These programs built on the prominence of the concept of *Tikkun Olam*, literally translated as "repairing the world," which has been a centerpiece of modern Jewish ethical discourse (key texts include Dorff, 2005; Jacobs, 2007; Kanarek, 2008; Krasner, 2013; see also critiques such as the now classic Wolf, 2001). The initiatives within the Jewish community also drew from the burgeoning literature on and practice of service and service-learning in the broader higher education community.

Initially, I approached the questions abstractly and with some distance, from my perch as a philosopher of education. What, I wondered, are the learning goals of Jewish service-learning in particular? What are the distinctive pedagogies around, for example, the common use of classical Jewish sources to inform, inspire, and in some cases problematize service? What are the particular conceptual or ethical challenges of doing service in a particularist context?[3] How does one learn to help another to serve, or to serve Jewishly, or in my shorthand, how does one become a "teacher of *tikkun olam*"?

I also wondered about the particular philanthropic dynamic that I observed, in which the objectives of those who were funding service and service-learning in the Jewish community were not always entirely aligned with the objectives of the grantees; while the latter were focused on serving those in need and in educating those who serve, the former were (also and sometimes primarily) interested in "building Jewish identity," where the scare quotes hint at the imprecision of this goal. I wondered about the deployment of so-called "private resources" toward the solution of social problems, and the assumptions that are built into that framing. And I wondered about the ever-present problem of donor fatigue in the development of the field.

Then, in 2011, these questions became less abstract and more concrete, when my involvement in various conversations with colleagues at other institutions of higher education as well as service and social justice activists led to an invitation to participate in a cohort of the Jewish Studies Service-Learning Initiative, a fellowship organized by an organization called, fittingly, Repair the World. This organization, still relatively new at the time, launched with an initial mandate to convene the relevant stakeholders and to build the field of Jewish service and service-learning. The purpose of the fellowship was to explore how academic Jewish studies could inform community-engaged pedagogy, and vice versa.

How did we actually do this work? The group of Jewish studies scholars met regularly over the course of a year, read literature about service-learning and community-engaged pedagogy, discussed its application to academic Jewish studies and pushed back on its assumptions, and workshopped our evolving course syllabi.

The fellowship provided material resources; the first time that I taught the course, I had funding from Repair the World for a course assistant to help with the organization and oversight of the service-learning strand (in subsequent iterations of the course, I had funding from an internal Brandeis grant or from reallocated research funds). But beyond material resources, it also provided intellectual companionship and legitimation. In retrospect, it seems important that I was able to frame my involvement in this work, when I spoke about it with my Brandeis colleagues, as an opportunity to participate in a national fellowship that also included a number of other respected figures in the academic field of Jewish studies. I participated in the fellowship just prior to my tenure and promotion. I actually taught the course for the first time only after my promotion—but that was coincidental, not intentional, and I did write explicitly about my involvement in the fellowship and my development of a new service-learning course as part of my tenure dossier. The structure of the fellowship and the involvement of these colleagues from other institutions lent an air of credibility to the enterprise. Would I have gotten any criticism about my involvement in this work without the fellowship? That's impossible to know. But it is surely the case that the fellowship helped. Rather than feeling vulnerable as an untenured assistant professor, I proceeded with confidence.

So I did not hear criticism from my Brandeis colleagues. But on the other hand, I am well aware that there are important and serious critiques of service-learning or community-engaged learning, from pedagogic, institutional, and indeed ethical perspectives. The fellowship provided the space to seriously consider these—and I know that a number of colleagues in the fellowship did encounter institutional resistance, for example, from those who wondered whether they might be crossing the line into advocacy or abandoning the core intellectual purpose of their work.

And even for those in favor of service-learning, integrating these pedagogies into Jewish studies is complicated. The most obvious paradigm for the use of service-learning in higher education is a course on a particular social problem, such as poverty or homelessness, typically in the social sciences. But scholars of Jewish studies are, mostly, historians of various kinds (although I am a philosopher by training, not an historian). It is not at all clear how to integrate service-learning into a course on the Hebrew Bible, or medieval Jewish poetry, or the history of Jewish music, or even something more contemporary like the history of the American Jewish community or of the Holocaust. Furthermore, the discourse around community-engaged pedagogy tends to assume that the "community" in question is an impoverished one that will benefit from partnership with the academic institution. Does this mean that a Jewish studies course should *not* partner with the Jewish community, which, in the contemporary American context, is mostly (although of course not entirely) fairly comfortable? Finally, there is a rather strong reluctance among academics, at least in certain areas, to cross the line between scholarly inquiry and advocacy or activism. We might think about a course on Israel/Palestine, for example. Would an instructor want their students to be engaged in service-learning on behalf of one side of the conflict, or the other, or both sides? Or might they say, rather, that the job of the classroom community is to set activism aside, at least for a few minutes each week, in order to actually learn something that they did not previously know? (On the specific challenges of integrating service-learning into Jewish studies, see Butin & Pianko, 2012, as well as the entire issue 87 of the *Journal of Jewish Communal Service* in which their article appears.)

My own approach to these very real issues was to sidestep them completely. That is, rather than figuring out my answers to the questions and structuring the course accordingly, I made these questions the very ones that we would investigate together. I made *Tikkun Olam* itself the focus of my new service-learning course at Brandeis, which I titled "*Tikkun Olam/* Repairing the World: Service and Social Justice in Theory and Practice."

We would investigate *Tikkun Olam* as a term and a concept. We would ask questions about service and social justice initiatives themselves, rather than using our service to learn about some other social problem. We would interrogate our own assumptions as people—Jews, if we identify that way—who desperately want to do good in the world. We would critically examine the woeful history of paternalistic interventions around the world and right here at home. And we would do so while paying very close attention to our positionality—both personal and institutional.

We would be sitting at Brandeis University, a private, relatively well-resourced research university. Brandeis is an elite school, in the sense that it is highly selective; while the school is proud of its ambitious efforts to provide need-based aid to students, it is also true that, in the 21st century, selectivity correlates with socioeconomic status. And Brandeis is also distinctively Jewish. What does this mean? There are no required Jewish studies courses at Brandeis (although there is a very strong Jewish studies department). There are certainly no required religious observances (although the University does close for some Jewish holidays to accommodate observant Jewish students). In fact, for the last 10–20 years, the undergraduate student population has become more diverse, intentionally so (it is now only about one-third Jewish). However, the University does continue to receive most of its philanthropic support from the Jewish community. And even more importantly, the University does think about "service to the Jewish community," through teaching and scholarship, as one of its objectives. The University tells its own story as one that is grounded in Jewish values and Jewish historical experience (Brandeis' Jewish Roots, 2023).

In the specific case of the classroom community that we would build, that community would be, I expected, largely if not entirely upper middle class, largely if not entirely white-presenting, largely if not entirely liberal-to-progressive politically, and largely if not entirely Jewish. Interestingly, I discovered that the approach that I adopted—the approach of making *Tikkun Olam* itself the focus of the course—disrupted some of the conventional wisdom about community engagement. According to that conventional wisdom, service-learning ought to be designed in collaboration with a community partner, under the conditions of an ongoing relationship, to meet real needs, in a collective and coordinated way rather than a fragmented way. There are lots of reasons why that conventional wisdom makes sense, in a lot of settings. I respect the integrity of that approach. But in my course, it would not do. Instead, I realized that the purpose of service-learning within the context of my course was to provide a set of case studies of what service can look like, what challenges it can generate, how it might "succeed," and how it might "fail."

I therefore wanted and needed the service opportunities that my students pursued to be as diverse as possible. Instead of working with one community partner, my students would choose different causes to serve. They would serve different communities. They would adopt different modes of service— direct service, advocacy, community organizing, philanthropy, etc. Then, when they brought these diverse experiences back to the classroom, all these differences would contribute to our learning, as we shared successes and failures, interrogated assumptions, evaluated purposes, and critically examined the very organizations that we are supporting with our service. There is surely an inevitable tension between the goal of service (helping others, repairing the world) and the goal of learning (the students' own growth). In my particular class, with its particular focus, I am willing to accept the possibility or even the likelihood that some of the students' service is going to be fragmentary, ineffective, or inefficient, in order that all of us might have the opportunity to learn from reflection on those experiences.

I can understand that this calculus might be problematic for some. But here it might be useful to introduce a religious argument, not necessarily to persuade the reader but simply as a different way of thinking about things. What I have in mind is that, for a religious person, it may be easier to think about service not (only) as an effort to solve problems, but as a way of being in the world. To make the normative stance explicit: *We ought to be in service of others.* Why? We might say that that's the best way to live, or perhaps, that serving others is the way to be fully human. Theists might say that that's what God wants of us. If that's our starting point, then we still do have a responsibility to think about how to do that work effectively, of course—but our focus has shifted. We don't go through the world trying to solve somebody's problem. We go through the world seeking to serve.

I have called this a "religious argument," and for some readers it may sound distinctively Christian. But I believe that there are Jewish roots to this way of thinking as well (see Levisohn, 2012a, and Levisohn, 2012b). More generally, the argument maps onto the philosophical divide between consequentialist ethics and virtue ethics. In my teaching, I have often called this "the Band-Aid Problem." The fields of social justice and philanthropy often dismiss certain interventions as merely placing a band-aid on a problem rather than addressing the underlying systemic issues or root causes. Movements like "strategic philanthropy" and "effective altruism" denigrate the allocation of resources—our money and time—in any way but that which brings the most good to the most people. These are often critically important perspectives to keep in mind. At the same time, when someone is bleeding, a band-aid is exactly what they need. The perspective that I hope to share with my students is this: We ought not to become so enamored of our analyses of systemic problems that we lose sight of responding to the human beings right in front of us.

Let me turn, finally, to the question of what it means to be sitting together, as a group of (mostly but not entirely) white-presenting, idealistic, and progressive upper-middle-class Jews, committed to *Tikkun Olam,* and serving those in greater need. I do not claim that this is the best educational setting. Its homogeneity is surely a weakness. But here it may be helpful to name another aspect of the environment, namely, the commitment of the institution itself—Brandeis—to the ideals of social justice and "repairing the world." (Brandeis' Jewish Roots, 2023). We may be cynical about the use of the slogan, about whether the institution walks the walk. Surely there are grounds for that cynicism. At the same time, as an instructor, I can confidently say that our work together in the class is an enactment of the expressed commitments of the institution. Earlier, I referred to the fact that the structure of the fellowship with Repair the World and the involvement of senior Jewish studies colleagues from other institutions lent an air of credibility to the enterprise, which insulated me—as an untenured assistant professor at the time—from any sense of vulnerability. At the same time, in the decade since the fellowship, I have had only positive interactions regarding my community-engaged teaching with Brandeis colleagues, including the senior leadership of the University. Even those who are unsure about how to proceed with community-engaged teaching themselves seem to respect and value my work. Most recently, Brandeis secured a major philanthropic gift to create a new center that "seeks to make ethical and respectful community engagement a central pillar of a Brandeis education" (Brandeis Compact, 2023). Those of us who have been involved in service-learning are now perceived not as marginal to the institution, but rather as a vanguard.

Moreover, when I look out at a class of 15 or 18 Jewish students, I choose to leverage that very homogeneity in the service of greater and deeper learning about power and privilege. There are questions that we can ask and conversations that we can have, as these Jewish students pursue their service and as they envision future lives of service, precisely because they do not feel that they are under attack for their privilege or morally culpable for their power. Those questions include, especially after 2016, an exploration of white supremacy in which Jews are both implicated (because American Jews are mostly white-presenting, and because Jewish communities also struggle with racism both structural and individual) and also, explicitly and unambiguously, targeted (for an analysis of antisemitism on the right, see Ward, 2017; for an analysis of antisemitism on the left, see Rosenberg, 2022).

To be powerful is not to be corrupt; to be powerless is not a state of moral superiority. We all have power; we are also all subject to the power of others; that is the human condition. Our ethical responsibility, I propose to my students, is to acknowledge that power and privilege, and to strive to understand it as best we can, in order to decide how to live.

Making It to Full by Elena Klaw, PhD, Psychology Professor, San José State University

I joined the faculty at SJSU in 2000 as a tenure line hire in Clinical Psychology, armed with a PhD in Clinical and Community Psychology, a postdoctoral fellowship from the Department of Veterans Affairs (VA), and a professional license that enabled me to supervise emerging psychotherapists. As the first grandchild of Holocaust survivors and refugees, I had a deep-rooted passion for pursuing social justice, promoting resilience, and preventing violence.

My graduate experience in Psychology at a major research university was both intellectually inspiring and morally depleting. I finished my program bracingly aware that the pressures to "publish or perish" led some faculty to justify exploitative practices in the name of science (Klaw, 2008). Despite my love of teaching, I had considered leaving academia many times. Fortunately, my mentor at the VA, an internationally recognized Stanford research professor, modeled how to translate research into public policy (Humphreys, 1996), and to work alongside grassroots organizations using quantitative and qualitative methods to amplify the voices of participants. My postdoctoral fellowship restored my faith in higher education, in my field, and in myself.

Despite the fact that there was, and still is, no Community Psychology division within my Department, I sought to integrate the topics, theories, and methodological approaches of community psychology into my role by focusing on the science and practice of violence prevention. Having paid my dues by teaching standard curriculum in my department for several years, I developed an undergraduate service-learning and a graduate-level course focused on intimate violence, the specialty area most central to my work. Developing the courses led me to reach out to all the local agencies and offices working in the areas of family violence, sexual assault, and partner abuse to invite stakeholders ranging from direct service providers, to county administrators, to advocates and prosecutors, to serve as coeducators in my classroom. In turn, the undergraduate students who participated in my course provided workshops and outreach on preventing violence and abuse to community organizations ranging from preschools and elementary schools to gang prevention programs and sober living houses, senior centers, and homeless shelters (Klaw & Ampuero, 2007). Further, they translated and delivered the curriculum and resource lists that we developed into a wide variety of languages, making deliberate linkages to underserved groups. As I became recognized as a local expert, I provided countless invited community trainings focused on intimate violence prevention, often partnering with the Assistant District Attorney who created the Domestic Violence unit for our county. I quickly saw her as my mentor.

Despite the popularity of my courses, the success of the various student clubs I advised, and my expansive service to the community and the field, my focus on intimate violence was sometimes challenged by departmental committee members and in formal peer evaluations as "political advocacy" and "not really psychology." I thus made sure to continue to publish in peer-reviewed journals and maintained a consistent program of research that was easily recognizable as valid in my discipline, along with continuing my more explicitly feminist and qualitative endeavors. I found strong mentors at SJSU within Sociology, Education, and Student Affairs, and in the College of Social Science Deans Office, who encouraged me to pursue internal release time opportunities to continue to create community engagement opportunities and to build a scholarship of engagement.

When I was invited to pursue solicited proposals for external funding, I worked with an assistant professor in our Public Health Department to secure Foundation grants to explore domestic violence risk in student Veterans, and I partnered with our University Advancement Office to establish a consistent stream of corporate funding for student Veterans to serve as peer leaders. To launch a new community-engaged course on this topic, an emerging and rewarding specialty area, I invited local Veteran serving-organizations and Veteran community speakers to work with me to educate my students about the needs and perspectives of military members and their families. Since there were few programs focused on student Veterans at that time, and my research documented the vast need for Veteran support, the Division of Academic Affairs helped me to establish an infrastructure for my work through a .2 release time and a distinct course number to offer an academic class to serve Veterans. While I was on sabbatical completing a research program regarding best practices for serving Veterans, I was invited to chair the campus University Veterans Advisory Committee that successfully advocated for the establishment of a staffed Veteran Resource Center.

Stepping outside of the boundaries of my field, my Department, and the Division of Academic Affairs as a tenure track faculty member, to join and form campus collaboratives that involve multiple disciplines, offices, and community organizations has been both unexpectedly challenging and boundlessly rewarding. The consistent enthusiasm, appreciation, and openness I have experienced from local community members, service-providers, and policy makers has encouraged me to persist in community-engaged work. Conversely, the pushback I have experienced from faculty and administrators who wanted to make sure to protect their fiefdoms instead of collaborating with mutual respect has exhausted me. When I have been challenged to define my work more narrowly, or others have taken credit for my work, I have relied on my mentors and friends within the academy to revive me. Further, I have been fueled to continue my efforts by the expressions of appreciation I receive regularly from students and community colleagues who work in the areas of Veteran support and violence prevention. Prior to submitting my application for tenure, my work in service-learning was recognized by an award established by the Center for Community Learning & Leadership and granted through the Provost's Office. Including this simple certificate in my tenure dossier allowed me to document Community Engaged Learning within my application and then elaborate as to how this work fulfilled the three categories of required achievement, categorized discretely as pedagogy, scholarship, and service. Ultimately, I reached both tenure and the status of full professor with unwavering support and received an unexpected and much-appreciated pay raise due to the advocacy of my College Dean. Her evaluation said something to the extent that "Elena enacts the values of her discipline by bringing the community into her classroom and her classroom into the community."

Following my initial promotion to tenured associate professor, I was hired as the Director of the University's Center for Community Learning & Leadership (CCLL) through a half-time release position. Although the primary mandate of the Center is to oversee, assess, and document service-learning, I continue to direct peer leadership efforts through CCLL, and in my departmental faculty role, I teach graduate-level courses about violence and social equity to clinicians. This semester, as a full professor with 22 years of service, I am on my third sabbatical leave, with a contract to complete this book project. I work with a team of exceptionally competent and committed higher education professionals through the Center. As we are currently a leadership group comprised of four feminist women, including a full-time assistant director, we strive to be nonhierarchical, collaborative (see Schnackenberg & Simard, 2021), and even celebratory. Having survived the past few dreary years of the COVID-19 pandemic and national division, we are heartened to work with the Democratic leadership in our state and to participate in substantive new grant funded efforts to support partnerships between universities and K-12 public schools. Since our work at the Center is mission driven, we remain flexible to pivot our focus to different topics and approaches as different societal needs emerge. As working mothers, our senior leadership team experiences all polarities between feeling entirely invincible and utterly depleted (sometimes on a daily basis) but we are always ready to support students and faculty who wish to explore, implement, or expand pedagogy and practice that is based on meaningful, just, and sustained involvement with local communities.

In our roles, we are acutely aware of the common obstacles faculty cite to including community engagement within their courses and we seek to ease barriers to adopting this approach. Common challenges mentioned by faculty in our humongous (36,000 students), ethnically diverse commuter university include perpetual overwork, escalating bureaucratic procedures, concerns regarding meeting course learning objectives, and pressure to meet criteria for retention, tenure, and promotion, as well as needing introductions to local community partners (Widaman et al., 2022).

Not surprisingly, during the quarantine mandates and school shutdowns instituted in response to the COVID-19 pandemic in 2020–2021, course-based service-learning was significantly reduced (Pfeiffer & Baker, 2021). Research by our team (Widaman et al., 2022) suggests that during this time period, faculty members were mainly concerned with their own safety and that of their students, challenges managing communication using only electronic modalities, expanded workloads, and a lack of support from their institutions of higher education. The uncertainty surrounding our daily lives in the pandemic, our own changing working conditions, and the shuttering of K-12 schools and child care resulted in cataclysmic levels of stress for educators, for college students, and for the vulnerable communities we serve (Cipriano, et al., 2020; Parks, 2022; Wang et al., 2020). Nevertheless, as evidenced in this book, many of us persisted and transformed our work to meet the challenges of the day. In fact, by listening to our students and collaborating with partners and staff members, we created new models of community engagement that allowed us to bolster our students, our communities, and our splintered nation. Concurrently, higher education faculty members worked even harder than before (Boyer-Davis, 2020; Ramlo, 2021) to forward our own academic disciplines, departments, and scholarship. Current literature suggests that the institutions of higher education need to do more to address the psychological and physical costs of the added burdens of work that educators have shouldered these past few years (Tugend, 2020; Zahneis, 2022). At SJSU, as part of the California State University system, the faculty union successfully bargained for back pay for the hours spent retooling our courses into remote formats. Educators must be recognized, supported (Boyer-Davis, 2020), and compensated for these added burdens.

As a full professor in the role of CCLL Director, I derive great satisfaction from helping fellow faculty members navigate the perilous trail to a successful and rewarding academic career. I hope that the scholarship I conduct contributes to the science of resilience (Walsh, 2015) and to the large body of findings indicating that mentoring is a key ingredient enabling people to achieve their life goals (Bruce & Bridgeland, 2014; Ghosh & Reio, 2013; Klaw & Rhodes, 1995). Just like the students, communities and collaborators we work with, we, as higher education faculty members, require and deserve support to thrive (Klaw, 2008). In this spirit of collegial mentorship, we hope you will draw some guidance and inspiration from this chapter as you move forward within the academy in a community-engaged career.

Common Themes

The case narratives provided in this chapter showcase the experiences of faculty who are diverse in their historical origins, current institutional contexts, and statuses. Despite these differences, faculty descriptions of their paths to community-engaged learning (CEL) share some common themes that illustrate the challenges and opportunities inherent in undertaking community engagement within a professorial career. These themes are summarized and explored here as they relate to developing and supporting community-engaged faculty.

1. **Identity and Values are Central to CE**: In line with existing literature (Stanton et al., 1999; Ward & Miller; 2016), the narratives illuminate that faculty efforts in community-engaged learning are inexorably tied to our own identities and values, values that may stem from our cultural backgrounds, our faith-based perspectives, and/or the immigration journeys of our families. For community-engaged faculty, our values and identities motivate us to envision a world as we think it should be and drive the pedagogies and approaches we employ in enculturating our students to become civic minded (Ward & Miller, 2016; Stanton et al., 1999). Ngo, for example, discusses her family's immigration from Vietnam and her pride in her grandfather's civic leadership, and Sandy refers to identifying connections between the posadas she participated in as a graduate student learning about the social justice struggles of immigrants to California, and the experiences of her family in immigrating from Europe to the Midwest. Mejia, in discussing the obstacles she has faced as a woman of color in a predominately white space, connects community engagement to centering the experiences

of BIPOC individuals, and challenging racist assumptions. Levisohn discusses Judaism as the framework for his work, and Klaw ties her passion for social justice to her family's experiences fleeing and surviving the Third Reich. Drawing from their own identities and values, as well as the guiding principles of the community engagement field that center social justice movements such as feminism, antiracism, and health care equity (Aguilar-Gaxiola, 2022; Saltmarsh & Hartley, 2016), faculty who "teach community" (hooks, 2003) value the role of higher education in producing critical thinkers who are aware of the world around them, consider principles of equity, and employ the tools that they acquire from coursework to participate effectively in a just and democratic society (Longo et al., 2016; Obama, 2022; Oluo, 2020; Welch & Plaxton-Moore, 2019).

2. **Mission is Made Meaningful with Institutional Support**: The narratives illuminate the ways in which the practice of community-engaged learning may or may not fit with the missions of academic departments, disciplines, and institutions. For some faculty members, the mission of their institution or of their departmental home may provide a perfect umbrella under which to justify, develop, establish, and expand community engagement (Green et al., 2016; Yamamura & Koth, 2018). Levisohn, for example, explains that the field of Jewish studies and the explicit mission of Brandeis as a Jewish institution provided a natural home for his work. He notes that as a selective private institution, his university is "relatively well resourced." For Ngo, the Global TIES program contained within the College of Engineering at a major research university provides a clear institutional structure for her efforts that is supported by staffing positions.

   For other faculty members, a rhetoric of community engagement embodied in a published mission statement may not match the actual level of institutional support required for such activities (O'Meara, 2016; Post et al., 2016; Yamamura & Koth, 2018). Simply put, integrated organizational structures are needed to support broad prevailing institutional missions such as "student success" and "civic engagement" (Saltmarsh, 2017; White, 2016). Even in the case of the Global TIES Program, for example, Ngo notes, an unwieldy bureaucracy stymies course enrollment. Klaw, Mejia, Sandy, and Ngo, all laboring at public institutions, describe ways in which faculty may be charged to enact values espoused by their institution without having resources needed, such as release time incentives, student assistantships, and funding for the staff, community partners, and even students who engage in the requisite daily activities of project implementation, site supervision, and relationship building. As the narratives from Mejia, Klaw, and Sandy suggest, administrators who espouse "community engagement" as a cornerstone of their institution or office without actually supporting or communicating their appreciation for faculty and staff who conduct these efforts, risk faculty attrition, and resentment from faculty members who seek to serve students, communities, and the university through this modality. In this vein, Mejia, Sandy, and Klaw all discuss considering an alternative departmental or institutional home for their work as community-engaged tenure track scholars.

3. **CE Pushes Epistemological Boundaries Within Disciplines**: In line with existing literature (Keith, 2015; O'Meara, 2016; Stanton et al., 1999; Welch & Plaxton-Moore, 2019), all of the narratives illustrate the ways in which community-engaged faculty continue to expand the boundaries of their disciplines, mandating that we translate and apply academic knowledge to benefit underserved groups (Saltmarsh, 2017). Inherent in this work is a modernizing and decolonizing of the curriculum to incorporate multiple perspectives, with particular attention to the ways in which some groups have been silenced, misrepresented, and disenfranchised. This imperative is inherent in the very founding of the service-learning movement (Stanton et al., 1999) and is emphasized within Mitchell's paradigm of "critical service-learning" (2008). As demonstrated by Mejia and Klaw, using the pluralistic lenses of social justice to engage students in critical thinking about their world, their education, and their field of study, a community-engaged faculty member risks negative reactions from students, committee members, and colleagues. In addition to upholding a principled stance with regard to pedagogy and practice, a nontenured faculty member needs to remain mindful of the requirements of their position with regard to teaching, committee work, and scholarship in order to keep their job (Barrenche et al., 2018; O'Meara, 2016; Welch & Plaxton-Moore, 2019). Managing these multiple requirements, Mejia discusses her "in betweenness" as a community-engaged faculty of color. These experiences mirror recent findings by Saltmarsh & Hartley (2016) that "For underrepresented faculty pursuing academic careers, the university was often a hostile place. The institution may have opened the door, but once inside, faculty found a narrow environment unaccepting of many ways of knowing and different habits of being" (p. 25). Ward and Miller (2016) also discuss common experiences of marginalization within the academy noting "our sense of wholeness becomes fragmented when we face resistance to our work." (p. 189). To support the retention and advancement of engaged scholars, recent books focused on faculty development in community-engaged learning offer guidance on accomplishing and documenting the required

benchmarks for the tenure process (Berkey et al., 2018; Welch & Plaxton-Moore, 2019).

4. **Collaborations Matter**: Awards from external fellowships and grants, internal release time programs, and Center based interdisciplinary appointments provide collegial support as well as credibility. These resources enable the development and maintenance of infrastructure for faculty to conduct community-engaged work (Green et al., 2018; Keith, 2015; O'Meara, 2016). For Levisohn, not only did a funded disciplinary fellowship provide resources and recognition of his work as important, useful, and valuable to his department and institution, but it also provided him with "intellectual companionship," that was integral to developing his ideas. Sandy mentions that "infrastructure in place through the campus-wide service-learning office has been very helpful with supporting community engaged scholars by connecting this group regularly, holding special events, and providing annual recognition of exceptional work." For Ngo, an anthropologist, who experienced transformational service-learning through an interdisciplinary concentration as an undergraduate, an award-winning program within the College of Engineering provided opportunities to enact this pedagogy. Klaw collaborated outside of her department in solicited proposals for external funding and applied to serve as CCLL Director, enabling her to work with administrators, faculty, and partners across disciplines. Sandy and Mejia both hold appointments in departments specifically related to CE and are navigating their way up the tenure ladder. Like Klaw, they have been made aware of the existing pressures for faculty to succeed according to traditional rubrics related to research and teaching (Barrenche, 2018; White, 2016), which are measured by committees that decide retention, tenure, and promotion, and have sought out allies in their work (Easter, 2021). In line with Klaw's early experiences in her academic department, Levisohn notes that "colleagues in the [Repair the World] fellowship did encounter institutional resistance, for example, from those who wondered whether they might be crossing the line into advocacy or abandoning the core intellectual purpose of their work." As the narratives attest, given the sustained labor required for mutually beneficial and reciprocal community engagement, it is incumbent upon community-engaged faculty members to identify, discuss, and garner recognition for the epistemologies and labor required in building a program of community engagement (Keith, 2015; Welch & Plaxton-Moore, 2019; Welch, 2016; Yamamura & Koth, 2018) so that they can advocate for their own careers and for the requisite resources to sustain community involvement. As documented in existing literature

(Welch & Plaxton-Moore, 2019; Stanton et al., 1999), without support from colleagues and mentors, engaged faculty may feel isolated, vulnerable to critique or misunderstanding (Easter, 2021; Green et al., 2018; O'Meara, 2016; Ward & Miller, 2016; Welch, 2016), and may feel compelled to find a new departmental or institutional home. In line with extant findings, Klaw and Sandy mention the important role of mentors both inside of and outside of the academy in the development of an academic career focused on centering marginalized perspectives (Green et al., 2018; Klaw, 2008). Ngo emphasizes the opportunities within her academic programs that led her to successfully pursue a career focused on community development in higher education; and Levisohn emphasizes the value of discussing the principles of community engagement with fellow scholars in his field through the Repair the World Program. Not surprisingly, just as science itself relies on scaffolded team efforts, the literature on community-engaged practitioners suggest that the development of this field has relied on academics working collaboratively (Saltmarsh, 2017), not simply solo faculty members working alone one project at a time with single community partners (Eatman, 2018). Building upon existing literature (Kiely & Sexsmith, 2018), the narratives suggest that bolstered by support provided by career mentors, fellowships, internal and external grants, and interdisciplinary appointments, faculty members can lead their departments, disciplines, and institutions in deploying the tools of higher education to create generations of college graduates who think critically and act civically (Green et al., 2018; Saltmarsh & Hartley, 2016).

5. **Rewards Outside of Academic Rubrics Matter**: For Ngo, expressions of student appreciation regarding the skills and opportunities they have gained from her course allow her to manage the frustration of institutional bureaucracies around limitations in resources that stymie community engagement efforts. For Mejia, community partners help "lift her up" above the "nonsense" of academy. For Sandy, participation in the posadas ground her in the central mission of her work. Levisohn embeds his work within a deep commitment to understanding and enacting Judaism, and Klaw discusses the unexpected and career changing rewards of working with Veterans. As the literature suggests, beyond the roles that are defined by their institutional appointments, community-engaged faculty continue to see themselves as mavericks and boundary spanners who are fundamentally committed to working in partnership with their communities (Guarasci & Eatman, 2022; Saltmarsh, 2017) in order to enact what they see as the democratic purposes of the academy (Eatman, 2016, xiii; Yamamura & Koth, 2018).

Conclusion

In total, the narratives suggest that CEL faculty are distinctly passionate about harnessing the frameworks and analytic tools of our disciplines to make an impact as educators. Because we view problems through the lenses of social justice, our shared priority is to develop students as equity-minded, analytical participants in a democratic society (Guarasci & Eatman, 2022; Saltmarsh & Hartley, 2016; Stanton et al., 1999). Simply put, just like the founders of the field, CEL faculty believe that the purpose of higher education is to create a more just world (Saltmarsh & Hartley, 2016; Stanton et al., 1999), and we are uniquely determined to match our pedagogy and scholarly practices to our values. It is our hope that the reflections embodied here urge us to move past the rhetoric of mission statements, strategic plans, and institutional recognition schemes, and beyond the mandates of individual departments, disciplines, divisions, and committees, to provide administrative support, concrete incentives, and compensation (Saltmarsh, 2017), along with sufficient staffing for developing, expanding, and institutionalizing a community-engaged model of higher education. As next-generation faculty (Guarasci & Eatman, 2022; Hartley & Saltmarsh, 2016), we believe that the community engagement model, which involves students in the application of classroom learning along with critical reflection, and develops knowledge to benefit the social good, is uniquely suited to the cascading challenges of our current time.

Notes

1 Rosa Martha Zarate defined the Nahuatl Aztec word "calpulli" as "that which belongs to us" (personal communication April 21, 2004). In Aztec society, she said the calpulli involved a group of people who worked in and shared property together. The Calpulli project of Libreria del Pueblo involved efforts for an alternative self-sustaining community for collective human dignity, involving microenterprise, affordable housing owned by the collective, child care, immigration support, and spirituality, health, and wellness activities.
2 "The Milwaukee Idea is the University of Wisconsin–Milwaukee's initiative to forge vital and long-lasting community-university partnerships. Started in 1999, the initiative has led to the expansion of service learning efforts, partnerships with local K-12 schools, and university participation in affordable housing development. Consortium activities include economic development projects, action-oriented research, and entrepreneurial training to help emerging and established entrepreneurs gain critical business skills."
3 In my teaching, I sometimes refer to the "paradox of particularism," i.e., the way in which our deepest ethical commitment to the Other often emerges from a particular ethical/religious tradition, but those same traditions also tend to prioritize the welfare of the communities that uphold them. I have avoided the adjective "religious" here, because one of the distinctive characteristics of Jewish service and service-learning programs and the field of discourse around them is that they are dominated by liberal Jews, i.e., those who are less traditionally

religious and also (overwhelmingly) liberal-to-progressive politically. This is just one of the many ways that terms and frameworks from one ethnic or religious context do not translate seamlessly to another. I mention this dynamic because it became important to our classroom discussions. Why is it, exactly, that liberal Jews embrace the discourse around liberal *Tikkun Olam* in a way that more traditionalist Jews do not? Surely the latter are no less committed to serving others—and according to some social scientific data, even more so? Shifting from religious ideology to political ideology, surely political conservatives share many goals with liberals (building healthy communities, supporting individual flourishing) but simply diverge on how to get there.

References

Aguilar-Gaxiola, S., Ahmed, S.M., Anise, A., Azzahir, A., Baker, K.E., Cupito, A., Eder, M., Everette, T.D., Erwin, K., Felzien, M., Freeman, E., Gibbs, D., Greene-Moton, E., Hernández-Cancio, S., Hwang, A., Jones, F., Jones, G., Jones, M., Khodyakov, D., Michener, J.L., Milstein, B., Oto-Kent, D.S., Orban, M., Pusch, B., Shah, M., Shaw, M., Tarrant, J., Wallerstein, N., Westfall, J.M., Williams, A., & Zaldivar, R. (2022, February 14). Assessing meaningful community engagement: A conceptual model to advance health equity through transformed systems for health. *Organizing Committee for Assessing Meaningful Community Engagement in Health & Health Care Programs & Policies.* https://doi.org/10.31478/202202c

Angotti, T., Doble, C., & Horrigan, P. (2012). *Service-learning in design and planning: Educating at the boundaries.* NYU Press.

Aronowitz, S. (2001). *The knowledge factory: Dismantling the corporate university and creating true higher learning.* Beacon Press.

Association of Public & Land-Grant Universities. (2020, February 4). *2020 Carnegie community engagement classification recipients announced.* www.aplu.org/news-and-media/blog/2020/02/04/2020-carnegie-community-engagement-classification-recipients-announced/

Astin, A. W., Vogelgesang, L. J., Ikeda, E. K., & Yee, J. A. (2000). *How service learning affects students.* Higher Education Research Institute. https://heri.ucla.edu/PDFs/HSLAS/HSLAS.PDF

Barrenche, G. I., Meyer, M., & Gross, S. (2018). Reciprocity and partnership: How do we know it's working? In B. Berkey, C. E. Meixner, P. M. Green, & E. A. Eddins (Eds.), *Reconceptualizing faculty development in service-learning/community engagement: Exploring intersections, frameworks, and models of practice* (pp. 241–264). Stylus Publishing, LLC.

Beck, K., Bush, A., Holguin, L., Morgan, D. L., & Orphan, C. M. (2016). Developing a community-engaged scholarly identity. In M. A. Post, E. Ward, N. V. Longo, & J. Saltmarsh (Eds.), *Next-generation engagement and the future of higher education: Publicly engaged scholars* (pp. 130–140). Stylus Publishing, LLC.

Berkey, B., Meixner, C. E., Green, P. M., & Eddins, E. A. (2018). *Reconceptualizing faculty development in service-learning/community engagement: Exploring intersections, frameworks, and models of practice.* Stylus Publishing, LLC.

Bose, P. (2012). Faculty activism and the corporatization of the university. *American Quarterly, 64*(4), 815–818.

Boyer, E. L. (1990). *Scholarship reconsidered priorities of the Professoriate*. The Carnegie Foundation for the Advancement of Teaching.

Boyer-Davis, S. (2020). Technostress in higher education: An examination of faculty perceptions before and during the COVID-19 pandemic. *Journal of Business and Accounting, 13*(1), 42–58.

Brandeis Compact. (2023). *Samuels Center for Community Partnerships and Civic Transformation (compact)*. Brandeis University. www.brandeis.edu/compact/

Brandeis' Jewish Roots. (2023). *Our Jewish roots*. Brandeis University. www.brandeis.edu/about/jewish-roots.html

Bringle, R. G., Hatcher, J. A., & Muthiah, R. N. (2010). The role of service-learning on the retention of first-year students to second year. *Michigan Journal of Community Service Learning, 16*(2), 38–49.

Bruce, M., & Bridgeland, J. (2014). *The mentoring effect: young people's perspectives on the outcomes and availability of mentoring. A report for MENTOR: The National Mentoring Partnership*. Civic Enterprises with Hart Research Associates for MENTOR: The National Mentoring Partnership. www.civicenterprises.net/Education.

BTW Informing Change. (2008). *Jewish service learning: What is and what could be*. A Summary of an analysis of the Jewish Service Learning Landscape. https://search.issuelab.org/resources/9944/9944.pdf

Butin, D. & Pianko, N. (2012). The integration of service-learning and Jewish studies. *Journal of Jewish Communal Service, 87*(1–2), 157–164.

Carnegie Elective Classifications. (2022, September 30). *The elective classification for community engagement*. https://carnegieelectiveclassifications.org/the-2024-elective-classification-for-community-engagement/

Celio, C. I., Durlak, J., & Dymnicki, A. (2011). A meta-analysis of the impact of service-learning on students. *Journal of Experiential education, 34*(2), 164–181.

Cipriano, C., Rappolt-Schlichtmann, G., & Brackett, M. A. (2020). *Supporting school community wellness with social and emotional learning (SEL) during and after a pandemic*. Edna Bennet Pierce Prevention Research Center, Pennsylvania State University.

Combs, B. H. (2016). Black (and brown) bodies out of place: Towards a theoretical understanding of systematic voter suppression in the United States. *Critical Sociology, 42*(4–5), 535–549.

Dorff, E. N. (2005). *The way into tikkun olam (repairing the world)*. Jewish Lights Publishing.

Easter, M. E. (2021). *Resilience: Bravery in the face of racism, corruption, and privilege in the halls of academia*. Marilyn Easter.

Eatman, T. (2016). Foreword (pp. xi–xv). In M. A. Post, E. Ward, N. V. Longo, & J. Saltmarsh (Eds.), *Next-generation engagement and the future of higher education: Publicly engaged scholars* (pp. 130–140). Stylus Publishing, LLC.

Eatman, T. (2018). Faculty as colearners: Community engagement and the power of story in faculty development. In B. Berkey, C. E. Meixner, P. M. Green, & E. A. Eddins (Eds.), *Reconceptualizing faculty development in service-learning/community engagement: Exploring intersections, frameworks, and models of practice* (pp. 59–84). Stylus Publishing, LLC.

Engberg, M. E., Carrera, L. F., & Mika, L. P. (2018). Utilizing domestic off-campus experiences to influence social justice awareness and career development. *Journal of Higher Education Outreach and Engagement, 22*(1), 63–86.

Ghosh, R. & Reio Jr, T. G. (2013). Career benefits associated with mentoring for mentors: A meta-analysis. *Journal of Vocational Behavior, 83*(1), 106–116.

Green, P. M., Eddins, E. A., Berkey, B., & Meixner, C. (2018). Exploring the borderlands through collaborative inquiry: A narrative introduction. In B. Berkey, C. E. Meixner, P. M. Green, & E. A. Eddins (Eds.), *Reconceptualizing faculty development in service-learning/community engagement: Exploring intersections, frameworks, and models of practice* (pp. 1–23). Stylus Publishing, LLC.

Green, P. M., Harrison, B., Jones, J., & Shaffer, T. J. (2016). Paving new professional pathways for community-engaged scholarship. In M. A. Post, E. Ward, N. V. Longo, & J. Saltmarsh (Eds.), *Publicly engaged scholars: Next-generation engagement and the future of higher education* (pp. 141–155). Stylus Publishing, LLC.

Guarasci, R. & Eatman, T. K. (2022, Jan 18). *Neighborhood democracy: A model for building anchor partnerships between colleges and their communities.* Stylus Publishing, LLC.

Hartley, M. & Saltmarsh, J. (2016). A brief history of a movement. In M. A. Post, E. Ward, N. V. Longo, & J. Saltmarsh (Eds.), *Publicly engaged scholars: Next-generation engagement and the future of higher education* (pp. 34–60). Stylus Publishing, LLC.

Hollander, E. & Hartley, M. (2000). Civic renewal in higher education: The state of the movement and the need for a national network. In T. Ehrlich (Ed.), *Civic responsibility and higher education* (pp. 345–366). American Council on Education/The Oryx Press.

hooks, b. (2003). *Teaching community: A pedagogy of hope.* Routledge.

Humphreys, K. (1996). Clinical psychologists as psychotherapists: History, future, and alternatives. *American Psychologist, 51*(3), 190.

Jacobs, J. (2007, June 7). The history of "tikkun olam." Zeek. www.zeek.net/706tohu/

Kanarek, J. (2008). What does tikkun olam actually mean? In O. Rose, J. E. G. Kaiser, & M. Klein (Eds.), *Righteous indignation: A Jewish call for justice* (pp. 15–22). Jewish Lights Publishing.

Keith, N. Z. (2015). *Engaging in social partnerships: Democratic practices for campus-community partnerships.* Routledge.

Kiely, R. & Sexsmith, K. (2018). Innovative considerations in faculty development and service-learning and community engagement: New perspectives for the future. In B. Berkey, C. E. Meixner, P. M. Green, & E. A. Eddins (Eds.), *Reconceptualizing faculty development in service-learning/community engagement: Exploring intersections, frameworks, and models of practice* (pp. 283–314). Stylus Publishing, LLC.

Klaw, E. (2008). *Mentoring and making it in academe: A guide for newcomers to the ivory tower.* University Press of America.

Klaw, E., & Ampuero, M. C. (2007). From "no means no" to community change: The impact of university-based service learning related to intimate violence prevention. In G. Stahley (Ed.), *Gender identity, equity, and violence* (pp. 181–200). Routledge.

Klaw, E. L., & Rhodes, J. E. (1995). Mentor relationships and the career development of pregnant and parenting African-American teenagers. *Psychology of Women Quarterly, 19*(4), 551–562.

Krasner, J. (2013). The place of tikkun olam in American Jewish life. *Jewish Political Studies Review, 25*(3–4), 59–98.

Kuh, G. D. (2008). *High-impact educational practices: What they are, who has access to them, and why they matter*. Association of American Colleges and Universities.

Levisohn, J. A. (2012a). Becoming a servant: How James Kugel's conception of *avodat hashem* can help us think about the dispositional goals of Jewish service-learning. *Journal of Jewish Community Service, 87*(1–2), 104–112.

Levisohn, J. A. (2012b). The goals of Jewish service-learning. *Compact Blog*. https://compact.org/the-goals-of-jewish-service-learning/

Longo, N. V., Kiesa, A., & Battistoni, R. (2016). The future of the academy with students as colleagues. In M. A. Post, E. Ward, N. V. Longo, & J. Saltmarsh (Eds.), *Publicly engaged scholars: Next-generation engagement and the future of higher education* (pp. 197–213). Stylus Publishing, LLC.

Mejia, A. P., Quiroz, O., Morales, Y., Ponce, R., Chavez, G. L., & Torre, E. O. Y. (2013). From madres to mujeristas: Latinas making change with photovoice. *Action Research, 11*(4), 301–321.

Mejia, A. & Taniguchi, M. Y. (2021). Art and heart to counter the one-hour-zoom-diversity event: Counterspaces as a response to diversity regimes in academia. *Present Tense: A Journal of Rhetoric in Society, 9*(2). https://doi.org/10.31235/osf.io/rxfkp

Mitchell, T. D. (2008). Traditional vs. critical service-learning: Engaging the literature to differentiate two models. *Michigan Journal of Community Service Learning, 14*(2), 50–65.

Mitchell, T. D. & Rost-Banik, C. (2019). How sustained service-learning experiences inform career pathways. *Michigan Journal of Community Service Learning, 25*(1), 18–29.

Obama, M. (2022). *The light we carry: Overcoming in uncertain times*. Hardcover Crown.

Oluo, I. (2020). *Mediocre: The dangerous legacy of white male America*. Seal Press.

O'Meara, K. (2016). Legitimacy, agency, and inequality: Organizational practices for full participation of community-engaged faculty. In M. A. Post, E., Ward, N.V. Longo & J. Saltmarsh (Eds.), *Publicly engaged scholars: Next-generation engagement and the future of higher education* (pp. 96–110). Stylus Publishing, LLC.

Orphan, C. M. & O'Meara, K. (2016). Next-generation engagement scholars in the neoliberal university. In M. A. Post, E., Ward, N. V. Longo, & J. Saltmarsh (Eds.), *Publicly engaged scholars: Next-generation engagement and the future of higher education* (pp. 214–231). Stylus Publishing, LLC.

Parks, K. A. (2022). The no-time bind: Examining the experience of faculty mothers during the COVID-19 lockdown. *Peabody Journal of Education, 97*(2), 212–227.

Pfeiffer, K., Baker, H., & Mascorro, A. (2021). Service-learning in a pandemic: The transition to virtual engagement. *Journal of Nursing Education, 60*(6), 362–363.

Pollack, S. S. (1996). Higher education's contested service role: A framework for analysis and historical survey. In K. Stanton (Ed.), *To strengthen service-learning policy and practice: Stories from the field. Interim report from a service-learning history project.* Haas Center for Public Service.

Post, M. A., Ward, E., Longo, N. V., & Saltmarsh, J. (2016). Introducing next-generation engagement. In M. A. Post, E., Ward, N. V. Longo, & J. Saltmarsh (Eds.), *Publicly engaged scholars: Next-generation engagement and the future of higher education* (pp. 1–11). Stylus Publishing, LLC.

Ramlo, S. (2021). The coronavirus and higher education: Faculty viewpoints about universities moving online during a worldwide pandemic. *Innovative Higher Education, 46*(3), 241–259. https://doi.org/10.1007/s10755-020-09532-8

Ramnani, A., Ramos, J., Lopez, A. A., & Klaw, E. (2016). Application: A social psychology experiment on learning by social immersion. In S. Randal (Ed.), *Social psychology: How other people influence our thoughts and actions [2 volumes]* (pp. 409). Greenwood.

Rosenberg, Y. (2022, February 19). Why so many people still don't understand anti-semitism. *The Atlantic.* www.theatlantic.com/ideas/archive/2022/01/texas-synagogue-anti-semitism-conspiracy-theory/621286/

Saltmarsh, J. (2017). A collaborative turn: Trends and directions in community engagement. In J. Sachs & L. Clark (Eds.), *Learning through community engagement: Vision and practice in higher education* (pp. 3–15). Springer.

Saltmarsh, J., Giles Jr., D. E., Ward, E., & Buglione, S. M. (2009). Rewarding community-engaged scholarship. *New Directions for Higher Education, 2009*(147), 25–35. https://doi.org/10.1002/he.355

Saltmarsh, J. & Hartley, M. (2016). The inheritance of next-generation engagement scholars. In M. A. Post, E. Ward, N. V. Longo, & J. Saltmarsh (Eds.), *Publicly engaged scholars: Next-generation engagement and the future of higher education* (pp. 15–33). Stylus Publishing, LLC.

Saltmarsh, J. & Johnson, M. (2020). Campus classification, identity, and change: The elective Carnegie Classification for Community Engagement. *Journal of Higher Education Outreach and Engagement, 24*(3), 105–114.

Schnackenberg, H. L. & Simard, D. A. (Eds.). (2021). *Women and leadership in higher education during global crises.* IGI Global.

Stanton, T., Giles, D. E., & Cruz, N. I. (1999). *Service-learning: a movement's pioneers reflect on its origins, practice, and future.* Jossey-Bass.

Taniguchi, Y. (2021, May 1). Running through. Touchstone Literary Magazine. www.touchstonekstate.org/nonfic/running-through-by-yuko-taniguchi

Tugend, A. (2020). On the verge of burnout: COVID-19's impact on faculty well-being and career plans. *The Chronicle of Higher Education, 7.* https://connect.chronicle.com/rs/931-EKA-218/images/Covid%26FacultyCareerPaths_Fidelity_ResearchBrief_v3%20%281%29.pdf

University of Colorado Boulder. (2022, September 15). *What is community-engaged scholarship?* www.colorado.edu/outreach/ooe/community-engaged-scholarship/what-community-engaged-scholarship

University of Minnesota Rochester. (2022). *UMR Vision.* https://r.umn.edu/about-umr

Walsh, F. (2015). *Strengthening family resilience.* Guilford.

Wang, X., Hegde, S., Son, C., Keller, B., Smith, A., & Sasangohar, F. (2020). Investigating mental health of US college students during the COVID-19 pandemic: Cross-sectional survey study. *Journal of Medical Internet Research*, 22(9), e22817.

Ward, E. (2017, June 29). *Skin in the game*. Political Research Associates. https://politicalresearch.org/2017/06/29/skin-in-the-game-how-antisemitism-animates-white-nationalism

Ward, E. & Miller, A. (2016). Next generation engaged scholars: Stewards of change. In M. A. Post, E. Ward, N. V. Longo, & J. Saltmarsh (Eds.), *Next-generation engagement and the future of higher education: Publicly engaged scholars* (pp. 184–194). Stylus Publishing, LLC.

Weerts, D. J. & Sandmann, L. R. (2010). Community engagement and boundary-spanning roles at research universities. *The Journal of Higher Education*, 81(6), 632–657.

Welch, M. (2016). *Engaging higher education: Purpose, platforms, and programs for community engagement*. Stylus Publishing, LLC.

Welch, M. & Plaxton-Moore, S. (2019). *The craft of community-engaged teaching and learning: A guide for faculty development*. Campus Compact.

White, B. (2016). Building an organizational structure that fosters blended engagement. In M. A. Post, E. Ward, N. V. Longo, & J. Saltmarsh (Eds.), *Next-generation engagement and the future of higher education: Publicly engaged scholars* (pp. 232–246). Stylus Publishing, LLC.

Widaman, A. M., Tully, A., Klaw, E. Ghavami, N., Moges, M., & Costa, C. (2022, April). *Facilitators and barriers for faculty implementing community-engaged learning during a global pandemic*. Presentation conducted at the virtual convention of the International Teaching & Learning Coalition.

Wolf, A. J. (2001). Repairing tikkun olam. *Judaism*, 50(4), 479–482.

Yamamura, E. K. & Koth, K. (2018). *Place-based community engagement in higher education: A strategy to transform universities and communities*. Stylus Publishing, LLC.

Yeh, T. L. (2010). Service-learning and persistence of low-income, first-generation college students: An exploratory study. *Michigan Journal of Community Service Learning*, 16(2), 50–65.

Yorio, P. L. & Ye, F. (2012). A meta-analysis on the effects of service-learning on the social, personal, and cognitive outcomes of learning. *Academy of Management Learning & Education*, 11(1), 9–27.

Zahneis, M. (2022, December 1). A rare survey of faculty morale shows that the pandemic's effects continue to ripple. *The Chronicle of Higher Education*. www.chronicle.com/article/a-rare-survey-of-faculty-morale-shows-that-the-pandemics-effects-continue-to-ripple

11
COMMUNITY-ENGAGED PARTNERSHIPS WHEN HEALTHY RELATIONSHIPS ARE THE PRIORITY

Jamilah Ducar and Daren Ellerbee

Introduction

At the University of Pittsburgh, neighborhood commitments and engaged capacity-building efforts intersect and overlap through the collective work of networks. The Office of Engagement and Community Affairs (ECA) works across internal and external stakeholders to advance community-engaged teaching, practice, and partnerships. In this chapter, we discuss how community-engaged learning and partnerships are advanced programmatically by the ECA team through shared channels with efforts to institutionalize Pitt's unique community-engaged identity. By serving as a convener, facilitator, and strategic collaborator, the Community Engagement Centers and ECA team educate, engage, and encourage faculty, staff, and students as learners and cocreators to further ethical, community-centered praxis.

Context: Who We Are

I am Jamilah (Jamie) Ducar and serve as Executive Director of The Engaged Campus for the University of Pittsburgh, also known as Pitt. As per my job description, I lead several key areas across community affairs, public service and volunteerism, and capacity-building functions. The reality of that charge is that no day looks the same. My priorities are to serve the institution as a bridge-builder, team cheerleader, and highly relational central point of contact for whoever comes my way. This means that I have the freedom to cultivate, convene, and activate networks of peers and partners toward

DOI: 10.4324/9781003448525-14

shared goals. It also means that I cocreate learning spaces for the entirety of our campus to consider lenses different from their own, prioritize community-centered approaches, and take action that makes Pitt a more responsive neighbor and collaborator. I also serve as the place-based lead for the neighborhoods closest to Pitt's campus and engage a wide group of resident, student, business, nonprofit, and anchor stakeholders to elevate the assets that encourage the community to thrive across lines of social difference. I bring my full self to my work: that means bringing my young children to community events (I have two), frequently airing dissertation writing frustrations (I defended my thesis in Summer 2022), and night-owl email writing.

As the inaugural director of the University of Pittsburgh Community Engagement Center (CEC) located in Homewood, I, Daren A. Ellerbee, coalesced neighborhood goals with institutional resources and sought mutual benefits through the activities of the center. Homewood is a historic African American community located 3.8 miles from campus in the City's East End. As lead of Pitt's place-based community engagements throughout greater Homewood, I drove forward an approach grounded in Asset-Based Community Development and Respectful and Effective Community Engagement, forging meaningful relationships and community-benefitting collaborations (Kretzmann & McKnight, 1993; Ohmer et al., 2017). As a Community Engagement Professional (CEP) who is a staff member and whose primary job is to support and administer community-campus engagement, I not only worked to ensure that the center filled gaps supporting the missions of community partners, but also championed social justice with an awareness of the area's challenges prevalent for many who look like me (Dostilio & Perry, 2017). In 2022 I transitioned into a new role at Pitt to direct the University Educational Outreach Center (EOC). Housed within the Office of the Provost, I continue to leverage strengths-based approaches to support K–12 pipelines to college. Overall, I am committed to seeing the socially marginalized thrive, especially in a city once considered the most livable in the continental United States (Smit, 2014).

Together, we, Jamie and Daren, work in varied but overlapping aspects of the University of Pittsburgh's anchor mission and engaging identity. We hold shared responsibility for institutional responsiveness, through fielding community concerns and requests for partnerships or support, and serving as willing and actively listening university ambassadors. We promote a culture of engagement by supporting how our colleagues situate their work within the broader context of our institutional priorities and infrastructure. We consider how our institutional identity impacts community experiences and place-based engagement. We prioritize conceptualizations of place and space as an important aspect of our university's praxis and investment.

We have created unique pathways for faculty, staff, and students to engage with community-centered priorities and do so from the perspective of practitioners with foundations outside of higher education. We are also both current scholar-practitioners and pursuing doctorates of education as part of the inaugural cohort of Urban Education scholars within the University of Pittsburgh's School of Education. Our orientation to the work of campus-community partnership deeply considers the potential contradictions in the aspirations of pedagogies of the academy with the priorities of communities. This chapter outlines where and how our university, the University of Pittsburgh, has been able to grow as a leader in effective community engagement and how like-minded and similarly positioned faculty, staff, and administrators may have opportunities to influence community-centered pedagogies without directly administering student programs or research projects.

Given our responsibilities and positionalities as Black women and institutional workers, those whose "purposive action is aimed at creating, maintaining, and disrupting institutions" (Lawrence & Suddaby, 2006), we acknowledge the heavy lift for CEPs, especially those who themselves are minoritized and represent Predominantly White Institutions (PWIs) in a city like Pittsburgh. Black people in Pittsburgh are significantly impacted by the social determinants of health according to the Howell et al. (2019) "Pittsburgh's Inequality across Gender and Race" report. Black women, in particular, are cited as living in an environment that has impacted their overall well-being with Black women's maternal mortality, employment, poverty, and college readiness named as areas of focus for policy interventions. "Pittsburgh is arguably the most unlivable for Black women," and as Black women, this devastates us (Howell et al., 2019). We carry the hope of positively impacting the people we serve, many of whom share the same cultural heritage and kinship, while understanding that:

> universities and African American communities are culturally different, and therefore, African American [university] members who have assimilated to university culture in terms of language, dress, and mannerisms often must also use culturally competent strategies to establish trust with community members.
>
> *(Briscoe et al., 2009)*

We are reminded of the duality of our position and grapple with this double consciousness of looking at ourselves through the lens of others (DuBois, 1903). We cannot escape race, power, and privilege, as well as the inherent differences between academia and the African American community whose historical interactions with universities were often more transactional than transformational. "This includes traditional research paradigms antithetical to community-based research, so efforts may not be well-received by community members until trust is established" (Briscoe et al., 2009). By understanding the history of prior university-community partnerships and leveraging strengths-based approaches, it is our desire to cultivate mutually beneficial collaborations that further our mission of teaching, research, and service and that improve the quality of life for residents. In practice and posture, we turn away from needs-based approaches which reinforce a community's deficits. For example, we steer clear of discursive framing of people of color as "disadvantaged" or "at-risk," or "proposing strategies aimed at compensating deficiencies" (Iverson, 2007). Though research institutions have been seen as providing more benefits to the researchers than to the people who are researched (Briscoe et al., 2009), we also recognize the potential for universities to serve as major assets in community development and community revitalization (Briscoe et al., 2009). As CEPs, one institutional facing and one place based in a community, we remain committed to advancing multifaceted approaches which are informed by the guiding principles and values established by a coalition of people from the institution and beyond, whose voices and capacities are intertwined to make a difference.

The ability to authentically engage with our practice as doctoral students of urban education and as professionals is a privilege afforded to many of us within academia. Beyond a positioning, as subject-matter-experts of "community" as in place, we are also experts of the "community" as in people. Given our positionality, we expose classmates and colleagues to best practices while providing an opportunity for community stakeholders to build relationships and align their priorities with university resources. In many ways, we are a hybrid of community and university with an intimate knowledge of what is at stake—trust. We build coalitions with key stakeholders representing diverse perspectives and goals. In this regard, as CEPs of color, we are embedded within diversity work—circulating information to reach diverse audiences while representing institutional diversity, ourselves, as black bodies embedded within the institution (Ahmed, 2012). We do more than use the institutional language of transformation found in strategic plans and public statements but work diligently to reflect this language in action, promoting transformative paradigms throughout the institution.

Pittsburgh is a unique city for this work, especially when you consider a few key points. Pittsburgh's culture considers deeply what is of a place, within a place, for a place, and what came before in places that have changed. Typically, as part of an introduction, the pedigree and depth of each individual's roots are challenged. The local epistemology is grounded in how many degrees of separation there are between people and the spaces they can reference. The iterations of the city are neatly cataloged by those that have seen new priorities, and people remove and rename what was once familiar. In Pittsburgh, your reference points can provide key local contexts for how seriously you should be taken, especially if your goal is authenticity or fluency within this hyperlocal culture. Those born and bred in this city consider who (and where) might "vouch" for you or claim you as an important part of even the most glancing interpersonal interactions. Pittsburgh is also a highly visible example of the polarities in place. It finds itself highly valued and praised for its affordability, innovation economy, and "livability" while also still home to a blue-collar base of conservatism that rails against progressive policymaking and actively tolerates contemporary segregation and racial exclusion. These contradictions in opportunity and access are persistent challenges that, to this day, drive the nonprofit sector toward reimagining what would be possible, given the political will and investment. Beneath the veneer of rapid redevelopment and private sector marketing is a simple truth: Pittsburgh can only progress if a strong network of anchor institutions leverages its assets to encourage full participation in the city's future. As a city that is 65% White, 23% Black, 6% Asian, and 3.5% Hispanic or Latino according to the US Census Bureau (2022), Pittsburgh is an urban area that is yet to meet its full potential. When considering the entirety of Allegheny County, the region our university inhabits looks less diverse with the proportion of the White population rising to about 84% of total residents (US Census Bureau, 2022).

There are about 30 colleges and universities in the Pittsburgh metro area. At least five of those higher education institutions have a presence along Fifth Avenue, a key corridor of the city that stretches across changing urban landscapes between the Allegheny and Monongahela Rivers. In a city of 90 unique neighborhoods, the 2 largest universities sit in close physical proximity to one another, separated more by identity, size, and discipline specialties than the brief one-mile walk between the Cohon University Center of Carnegie Mellon University and William Pitt Union. As a state-related institution, the University of Pittsburgh has a unique orientation to its anchor identity. The charge to be a broad and catalytic partner within the region stretches beyond the impetus for public missions to be embedded within public institutions. As coauthors and colleagues, we believe that Pitt aspires to be truly of and for the city of Pittsburgh; from our roles, we consider the ways in which people, programs, and purpose come together to build shared opportunity. Alongside that belief sit some core challenges—one of which is that Black students and faculty continue to be underrepresented, making up less than 10% and 4% of their respective communities. When examining tenured professors, that number drops to about 2% (Harris, 2021).

The Work of Our Unit

At the University of Pittsburgh, engagement functions are both distributed throughout academic units and centralized through the Office of Engagement and Community Affairs (ECA). Officially, ECA's mission is to champion community engagement efforts across the Pitt system. ECA facilitates strategic community initiatives, leads the university's place-based engagements in the city of Pittsburgh, collaborates with the Provost's Office to support engaged scholarship, maintains positive relationships with the neighbors and organizations closest to our campus footprint, and ensures that Pitt is a partner and asset to communities, locally and globally. As an administrative unit that reports directly to the Chancellor, ECA maintains and grows its institutional value through relationship management, convening, and connecting a diversity of stakeholders interested in the power of partnered efforts.

The positioning of ECA as a chancellor-reporting unit with the unique charge of cultivating place-based engagement partnerships provides it with a landscape view of the institution and quick connectivity with community-based partners. Key to the core structure of ECA is a set of neighborhood-embedded Community Engagement Centers (CECs). The CECs are one of many resources of the University which make tangible its expressed Neighborhood Commitments to help *strengthen communities,* which included three main actions as noted on the Center's website: 1) A long-term 15-year commitment to infrastructure, staffing, and coordination; 2) shaped and led by a network of collaborators including neighborhood leaders, residents and Pitt faculty, staff, and students; and 3) a dedicated space rooted in the community in the form of the Community Engagement Centers.

ECA and the CECs have a broad reach that creates points of connection across the university and into communities. An example of the ways in which we leverage our relationships toward action is the quick development of a community-informed engagement model during the COVID-19 pandemic. In 2020 when stay-at-home orders were released and it seemed like the entire country was asked to shelter in place, key partners across the engagement function of Pitt considered who might be left behind, overlooked, or at risk due to a lack of options. To maximize our internal capacity for outreach, we removed bureaucratic silos and worked across public health, volunteerism, and information technology units among others to create the Pitt Pandemic Service Initiative (PPSI). PPSI's first primary use was as a listening body. We reached out to grassroots and neighborhood-level organizations to hear how they were supporting residents and identified gaps in network services, staffing, and knowledge that Pitt would be able to fill relatively quickly. We very quickly created a website that would allow any member of the public to request Pitt support using a low-barrier form that asked for relevant details and if any specialized knowledge was necessary. Our efforts channeled significant energy across the university community into direct service. Through PPSI, more than 800 staff, student, and faculty volunteers assisted 30 regional organizations and efforts to meet critical needs arising from the COVID-19 pandemic resulting in over 2000 hours of service. These assistance efforts included:

- "Care and Connection" caller volunteers made 6,000+ calls to support initiatives including check-ins with resource referrals at the beginning of the pandemic, rent relief, voter registration, and vaccination registration.
- 6,000 pounds of food were distributed in neighborhood locations via Farmers to Families events held in partnership with our campus food service provider Compass/Chartwells.
- The community affairs team of ECA cocreated Civic Action Week (CAW) with the Office of PittServes, engaging the campus community via 39 educational sessions, 6 DIY service opportunities, 3 donation drives, and 12 in-person service projects across 10 neighborhoods, with over 400 volunteer hours. Key to the CAW framework was a partnership, resulting in 100% of featured sessions being inclusive of external collaborators.

To do all this, the cross-functional volunteer management team leveraged the full support of the institution across our business and operations leadership, legal team, and the COVID-19 Medical Response Office. Our efforts required review by multiple layers of institutional risk management before opportunities could be offered to the campus community. The unique and time-sensitive nature of standing up for a pandemic-related response meant that volunteers had to either affirm that they were willing to take on the personal risk of in-person direct service or that they should look for virtual and phone-based opportunities to contribute to what ended up as a significant mobilization. Many of the volunteer roles we posted included limited or no contact tasks, which mitigated the risk of community spread. Staff was given, via official university policy drafted in partnership with ECA, up to 8 hours per work week to participate in volunteerism. That policy was broadly communicated by human resources, the Office of the Chancellor, and our engagement team in ways that encouraged the Pitt community to serve in any capacity they were able to. We are proud to say that our experience in crisis response mobilization contributed to the University of Pittsburgh creating a permanent policy for staff volunteerism and professional development. Pitt is now a national leader within higher education institutions, allowing one fully paid day per month for service to self or communities.

While the focus of this chapter is not centered strictly on the University of Pittsburgh's pandemic pivot and crisis response frameworks, they are shared to note the variety of ways in which ECA was able to lead or collaborate for community impact. None of those efforts would have been possible had Pitt chosen to be prescriptive in the ways it chose to be of service, nor would we have had access to time-critical information on what was happening within communities without the strong relationships established before the crisis. Notably, all of the efforts described sit outside of curricular opportunities; as a team of staff administrators, cocurricular involvement is our primary wheelhouse. Unlike other highly community-engaged institutions that have infrastructure which supports faculty in using engaged pedagogy, Pitt does not. At Pitt, support for community engagement is found in many places. Faculty that choose to pursue community-engaged learning typically do so with the internal support of their departments, but without the benefit of a centralized or Provost-embedded role to provide technical assistance or development. This may change soon as the University of Pittsburgh recently convened a workgroup on institutional progress on community engagement and was able to create and implement institutional definitions and course attributes to designate "civic learning" and "civic learning plus engagement." Interdisciplinary transcript distinctions have also been launched at the University and there are hopes that the field of civic and community engagement may be able to find an appropriate academic sponsor that can champion their inclusion. Currently, ECA champions academically centered community-engaged learning by connecting faculty with like-minded peers and collaborating as key partners for internal funding opportunities when they align with our office's goals and orientation within the communities with which we partner most closely.

When pandemic-related restrictions hit our institution, there were immediate strains on learning delivery including the rapid shift to fully virtual coursework, and the immediate pause on in-person community-embedded experiences. Fortunately, community-engaged faculty were able to seek out and elevate community partners with our assistance. As a shared volunteer management team across students, faculty, and staff, we deployed groups of our campus community toward civic efforts such as phone banking to turn out the vote and to sign-up community members for COVID-19 vaccines. Faculty also served as subject-matter experts in the community and local news outlets, thus providing a public service by sharing their expertise at the intersections of policy, public health, law, and more. With the help of a targeted website, our team also openly explored the available data on the potential impacts of the worsening conditions for our neighbors.

Building on the lessons learned through our immediate crisis response, the team developed a theory of action in partnership with a local consulting group and The Pittsburgh Study (a large, longitudinal study that brings community and academic partners together to learn about child health and thriving and address root causes of inequity). That theory of action generated a set of resources to educate the campus community on the intersections of lived experiences, research insights, and collective action. We paid for the consultant's time out of the modest ECA departmental budget, but the process was completely managed and informed by the cooperative, or brain trust, of ECA, the Office of PittServes, and key leaders from the Pittsburgh Study research and implementation team. Our exploration suggests that there are always new potential allies in the work, both across our university system and within communities, and that we must collectively prepare ourselves for growing community-engaged praxis while also remaining attentive to our organizational learning so as to minimize future harm in careless practice that stigmatizes and problematizes community concerns. We do all these things in collaboration but mostly through the steadfast time and attention of a team of 2–6 people including graduate student fellows, all housed across multiple offices that focus on capacity-building in addition to other duties.

The University of Pittsburgh is an urban, community-embedded higher education institution with a high level of research activity. While we understand that the ECA team cannot take full responsibility for every member of our campus community and the ways in which they approach those outside of the academy, we have taken proactive steps in elucidating and transforming some of the tensions between traditional research culture and what we hope to cultivate through the CECs. Yamamura and Koth (2018) expressed the need for universities to provide faculty with professional development opportunities that directly engage issues of race and culture and develop competencies in an asset-based approach to community partnerships. Toward that end, the CEC began a collaborative process to develop a means of providing Pitt stakeholders access to resources, methods, and epistemologies which would introduce and integrate them into the local community in a way that affirmed resident voices and existing assets. These assets include the people, civic associations, and institutions actively working to address the challenges of the area. Asset-Based Community Development (ABCD) was leveraged as a primary lens to view CEC communities who have experienced disenfranchisement such as Homewood, to avoid problematizing community concerns (Kretzmann & McKnight, 1993). Past approaches to community engagement, in contrast, have prioritized University research agendas. "A consistent criticism of the town-gown relationship is that the university tends to only see the community as a laboratory for studying needs and pathologies, not as a place of assessing assets and capacities on which to build" (Soska, 2015).

ABCD teaches that the most valuable asset in any community is its people, and that everyone's contributions and "gifts" should be valued (Kretzmann & McKnight, 1993). This includes residents, youth, elders, organizational leaders, government officials, philanthropists, faith-based groups, and more. Building on a community's strengths and turning away from a "deficit-perspective" considers all of the assets of African American families and communities including "financial, structural, organizational, human, and interpersonal assets" (Briscoe, et al, 2009, p. 208). Given this, ABCD was an ideal strengths-based framework to build from and provided a means for Pitt stakeholders to learn about the community's history and preferences.

A PWI-led place-based engagement center within a predominantly African American neighborhood must ensure that residents do not feel "researched." This meant emphasizing the importance of relationships and existing hyperlocal assets, as well as promoting effective, respectful engagement values and principles. A center rooted with a strong sense of place and context positions the institution to have a better awareness of community priorities and points of alignment, which will ensure that the center's offerings are not replicating existing community assets and duplicating programming. For instance, CEC staff including the director, outreach coordinator, receptionist, and greeter were hired in part due to their connections to the neighborhood such as familial, faith-based, and social ties. The staff of four, plus a small group of student interns and fellows, can be found at various events both large (festivals, summits, rallies, and events) and small (civic association and other local meetings and discussions) and are often identified as community members more than as Pitt representatives. In addition, CEC staff are invited to participate in regular community planning meetings. In Homewood, the CEC director was an active participant in the development of the "Homewood Community Comprehensive Plan," which brought a coalition of stakeholders together including residents, community leaders, activists, governmental officials, local institutions, and philanthropists to envision the community's future. Directing those from Pitt interested in working within CEC communities to relevant neighborhood plans prioritizes the expressed desires and voices of the people who contributed to the planning process while avoiding duplicating existing initiatives. Ensuring that institutional practitioners were well educated about Homewood's history and resources allowed an asset-based entry point to the community.

To set the tone and framework for our engagement, Dr. Mary Ohmer, a well-known and respected associate professor within Pitt's School of Social

Work and community organizer, led a community-based participatory research (CBPR) project in Homewood that sought to identify what Pitt stakeholders should and do know to engage residents respectfully and effectively. Building on her vast experience and meaningful relationships throughout the community and the university, she engaged youth and adult residents to facilitate civic engagement discussions and activities around equitable development. Dr. Ohmer's Fall 2017 master's level class interviewed 18 participants including community leaders, residents, and Pitt community-engaged faculty and staff, with each participant having had a connection to Homewood. Every interviewee had past experiences living, working, studying, or worshiping in the neighborhood. Some were Westinghouse High School alumni—the Pittsburgh Public School serving the area, and/or as members of Homewood African Methodist Episcopal (AME) Zion Church. Participants included a long-time resident active in community affairs and CEPs whose work in the area spans decades.

We were fortunate to have the voice of a griot, a community storyteller who proudly continued Homewood's robust oral tradition, one of many who maintained its history and culture. His counsel was valued and was highly sought by many higher education institutions in the area. By interviewing the griot, graduate students not only learned about the depth of Homewood's history (which included a once thriving and diverse middle-class neighborhood of 30,000 in the 1950s), but they also learned about its many challenges since the 1950s including redlining, the fall of the steel industry, the rise of drugs, gang violence, and crime (in 2017, for instance, 15% of Black homicides in Allegheny County happened in Homewood), compounded with failed community revitalization efforts and the current fear of gentrification. Moreover, they learned about how residents persevered through these seismic historic changes. We were also fortunate to be invited into the home of a long-time resident and community leader. She asserted that outsiders have come into the Homewood community with the language of collaboration but not a posture of collaborating and reminded graduate students that the community has a lot of knowledge to offer, "Seek to learn first ... be a learner before anything" (Ohmer et al., 2017).

Community-identified Priorities for University Members Seeking to Partner with Homewood Residents and Organizations

Their CBPR project identified three overarching themes for community engagement participants to consider. These themes included 1) Ways to Approach and Effectively Engage the Community, 2) Factors Impacting Engagement, and 3) Mutual Benefits and Sustainability. Based on our findings, behaviors that were recommended for Pitt faculty, staff, and students to adopt when engaging the Homewood community include:

- Transparency
- Cultural humility
- Collaboration
- Active listening
- Offer mutual benefits
- Intergenerational inclusion
- Utilizing existing community assets
- Sustainable planning
- Nonjudgmental

At the CEC, these behaviors are enacted in several ways:

- **Transparency** is seen in the language we use to describe our collaborative nature of work and was noted in the aesthetics of the community engagement center, itself, designed with big windows so that passersby can see what's happening in the space and feel welcomed to explore.
- **Cultural humility** is uplifted and acknowledged as "a lifelong process of self-reflection and self-critique whereby the individual not only learns about another's culture, but one starts with an examination of her/his own beliefs and cultural identities" (Yeager & Bauer-Wu, 2013). Reflection spaces were cultivated allowing Pitt faculty, staff, and students to unpack community experiences while exploring their own cultural identities and belief systems.
- **Collaboration** is reflected in not only the language to describe the CEC's mission and values, but also in the center's activity areas (Enhanced Health & Wellness, Strengthened Cultural Arts, Innovation & Business Growth, Data Access & Organizational Capacity, Enriched Education & Youth Experience, and Economic Prosperity & Family Support) and opportunities. In Fall 2021, for instance, university-community collaborations at the CEC included Pitt working alongside CBOs such as the Homewood Children's Village, Homewood Community Sports, Pittsburgh Public Schools, Homewood-Brushton YMCA, The Oasis Project, Operation Better Block, Primary Care Health Services, Inc., Sanant Counseling, Catalyst Connection, Toyz Electronics, Community Empowerment Association, Trying Together, and Neighborhood Legal Services.
- **Active listening** is seen in our responsiveness. For instance, we heard feedback from older residents that they wanted educational opportunities through the Center. In response to this, CEC staff-built relationships

with the Osher Lifelong Learning Institute at the University. Osher became one of the Center's most committed partners and has conducted no-cost programming at the center based on additional feedback from residents. An outcome of active listening is action, which can be seen in how CEC staff interact with visitors.
- **Mutual benefits** are carefully identified and offered to ensure that residents are not left seeing little of the benefits from the engagement. CEC staff help to facilitate discussions to define goals and to advocate for what is in the best interest of both community and institution, ensuring that planning processes are inclusive and accessible. If the institution is gaining something from the interaction, ensuring mutual benefits in return builds trust.
- **Intergenerational** opportunities are cultivated at the Center with an understanding that all members of a community have wisdom to offer. There are not only offerings for young and old but also opportunities which can be collectively embraced together regardless of age. The Center is a family-friendly facility and is welcoming.
- **Utilizing community assets** as a fundamental piece of the strengths-based approaches exhibited through the Center, including ABCD and CBPR.
- **Sustainability** is not only seen at the CEC through the institution's long-term investment in the space, but residents are included so that they feel a level of ownership over projects while also addressing long-term neighborhood challenges.
- **Promoting a nonjudgmental environment** at the Center includes making all visitors feel welcomed, being responsive to requests, and creating a space that feels more like the community, and less like campus.

To ensure that Pitt faculty, staff, and students had access to resources which would ground them in these behaviors, our online Orientation & Preparation Module was created and launched through the CEC's website. Supplemental readings, video clips and case studies were activities included within the 45-minute training. Though not all encompassing, the module was one of the initial CEP development pathways shaped and implemented throughout the University and led by ECA as a means of grounding our work in equity and social justice. While not mandatory, it is a tool used as a precursor to more detailed discussions with CEC staff. Some faculty have leveraged the module as a mandatory component of their classes, and CEC staff made referrals to the site which houses a plethora of resources pertaining to effective and respectful community engagement practices including a tip sheet for professional and respectful community engagements, a repository of neighborhood reports and plans, and interviews from stakeholders, in addition to the orientation. By using the module, students are able to better prepare themselves for community-engaged learning and research, strengthening their understanding of the culture and norms the CEC upholds. All resources are available for easy access online by those within and outside of the institution.

ECA also developed Faculty & Staff Open Houses which provide a structured opportunity for colleagues to tour the facility, meet center staff, and learn more about the history of Homewood and the community's goals. For residents, CEC Community Dinners & Conversations have brought collaborators from Pitt and the community together to "break bread," share experiences, and demystify the center and the neighborhood. The dinners have become an important social event for residents who have expressed a desire to meet Pitt people and to stay apprised of the activities of the CEC, as well as for members of the campus community interested in learning more about the community. Student workers through the CEC gain critical direct touchpoints with nonacademic environments and gain interpersonal skills with a wide breadth of stakeholders including faculty outside of their discipline, administrators, and residents. These opportunities break down barriers and build bridges toward meaningful collaborations. Providing a platform to bring coalitions of like-minded people together to cultivate ideas and combine their resources has built relationships which have resulted in additional community-benefitting collaborations, such as the PittEnrich tutoring program for elementary-aged youth.

While the CECs offer a distinct physical space, the full body of ECA's work includes being on-campus to collaborate and connect. A major portion of our practice centers acting as both concierge and diplomat with key stakeholders to smooth and reshape the boundaries of community-partnered efforts. Through our center, students gain access to nonacademic staff and nonuniversity leaders that serve as technical advisors and mentors for community-based, experiential curricular, and cocurricular opportunities. This unique positioning also enables ECA to address systemic challenges to mutually beneficial engagement.

The lift of ethical engagement requires a willing coalition of formal and informal champions that center community praxis as necessarily critical, as well as committed partners that believe in the potential for the university to bring immediate value to the communities they serve. Higher education engagement praxis has a practical component that supports some of the more immediate concerns that come with living near a large, urban, landlocked institution. To that end, ECA also works to support Pitt's identity as a responsive neighbor by partnering across the university to support the off-campus student experience. A team of professionals across community affairs, student affairs, and housing educate, engage, and encourage students to "Be

A Good Neighbor" by better understanding their rights, responsibilities, and the resources available to them as renters. Student leaders placed with partner organizations, or that serve as student organization officers, serve as ambassadors that encourage two-way communication between students and long-term residents. In this way, students can flex their skill set as boundary spanners, gaining confidence in public arenas and engaging in the civic life of the neighborhood.

One of the University of Pittsburgh's visible strengths is its CEPs, which serve as a significant asset for our ability to activate across multiple modalities of public service and civic engagement. CEPs operate in a loosely facilitated alliance, kept together by shared interests in how we can learn from one another and share resources. To that end, I (Jamie) colead two closely interrelated spaces: an Engagement Community of Practice for staff (and professors of practice) that are interested in sharing and growing aspects of Pitt's engaged identity in a supported space and the annual Community Engaged Scholarship Forum which serves as Pitt's institutional touchpoint to elevate, celebrate, and reflect on the efforts of our faculty and researchers to advance sustainable, scholarly partnerships. My membership in an affinity community for CEPs was guided largely by my mentor, a now-retired beacon of decades of institutional knowledge and far-reaching relationships. He introduced me to the people that would inspire my desire to more formally connect with others that hold roles like mine or were responsible for partnership in some way. An open call for participation quickly led to an opt-in email distribution list of about 100 staff and a set of enthusiastic pre-COVID meetups. I now compile and distribute a biweekly newsletter for outreach and engagement with the support of a Master of Social Work (MSW) Engagement Fellow. That point of contact provides local and national resources as well as brief updates from the CECs. Realizing the full potential of these spaces is ongoing, but I give most of the credit for their creation to many years of effort from many supporters that have advocated for the institutionalization of engagement. My hope and dissertation inquiry explores the potential in an engagement architecture that is informed by the experiences and professional conditions of those closest to the work.

Convening power is also built into the core framework of the CEC model at Pitt. The CECs are shaped and led by two advisory councils: an internal council made up of stakeholders appointed by deans of each school, and a Community Advisory Council made up of community leaders including organizational heads, residents, faith-based leaders, and government representatives. Their voices have contributed to not only the CEC's visual aesthetic but to its culture ensuring that the programs of the Center are aligned with the community's goals. Members of the Community Advisory Council were either invited to join or were nominated. The hiring process for the CEC director was led by the Community Council who ultimately selected Daren Ellerbee to be the inaugural director. Having community input and guidance at every stage of the CECs' development created an environment that celebrates institutional culture, as well as the unique culture of Homewood.

As cowriters of this chapter, we, Jamila (Jamie) and Daren, acknowledge that we are only two CEPs in an ecosystem that stretches across our Pitt University system. Through both collaborative and independently conversant bodies of work, we serve Pitt as ambassadors for the power of networked planning and action. We also recognize that they might advance a unique community-engaged praxis just by nature of being Black women in an institution and sector that perpetuates white normativity as the standard by which community impact is oriented (Morris, 2016). White normativity is sometimes difficult to recognize as it can present the conditions, ideas, practices, and culture by which an entire society operates. In practice, it can be the use of "community" as a synonym for black spaces, by the assumption that black and brown spaces lack wealth or expertise, or even simply that non-whiteness needs to be named as novel or central to others' conceptualization of themselves and their positionality. Critical roles and networks create spaces for BIPOC-CEPs where they are less likely to be in the minority, even if they continue to be disproportionately affected by institutional norms that marginalize their partners and their chosen epistemologies. By having a direct influence on the andragogy (the methods and principles of adult education which highly value purposeful, experiential modalities, self-efficacy and self-direction for learners, and intrinsic motivators) and organizational development of the University of Pittsburgh broadly, we have been able to influence pedagogy and practice in very tangible ways. These efforts make the civic life of engagement less isolating for ourselves and our allies. From our perspective, some of the most critical action steps CEPs, faculty, and administrators can take to affect positive change in our new reality are to:

- Assemble allies across as many of the core functions of the institution as possible (academic, research, cocurricular, engagement/community affairs, business and operations, marketing and communications). Meet them by paying attention to your institutional news outlets and artifacts of engagement. Review internal and local newsletters. I congratulate colleagues whose achievements are shared as University highlights and ask questions of those whose community-engaged efforts I am unfamiliar with. It is an easy way to initiate relationships in a world still on Zoom and Microsoft Teams.
- Think about what permissions are necessary for your colleagues to contribute in ways that are meaningful. Encourage your institutional

leaders to visibly participate, even if official policies lag. While flex work policies are popular and acceptable, our team reached out to new partners, located closer to where employees live, rather than in proximity to campus. Our team celebrates volunteerism publicly with regular stories in our PittWire news service and sends personal invites to senior leaders to join us in signature events. Be respectful of others' right not to participate as well. Personal and professional complexities should not be exacerbated by well-intentioned opportunities.
- Cut through bureaucracy by elevating community voice, priorities, and data. Even the most trusted academic or administrator is less compelling than those closest to community knowledge. Community researchers and advocacy groups publish reports regularly. Share those reports with your peers and supervisors as examples to act on, not duplicate or offer a counterpoint to.
- Combat the disenfranchisement inherent in lacking positional power by leveraging the coalition power of allies and be willing to bootstrap your own ideas quickly with internal fundraising and a clear theory of action. Find the friends you made earlier and pass the hat around. Most units can spare $100–$500 dollars as a transfer without too much red tape and with enough units participating, those dollars add up.
- Prepare students to enter community spaces by encouraging them to take up the work of humility and decentering. Do not leave it to your peers and partners to "teach" them inclusive mindsets. If you must do so, take care to position partners as experts and coleaders in the work you seek to advance. Give homework in advance of stepping in front of external communities, ask students to provide reflection and areas of further learning based on what they have researched. High-impact, experiential practices will deepen their understanding of ethical intergroup relationships.
- Partners without academic or positional titles offer significant cultural wealth and context. Make it clear that community-engaged learning is not possible without them.
- Step into existing gaps and serve as a protective factor for the communities with which you partner. Get more information before assuming that access and engagement should be granted to your colleagues or students. Be explicit about that orientation with your peers and establish clear expectations with your partners for when collaborations are challenged. Do not be afraid to slow down partnerships and speak truth to power. Holding relationships with communities is a privilege, not a right.
- Address power and positionality with honesty. Community-based organizations, BIPOC CEPs, and students with marginalized identities often take on under-compensated labor to maintain valued relationships. Be open and honest with partners that you understand and acknowledge

that there may be pressure to participate in university partnerships due to fear of negative consequences, such as omission from other institutional areas of potential resourcing and opportunity. Provide nonpunitive frameworks and clearly provide an exit clause if community capacity needs to shift away from the academy and its priorities.
- In trainings with faculty members and students, openly discuss exploitation and saviorism as barriers to the efficacy and ethics of community engagement. Discuss that a deficit-based stance, and viewing community members primarily as research subjects, sabotage long-term partnerships and knowledge sharing.
- Consider how you can shift compensation in your work, who receives it, how, and by whom. There are creative ways you can consider diverting allocations for project funds toward urgent community needs rather than investments that center on academy norms. Request what you would consider a fair, living hourly wage within your funding model, consider selecting front-line community workers rather than those that hold formal positional power as your primary partners.
- Develop intentions and specific plans regarding the types of students and community partners that are able to engage in community-engaged learning. Consider nontraditional perspectives, such as dissenting voices, individuals not normally accorded power or recognition, and those that are primarily focused on keeping food on the table through (nonflexible) hourly employment, and/or the 24-hour demands of caring for a family. Recognize the unique perspectives of individuals from different generations or chronosystems. Work to compensate or connect valued stakeholders with lower socioeconomic status through honorariums, fellowships, federal work-study, and other paid complements to curricular CEL that will allow them to participate in community-based pedagogies.
- Wait to engage in community-embedded work until you are confident that your professional priorities can integrate stakeholders ethically and with intention so that you do not do a disservice to your students and partners. Consider researching or refreshing yourself on the fundamentals of engaged scholarship and community partnership (even if you are a midcareer or a senior educator) before putting others in a position to be careless with relationships that should be considered long term and mutually valued.
- Consult your institution's center for community engagement, or seek out formal and informal peer experts for resources and best practices in community-engaged learning. It takes time, preparation, courage, and humility to engage effectively in mutually beneficial relationships with communities that may differ from your personal or institutional culture and conditions. We caution you to be aware of the hubris you may bring

from the academy and to instead take joy in the practice of collaboration and knowledge sharing. Better oriented and mindful faculty, staff, and students have greater potential to support and encourage thriving communities.

References

Ahmed, S. (2012). *On being included: Racism and diversity in institutional life*. Durham: Duke University Press.

Briscoe, R., Keller, H. R., McClain, G., Best, E., & Mazza, J. (2009). A culturally competent community-based research approach with African American neighborhoods: Critical components and examples. In S. Evans, C. Taylor, M. Dunlap, & D. Miller, *African Americans and community engagement in higher education* (pp. 205–239). State University of New York Press.

Dostilio, L. D., & Perry, L. G. (2017). An explanation of community engagement professionals as professionals and leaders. In L. D. Dostilio (Ed.), *The community engagement professional in higher education: A competency model for an emerging field* (pp. 1–26). Campus Compact.

DuBois, W. E. B. (1903). Of our spiritual strivings. In W. E. B. Du Bois (Ed.), *The souls of Black folk* (pp. 2–7). Coterie Classics.

Harris, J. L. (2021). Black on Black: The vilification of "me-search," tenure, and the economic position of Black sociologists. *Journal of Economics, Race, and Policy*, 4(2), 77–90.

Howell, J., Goodkind, S., Jacobs, L. A., Branson, D., & Miller, L. (2019). *Pittsburgh's inequality across gender and race [Review of* Pittsburgh's inequality across gender and race*]*. University of Pittsburgh School of Social Work. City of Pittsburgh's Gender Equity Commission. www.socialwork.pitt.edu/sites/default/files/pittsburghs_inequality_across_gender_and_race_07_19_20_compressed.pdf

Iverson, S. (2007). Camouflaging power and privilege: A critical race analysis of university diversity policies. *Educational Administration Quarterly*, 43(5), 586–611.

Kretzmann, J. P. & McKnight, J. L. (1993). *Building communities from the inside out*. ACTA Publications.

Lawrence, T. & Suddaby, R. (2006). Institutions and institutional work. In C. Hardy, S. R. Clegg, T. Lawrence, & W. Nord, *The Sage handbook of organization studies* (pp. 215–254). SAGE Publications.

Morris, M. (2016). Standard white: Dismantling white normativity. *California Law Review*, 104(4), 949–978. www.jstor.org/stable/24758741

Ohmer, M., Baker, S., Carroll, B., Cosoleto-Miller, K., & Piotrowski, J. (2017). *Respectful and effective community engagement: Results from interviews with Homewood stakeholders*. University of Pittsburgh Community Engagement Centers.

Smit, D. (2014, August 25). The economist names Pittsburgh the most livable city (on the mainland) again. *NEXTpittsburgh*. https://nextpittsburgh.com/business-tech-news/economist-names-pittsburgh-livable-city/

Soska, T. M. (2015). University and communities in partnership: Exploring the roots and current trends of higher education community engagement in the United

States. In J. W. Jacob, S. E. Sutin, J. C. Weidman, & J. L. Yeager, *Community engagement in higher education: Policy reforms and practice* (pp. 105–125). Sense Publishers.

U.S. Census Bureau. (2022). *QuickFacts Pittsburgh city, Pennsylvania*. The Census Bureau. www.census.gov/quickfacts/fact/table/pittsburghcitypennsylvania/PST045222

Yamamura, E. & Koth, K. (2018). *Place-based community engagement in higher education*. Stylus Publishing, LLC.

Yeager, K. A. & Bauer-Wu, S. (2013). Cultural humility: Essential foundation for clinical researchers. *Applied Nursing Research: ANR, 26*(4), 251–256. https://doi.org/10.1016/j.apnr.2013.06.008

12
ODE TO EDUCATION THAT LIFTS US HIGHER

Shandela Contreras

Do you want to go to college?

Your mom still wraps ham and American Swiss cheese in bolillos
No matter how hard the surface is at first to slice open
Because she knew inside there was a token

Texture so soft and so rich, the need to knead, in hopes it rises
She takes a look at her child, in hopes
She, he, they
rises

Your papa, baba, carries two dangling feet near the edge of his ears
And he hears
    the blending sound of sirens and your laughter
In the cross section of Vermont and King Boulevard
The plaza,
taking you to Payless to buy a pair of All-Star Converse
In every hallway, he hopes you don't converse in nonsense
and know that it doesn't matter the brand of the outsoles you wear on
    your feet
the sulcus in your brains are worth much more than that,
He wonders what brand will you become and represent at the front seat

DOI: 10.4324/9781003448525-15

Ten years old, just size six youth in shoes
You're taking steps closer, yet you're still so far to decide
To choose

Do you want to go to college?
At ten, they hope your answer is yes, si, shi de
At every age, they hope you continue to say yes
Knowing that in every y-e-s, you will be blessed
Because both e & s is written in success
Leaving out just the "y"

Why?
Because you will be the first in generations of the millionth generation
To have a more accessible access to higher education written in fine print
With names like
Castanon, Mendoza, Rodriguez, Dixon, Moore, Lagos, Alfaro, Rivas, Andrade, Nguyen, Solis
And within that certainty, there is a solace
That in the state of soaring angels, your wings fly in sync through the magic of each awakening day
that you will find your place
   in heights, hundreds of acres,
the ceiling of lecture halls you can't touch
But you are a vessel in the molding of the brick structure,
even if you didn't come from much
Or so you think
But El Mercadito, the heights you reach in Boyle Heights of East LA,
the walls of Gonzalez's Chicano Art
In La Placita Olvera, where the confetti blooms,
ancestry cheers to your future that has yet to start

Who do we owe our futures to
To the weekdays, we learned what it was to be empathetically amiable, consciously loquacious, infatuated with language
The core of words so elongated, we dared to share with our families the vocab lineage

To steer ahead
We were closer to catching up with the rest
Even with our disadvantages
We aimed to be the best
Because we were the scholars of California
The sensation of our family development

The residue of unfound treasure gutted out the bottom hole
The hubs that bridge the border of our experiences
The wheels that kept arriving at Riverside, San Jose, Sacramento, Compton, Costa Mesa, Bakersfield, the Bay
And nearer to all the forty-six partner campus that spread across the array
To show up and stand out like Chewbacca on Solo's ship
Roaring our code of ethics
For our rebel alliance, defying the odds
That as many as 3200 youth have a choice
to be a leader

A bobcat, a ram, an anteater,
a gator, a golden eagle, a trojan, a wave
Becoming a new wave of fresh souls that took
the initiative in their neighborhood to grace
all the cement that is paved

For today,
when anyone ask
Do we want to go to college
We say,
we made the choice
On a galaxy far far away
A while ago
To say
yes

Because to whom do we owe our futures to
To the acceptances and rejection
The donors who believed in us, that we never fail to mention
Our adversaries that may see our prosperities as a transgression
The murals that kept us smiling at all state intersections
Our mothers and fathers, abuelas and abuelitos advice we had to listen to with no objections
To ourselves

Because when anyone ask if we went to college
We say
We did

With our nooks and public library shelf books
our minds secluded with mamba mentality
We face our reality

That today we start the road ahead
But tomorrow we begin the initiative again

The College Corps we commend
For giving us an opportunity to answer—
Yes, in our quest
   to ascend

13
CONCLUSION

Elena Klaw, Andrea Tully, and Elaine K. Ikeda

When we started this project, our beautiful home state was literally burning down. Now, as we prepare this book for submission, the Supreme Court has stripped women of fundamental rights over their own bodies, a Supreme Court Justice called for a reversal of rulings protecting same-sex marriage, and, while the nation was still grieving the massacre of a class of fourth graders, a 21-year-old man used a legally purchased automatic weapon to slaughter seven people at an Independence Day parade. As our collective sense of safety in our country and on the earth, itself, has been diminishing, hope has somehow remained on the horizon. Higher education professionals across the nation have fought tirelessly alongside our students and our community partners for social change, to prevent ceaseless cycles of violence, and to "get out the vote," aiming to usher in a new cohort of elected officials who will commit to equity.

We have all been sobered, challenged, and worn down by the effects of the global pandemic and the constant upheaval within the United States. Despite our collective exhaustion, we concur with William G. Tierney (2021) who stated, "As institutions that ostensibly are committed to the search for truth, [institutions of higher education] should be central to the efforts to protect and enhance democracy." We believe that the contributors to this book have demonstrated the ways in which community engagement enacts the four functions of American higher education identified by Daniels et al. (2021), as essential to democracy, specifically, social mobility, citizenship education, the stewardship of facts, and the cultivation of pluralistic, diverse communities.

DOI: 10.4324/9781003448525-16

So, how do we, as educators, continue to act in the face of the forces of injustice, domination, political corruption, greed, and extremism? We act because we have no choice. We act because we want an earth for future generations to live in. We act to stand up for those who would otherwise be silenced. We act because we want safety for all people of the world and know that guns, wars, droughts, cages, abuse, and toxic chemicals kill. We act because we believe that freedom, peace, equality, liberation, and love must triumph. We act because we are angry and because we are scared but mostly because we are principled and refuse to be silent. As the pioneers of the community engagement field suggest, we, too, are "a part of the social and political struggles of our time" (Stanton et al., 1999, p. 243). We still, and likely always will, face crosswinds that make it difficult to continue on our path. Yet, we persist, because our students, our community, and our democracy are counting on us.

> If I am not for myself, who is for me? When I am for myself, what am I? If not now, when?
> *(Hillel, n.d., Pirkei Avot 1:14; cited in Loevinger, 2017)*

All of the contributors to this book are changemakers and liberators (Friere, 1970). All of the authors believe that the students we serve can and will create a better future, given the education and the confidence to do so. As three women leaders who occupy different roles in higher education, we hope that you have found inspiration, support, and guidance somewhere in these pages, either as a student, staff, faculty member, administrator, policy maker or a community partner, to engage students in iterative processes of reflection, action, and assessment involved in community engagement.

We know firsthand that this work is not easy. Even coming together to complete this project as a faculty member, staff member, and a state-wide nonprofit director posed challenges. As collaborators, we became painfully aware of the differences in our work schedules, our structural supports for project management, and our distinct networks of colleagues, disciplinary affiliations, and professional associations. We even came across differences in our perspectives as to who has influence and who "does the work" within colleges and universities. As seasoned professionals in community engaged learning, it was humbling to realize that such common terms as "the university," "the literature," "the community," and "the field" connote entirely different things to different stakeholders working within community engagement. Despite periods of misunderstanding, frustration, and overwhelm related to health and caretaking challenges during a global pandemic, and multiple distinct competing priorities, we have been buoyed by a shared feminist vision, a commitment to social justice, and a belief in higher education as a cornerstone of democracy, as we have completed this project. We have remained committed to the belief that our different positions and backgrounds have afforded us distinct vantage points related to forwarding the field of community engagement during these tenuous times. We appreciate that the contributors to this book were brave enough to share their histories, experiences, challenges, dilemmas, milestones, and accomplishments in discussing their community engagement work.

Some authors highlighted the slow and arduous nature of engagement. Indeed, for many of us in this field, our efforts to change structures, policies, attitudes, and behaviors have required reservoirs of patience and a commitment to a long-term view. Navigating campus politics and confronting unjust structures or policies while holding true to our integrity and values requires resilience and perseverance, as well as audacity and a bold vision of social justice. It is clear to us that the contributors included in this book care deeply about their students, their communities, and their colleagues and that they model their commitment to equity through their professional roles.

A wide range of topical issues are addressed in this compendium including racial injustice, the marginalization of immigrant perspectives, educational disparities, interpersonal violence, and climate crises. We hope you have found guidance related to implementing community engaged learning (CEL) that both stirs you to act and fits within your disciplinary training. We hope that you have received signposts for your career trajectory as a CEL practitioner or researcher. We also hope you have seen your institutional context represented, whether you toil at a well-funded research university, a selective faith-based private college, or a comprehensive public institution. Most of all, we hope that we, in at least some small way, helped you to continue along the path toward implementing and instituting a pedagogy of hope, freedom, and action (Friere, 1970) as we all work together to empower this generation of college students to heal the world (Levisohn, 2012).

> For there is always light if only we're brave enough to see it, if only we're brave enough to be it.
>
> *(Gorman, 2021, p. 28)*

References

Daniels, R., Shreve, G., & Spector, P. (2021). *What universities owe democracy.* Johns Hopkins University Press.
Friere, P. (1970). *Pedagogy of the oppressed.* Continuum.
Gorman, A. (2021). *The hill we climb.* Viking Books.

Levisohn, J. A. (2012). Becoming a servant how James Kugel's conception of avodat hashem can help us think about the dispositional goals of Jewish service-learning. *Journal of Jewish Communal Service, 87*(1), 104–112.

Loevinger, N. J. (2017). *If not now, when?* My Jewish Learning. www.myjewishlearning.com/article/if-not-now-when/

Stanton, T. K., Giles, D. E., & Cruz, N. I. (1999). *Service-learning: A movement's pioneers reflect on its origins, practice, and future.* Jossey-Bass Publishers.

Tierney, W. G. (2021, December 6). *Academe's neglected responsibility.* Inside Higher Ed. www.insidehighered.com/views/2021/12/06/colleges-are-shirking-their-responsibility-support-democracy-opinion

ABOUT THE CONTRIBUTORS

Roni Bennett, B.B.A., is a cofounder and the Executive Director of South Florida People of Color.

Courtney A. Berrien, M.A.T., is Director of the Adrian Dominican Institute for Mission and Leadership at Barry University.

Glenn A. Bowen, Ph.D., is Associate Professor and the Executive Director of the Center for Community Service Initiatives at Barry University.

Shandela Contreras is an undergraduate student at the University of Southern California majoring in Creative Writing. She is a Finalist for the California Youth Poet Laureate 2023 and a Los Angeles County Youth Poet Ambassador.

David M. Donahue, Ph.D., is Professor of Education in the School of Education at the University of San Francisco.

Jamilah Ducar, EdD., is Executive Director of the Engaged Campus at the University of Pittsburgh.

Daren Ellerbee, M.S., is the inaugural Director of the University of Pittsburgh's Educational Outreach Center (EOC). She is currently earning a doctorate in Urban Education at the University of Pittsburgh's School of Education.

About the Contributors

Bryant Fairley, M.A., is Director of the Innovation Incubator and the Interim Director for the Center for Community Engagement, California State Polytechnic University, Pomona.

Henry Fan, A.S., is an undergraduate senior studying Computer Science and Humanities while serving as a #CaliforniansforAll College Corps Fellow at San José State University.

Mark Felton, Ph.D., is Professor of Teacher Education and Faculty Associate Dean for Research at the Lurie College of Education at San José State University.

Daniel Fidalgo Tomé, Ed.D., is Engaged Civic Learning Program Coordinator in the Division of Diversity, Inclusion & Civic Engagement at Rutgers, The State University of New Jersey–Camden.

Josh Fryday, J.D., serves as California Chief Service Officer within the Office of the Governor. He is a military Veteran and the former Mayor of Novato, California.

Elaine K. Ikeda, Ph.D., is Executive Director of LEAD California.

Elena Klaw, Ph.D., is Professor of Psychology at San José State University. She serves as the Director of the Center for Community Learning & Leadership at San José State University.

Kent Koth, M.A., is Executive Director of the Seattle University Sundborg Center for Community Engagement.

Jon A. Levisohn, Ph.D., is Jack, Joseph and Morton Mandel Associate Professor of Jewish Educational Thought at Brandeis University.

Angie Mejia, Ph.D., is Assistant Director of the Community Engagement and Education (CEEd) Hub at the Masonic Institute for the Developing Brain at the University of Minnesota.

Ellen Middaugh, Ph.D., is Associate Professor of Child and Adolescent Development at the Lurie College of Education at San José State University.

Chris Nayve, J.D., is Associate Vice President for Community Engagement and Anchor Initiatives at the University of San Diego.

About the Contributors

Anh-Thu Ngo, Ph.D., is Lecturer in the Global TIES Program at the Jacobs School of Engineering, University of California, San Diego.

Pilar Pacheco, M.A., is Director of the Center for Community Engagement, California State University Channel Islands.

Star Plaxton-Moore, Ed.D., is Director of Community-Engaged Learning and McCarthy Center Programs at the Leo T. McCarthy Center for Public Service and the Common Good at the University of San Francisco.

Patricia D. Robinson, Ph.D., is Professor of Sociology at the College of the Canyons. She serves as Faculty Director, Civic and Community Engagement Initiatives.

Verdis LeVar Robinson, M.Div., is Associate of the Kettering Foundation and Adjunct Professor for the Urban College of Boston.

Marie Sandy, Ph.D., is Associate Professor in the Department of Administrative Leadership, School of Education at the University of Wisconsin-Milwaukee. She is the Wm. Collins Kohler Endowed Chair of Systems Change and Peacebuilding.

Andrea Tafolla, B.A., is Community Engagement Coordinator for the Community Engagement Center at the University of California, Merced.

Andrea Tully, M.Ed., is Assistant Director of the Center for Community Learning & Leadership at San José State University.

Erica K. Yamamura, Ph.D., is Higher Education Consultant. Previously, she was Director and Professor of the Student Development Administration Master's Program in the College of Education at Seattle University.

INDEX

Note: Endnotes are indicated by the page number followed by "n" and the note number e.g., 206n3 refers to note 3 on page 206. Page locators in **bold** and *italics* represents table and figures, respectively.

AAC&U's Integrative Learning and Signature Work Institute *see* Institute on Engaged and Integrative Learning
A Call to Action: An Initiative for Civic Engagement, Self, and Society (2015) 59
A Crucible Moment: College Learning and Democracy's Future (2012) 59, 67–8
active listening 224–5
Adichie, Chimamanda 40
African Americans *see* Black Americans
Ahmed, Sara 45
Allen, Mike 18
ALL IN Campus Democracy Challenge 69–70
Alternative Spring Break Programs 168
American Association for Higher Education (AAHE) 108
American Association of State Colleges & Universities (AASCU) 17, 172
American College Personnel Association (ACPA) 172
American democracy 12–13, 57, 60, 63
American Democracy Project (ADP) 172
American Dream 57
American higher education 11, 62, 177, 237; institutions of 11; traditional model of 62
AmeriCorps 120, 122, 124, 129, 131, 171; Volunteers in Service to America (VISTA) 127
Anh-Thu Ngo 181–4
antiracism education, recommended resources for **28–9**
antiracism, imperatives of 14–16
antiracist policies and practices 22
anti-Semitic movement 12
arguments 86; coalescing 88; coconstructing 88; critiquing 88; persuasive 87; religious 195; surfacing 87
Aschheim, Deborah 71
Ashoka U Changemaker Campus 140, 183
Asian Americans: minority-serving institution 151; racism targeted toward 79
Asset-Based Community Development (ABCD) 66, 72, 214, 221–2
Asset-Based Community Development and Respectful and Effective Community Engagement 214

Associate Vice President (AVP) for Academic Innovation 169
Association of American Colleges and Universities (AAC&U) *see* American Association of State Colleges & Universities (AASCU)
Astin, Alexander "Sandy" 111
Atlantic, The 120

Barry Service Corps (BSC) 19–20
Barry University 18–19, 23; Center for Community Service Initiatives at 18, 21; Deliberative Dialogue Series 21
Bastide, Xiye 90
"Bittersweet Harvest, The Bracero Program 1942–1964" bilingual exhibition 160–1
Black Americans: killing of 12; lynching of 23–4; racial terror perpetrated against 23; studies at community college 59; university culture 215
Black homicides, in Allegheny County 223
Black, Indigenous, and People of Color (BIPOC) communities: 187, 188, 202, 228–9; college presidents 135; social and racial injustices 161
Black Lives Matter movement 1, 12, 79, 90, 115
Black women 215, 228
bodies out of place (BOP) phenomena 185
book clubs 44
bookmarking 84
Boyer, Ernest 32, 40, 62
Bracero Oral History Project 161
Brandeis University 191–4, 196, 202
Bratton, Mandy 183
Bridgewater State University 15
Brown, Adrienne Maree 36, 45

California Assembly Bill 963 70
California Campus Compact (CACC) 4, 102, 111, 190
California College Corps *see* #CaliforniansForAll College Corps
California Community College (CCC) system 61–2, 65; current priorities of 67; racial and ethnic composition of 62
California Department of Education 115
California National Guard 124

#CaliforniansForAll College Corps 120, 121–6; benefits and challenges 130–1; Food & Supplies Taskforce Workgroup 124; prototypical quotes 130; service and college 122–3; win for communities 124–5; win for students 123–4
Californians for Civic Learning 115
California State University San Bernardino (CSUSB) 167–8
California State University (CSU) system 4, 80, 90, 158, 200; Center for Community Engagement 115; Chancellor's Office of 129
California Volunteers 115, 120–3, 122, 126–7, 129, 131
campus-community partnerships 67
Campus Compact 4, 41, 90, 102, 104, 108, 113, 116, 117, 162, 190; founding of 111
campus culture 59, 63, 65, 105; and organizational structures 104–7
Campus Democracy Project (CDP) 19
campus politics 105, 239
"Care and Connection" caller 219
Carnation Revolution 170
Carnegie Classification for Community Engagement (CE) 178
Carnegie Classified Community Engaged University 140
Carnegie Elective Classifications 2, 17, 178
Carnegie Elective Community Engagement Classification 107
Carnegie Foundation 17–18, 48, 63, 178
Carnegie Foundation for the Advancement of Teaching: Community Engagement Classification (2015) 18; definition of community engagement 17
CCNY's CityServ program 171
Center for Civic Engagement (CCE) 58, 69; Center for Community Engagement 138–9, 158–9, 166, 169, 230
Center for Community Learning & Leadership (CCLL) 4–5, 126–8, 199
Center for Excellence in Early Childhood Education (CfE) 159
Center for Learning Innovation (CLI) 186

Chicano Latino Youth Leadership Conference 163
citizenship education 67, 237
civic action: to address climate change activity 97; within a community engaged learning course 88–90
Civic Action Fellows 123, 129, 130
Civic Action Fellowship 123, 125, 127–9, 131
Civic and Community Engagement Initiatives 58–9, 220
civic and social responsibility, sense of 102
civic dialogue 70, 86–8
civic empowerment gap 60, 64
civic engagement, in higher education 62–3; campus-wide 58; CLARION conceptual framework for 78; concept of 58, 63, 65; definition of 63; practices of 78
civic equity: issues of 64, 71–2; pedagogy of 64–5; shared values of 59
civic inquiry, about climate change 77, 84–6, 88
civic learning 4, 11, 18–20, 30, 34, 60–8, 72, 172, 220
Civic Learning and Democratic Engagement (CLDE) Annual Conference (2016) 59
civic learning and democratic engagement (CLDE) programs 11, 18–20, 64–7
civic learning plus engagement 220
civic mission, of higher education 62; community college commitment to 69; of Democracy's College 60, 65, 72
civic opportunity gap 63–4
Civics in Action: Recognizing College of the Canyons' Obligation to Self and Society (2013–2014) 58
Civilian Conservation Corps (CCC) 125
CLARION (Civic Learning and Reasoning in Online Networks) project 77; for community-engaged learning 88; framework for civic engagement 78
Climate Action module 86; deliberation dialogue on 96–7
climate change, issue of 77, 80, 82
#climatecrisis 76, 90

#climatestrike 89
Clinton Global Initiative University 183
Coalition of Immokalee Workers' (CIW's) Fair Food Program 20
coalitions, building of: developing resources that support 114–15; evolutions for continuous improvement and impact 116–17; on individual campuses 102–3; to influence the state and national community engagement field 110–12; learning and community engagement 113; to leverage resources and maximize impact 115–16; through dialogues and networking 112–14
cognitive biases 87
cognitive skills, students' development of 48
collaboration 5, 11, 67, 81, 111, 113, 117, 120, 129, 160–1, 178, 186, 195, 204–5, 221, 223–4, 229, 231; between communities and institutions of higher education 2, 17, 48; community-benefitting 214, 226; mutually beneficial 43, 216; with stakeholders 35
collaborative teamwork 68
college education 135
College of the Canyons (COC) 69; Basic Needs Center (BaNC) 71; Civic and Community Engagement Initiative 58–9; culture change at 70–2
Combs, Barbara Harris 185
communities of color 21, 148, 151
community assets, utilization of 225
community-based participatory research (CBPR) project 223
community-based research 135, 190–1, 216
community-based work 187, 189–90
Community Collaborative 184
community college 57; African American studies at 59; in America 61; in California 61–2, 65; civic gaps and community college students 63–4; civic power 60; commitment to the "civic mission" of higher education 69; deliberative pedagogy 69; Democracy's Colleges and its

Index **247**

civic mission 60–1; four pillars of 65; impact of the COVID pandemic on 68; impact on the future of democracy 64; Patty, story of 57–8; as people's college 67; reimagining teaching and learning 67; role of 60; student-centered practices 67; Verdis, story of 59–60, 68
community development 205, 216; asset-based 66, 72; link with civic learning 4
community-engaged institutions 220
community-engaged learning (CEL) xiii, xv, 4, 31, 33, 79–80, 88, 128–9, 131, 169, 177, 179, 184, 186, 193, 201, 203, 213, 220, 226, 229–30
community-engaged pedagogy 171, 181, 192
community-engaged scholarship 172, 189–91; on racial justice 22–3
Community Engaged Scholarship Forum 227
community-engaged teaching xii, 181, 196, 213
Community Engagement and Social Justice Faculty Fellows Program 161, 174
Community Engagement Centers (CECs) 102, 106, 115, 213, 218; Community Dinners & Conversations 226; University of Pittsburgh 213–5, 217–21, 227, 228
community engagement, in higher education 4, 7, 102, 113, 120, 150; applications and implications of 48; benefits of 17, 123, 129, 165; change-making practices 46–7; for creating more possibilities 36; critical feminist aspirations for 39; critical feminist principles for 55–6; defined 17; feminist praxis as the starting point 48–50; fractals 36; framework development for 35–7; initiatives for 151; institutionalization of 110; interdependence and decentralization 36; literature review of 32–5; method for 68–72, 105; as a mission-centered pedagogical method for faculty 141–2; national example for 68–9; nonlinear and iterative 36; Patty's campus for 69–70; place-based 42, 116, 136, 214, 218, 222; practice of 47, 179, 202; principles of 33, 202, 205; resilience 36; scholarship xiv–xv, 17–8, 22–3, 26, 35, 40, 42, 53, 161, 172, 181, 187, 189–91, 198, 227, 230; strategy of 2, 14–5, 17–18, 20–1, 35, 102, 105; by universities 2; university impact on 142–3; as valuable mission work 140–1; as a vehicle to actualize mission 140–4
community engagement professionals (CEPs) 3, 21, 30–53, 103, 157–8, 173–175, 214–16; bloom of possibility 47–9 ; capacities for disruption and creation 53; community empowerment 46; ecosystem of critical feminist praxis for 30–2, 35, 37–9, 48, 52–3; feminist praxis as emergence 50–2; foundations of 39–41; mentorship programs 173; ways for promoting transformational education 173–5
community engagement programs 106, 108
Community Engagement Student Fellows program 70
community health and social well-being 102
community knowledge 161, 229
community partnerships, asset-based approach to 221
community service, institutionalizing of 102
community–university relations, colonialist structures in 22
community voices, opportunities for 47
Cone, Richard 112
Conservation Corps 124
Continuums of Service Conference (2015) 116, 157
Cook College–Rutgers University 171
Copeny, Mari 90
course-based curricular service-learning 2
COVID-19 pandemic 1, 6, 63, 114, 124, 134, 136, 141, 146–7, 157, 161, 199–200, 218, 220; on Black and Brown communities 21; constraints associated with 49; creating a service fellowship during 126–131 ; destructive impacts of 117; disparities in healthcare access

12; impact on community colleges 68; Medical Response Office 219; shutdowns due to 128–9; and sociopolitical strife 25; vaccine clinics on campus 146
CRAAP test 86, 95
Crenshaw, Kimberlé 45
critical consciousness 65, 82, 83, 161
critical feminist praxis worksheet, ecosystem of *51*
critical service-learning, theory of 151, 178
critical thinking 67, 179–80, 203
Cronon, William 62
Crow, Jim 23–4
Cruz, Nadinne 33
CSU Channel Islands (CSUCI) 158
cultural humility 224
cultural identity 65, 224
culturally responsive teaching 64–5
curriculum, decolonization of 15–6

Davis, Angela Y. 15
De Anza College, Northern California 58
decision-making: community-centered policies in 34; institutional 52
Deferred Action for Childhood Arrivals renewals 165
Defiance College in Defiance, Ohio 140
deliberative dialogue 20–1, 79, 82, 86–8; on climate action 96–7; Deliberative Dialogue Series on "Race Matters" (2020–2021) 21
democracy xiii, xv, 1, 3–4, 12–3, 16, 19, 21, 57–72, 90, 101, 105, 111–12, 116–18, 120, 122, 129, 131, 168, 170, 237–9; role of dialogue and deliberation in advancing of 69
Democracy's Colleges 61, 72; civic mission of 60–1, 65, 72; contribution of civic actors in betterment of 67; reinvesting in 67–8
democratic citizens 62, 67
Democratic Dilemmas of Teaching Service-Learning 114
democratic engagement programs 18–20, 65; civic learning and 18–20
democratic learning 62–3
democratic society 5, 61, 103, 177, 179, 202, 206; constructive citizens of 61

Department of Veterans Affairs (VA) 197
Dewey, John 32, 40, 72, 101
direct volunteer service 135
Dissertation Dish 113
diversity, equity, and inclusion (DEI), through higher education xiv, 11, 13, 14, 20, 26, 60, 64–6, 150, 142, 144, 146–8, 150–2, 188
diversity training, for staff of higher education institutes 13–14
DIY service 219
Donahue, David 2, 114
donor identification 143
Dostilio, Lina 30, 34, 157–8, 173–4, 214
Ducar, Jamilah (Jamie) xiv, 3, 213
Dust Bowl Okie migration 57

echo-chambers 84
Ecosystem of Critical Feminist Praxis for Community Engagement Professionals (ECFP, 2021) 31–2, 35, 37, 38, 48, 52
"effective altruism" movement 196
Ehrlich, Thomas 63
Ellerbee, Daren A. xiv, 3, 214, 228
Emergent Strategy: Shaping Change, Changing Worlds (2017) 36
emerging economy 68
Encanto (movie) 166
Engagement Community of Practice 227
Engineers Without Borders irrigation project 183
environmental justice 90, 171; fellowship 81–2, 97
Equal Justice Initiative (EJI) 23
equity-focused community partnerships 139
equity-minded inquiry 15
evidence-based dialogue 81

Fairley, Bryant 157–8, 166–7, 173–5, 242
faith-based higher education 134, 148, 150
faith-based institutions 126, 134–7, 144, 148–152; future of community engagement at 148–50; personal leadership in 144–6
fake news, problem of 79, 85
federal service program 120

First 5 funded programs, for Ventura County 159
Florida Legislature 19
Floyd, George 12
food insecurity 19, 124, 168, 174
Food Stamp Nutritional Education Program 171
forced labor camp 182
fostering networks, importance of 111
framing, importance of 89
Freire, Paulo 32, 37, 40, 65, 68, 83, 160, 161
#fridaysforthefuture 89
Fryday, Josh xiii, 3, 120–1, 242
Furco, Andrew 107, 160
future leaders, development of 101, 125, 159

gang violence 223
Global TIES 183, 202, 243
global warming 82, 85, 94
Gold Standard: Project Design Elements 66
good citizenship, promotion of 101
Google 79, 85, 94–5
Governor's Office of Service and Volunteerism *see* California Volunteers
Great Depression 57, 125
Greensboro Truth and Reconciliation Commission (2004–2006) 16
Grounded Theory approach, for coding and analyzing qualitative data 129

Harkavy, Ira 61
Harris III, James T. 137, 1 40, 141
Harvard University 182
higher education xiii, xv, 1–4, 6, 11, 102; bureaucratic system of 67; characteristic of 33; community engagement 157; community engagement in xiv, 4–5, 7; dominant norms and narratives in 33; public purposes of 104; role in producing critical thinkers 202
higher education institutions 3 , 6, 11–3, 15, 17, 23, 25, 35, 39, 48, 111, 118, 134, 148, 217, 223 ; diversity training for staff of 13–14; failure to address racism 13; as producers and distributors of knowledge 48; serving of communities of color 147–8; as source of light and heat 43–4, 49–50
higher education professionals 1, 174, 199, 237
Hispanic-Serving Institutions (HSIs) 61, 168
historically Black colleges and universities (HBCUs) 33
holistic learning model, need for creation of 66
Homewood African Methodist Episcopal (AME) Zion Church 223
Homewood Community Comprehensive Plan 222
Homewood residents and organizations: community-identified priorities for university audiences seeking to partner with 223–31; Faculty & Staff Open Houses 226; themes for community engagement participants 223–4
Hook, Van 58–9
Horizon Project 137
human rights abuses 16

identity, community-engaged 213
Ikeda, Elaine K. xiii, 3, 4, 6–7, 101, 157, 237, 242
Imagining America 113
IMPACT Conference 168
Indigenous peoples 14, 16, 146, 161
inquiry-based learning 67
Instagram 79, 94
Institute on Engaged and Integrative Learning 70
institutional identity 178, 214
institutional invisibilization 186
institutional racism 117
integrative learning 70
intellectual companionship 192, 204
intergenerational opportunities 225
Intergovernmental Panel on Climate Change (IPCC) 84, 94
International Association for Research on Service-Learning and Community Engagement (IARSLCE) 41, 113
interpersonal skills 14, 178, 226
interpersonal violence 239
intersectional power analysis 36, 45

Jacoby, Barbara 62
Jesuit Catholic university 137

Jewish Studies Service-Learning Initiative 191–4 , 196, 202
Journal of Jewish Communal Service 194
Judaism 202, 205

K–12 education 115; and higher education 115; public schools 200; teacher 44, 81
Kendi, Ibram X. 20
Kennedy, Donald 2
Kettering Foundation 69–70, 243
Klaw, Elena xiii, xiv, 1–5, 120–1, 126–9, 177, 197–205, 237, 242

land grant universities 177–8
Lands Recognition Statement (2020) 14
LEAD California 4, 70, 102–4, 111–15, 117, 242; strategic goals 112, 114
leadership: development workshops 171; key challenges 103–4; personal 144–6; skills 102; in times of crisis 146–7
learning: civic learning 4, 11, 18–20, 30, 34, 59–8, 72, 77, 115, 172, 220, 242; community-engaged xiii, 79–80, 186, 220; course-based curricular service-learning 2; critical service-learning, theory of 21, 33, 151, 161, 203; inquiry-based learning 67; integrative learning 70; presidential *see* presidential leadership, in higher education; problem-based learning 102; project-based learning (PBL) 60, 66–7, 70–1; remote learning 68; service-learning programs *see* service-learning programs; transdisciplinary teaching and learning 66
Levinson, Meira 60, 64
Levisohn, Jon A. 177, 191–7, 202, 204–5, 239
liberal education 62–3, 72
life skills 102
Lorde, Audre 45, 172
Lurie College of Education (San José State University) 77, 242
lynching, of African Americans 23–4

maker's mentality, notion of 66
marginalized communities 15, 34, 117; lived experiences of 22

Martin Luther King Jr. (MLK) Day of Service event (2021) 166
Martin, Trayvon 12, 18
Master of Social Work (MSW) Engagement Fellows 227
McIntosh, Peggy 25
McMaster School for the Advancement of Humanity 140
Mejia, Angie 177, 184–8, 202–5, 242
Mellon Foundation grant 70–1
Michigan Journal of Service Learning, The 107
Mill, John Stuart 15
Minnesota Campus Compact 113
Mitchell, Tania 21, 33, 72, 113, 131, 135, 151, 16–1, 178–9, 203
Murphy, Brian 58
Musil, Caryn McTighe 67–8
mutual benefits 214, 223–5

Nader, Ralph 182
narrative inquiry 66
narrative regeneration 17
NASPA 19
National Aeronautics and Space Administration (NASA) 84
National Conference on Race and Ethnicity in Higher Education (NCORE) 115
national consciousness 13
National Issues Forums (NIF) 69
National Service-Learning Clearinghouse Higher Education Project 111
National Task Force on Civic Learning and Democratic Engagement 61, 63
natural disaster, climate-related 80
Nayve, Chris xiii, 134, 138, 242
New Deal to Civil Rights activism 177
Newsom, Gavin 120, 122, 125
New York Public Interest Research Group (NYPIRG) 171
New York Times, The 84, 120
Next Generation Garden Environmental Justice Fellowship 81
nonjudgmental environment, promotion of 225

Office of Engagement and Community Affairs (ECA) 213, 218
Ohmer, Mary 214, 222–3

one-semester service-learning courses 187
online activism 76
online public sphere 77
Operation Tomodachi 121
organizational chart 106
organizational leadership 31, 222
Orientation & Preparation Module 225
Osher Lifelong Learning Institute 225

Pacheco, Pilar 157 –62, 173–5, 243
Pacific School of Religion, Berkeley 138
Padrón, Eduardo 64
participatory democracy 64, 66, 72
particularism, paradox of 206n3
partnerships: and relationships matter 108–10
Partnerships for Listening and Action by Communities and Educators (PLACE) 69–70, 72; Student Action Team 71
Patty, story of 57–8
Peace Corps 122, 158, 162, 173
Pedagogy of the Oppressed (1970) 40, 160
peer-leadership, student program focused on 52
people of color 12, 15–16, 18, 20, 24–5, 65, 135, 137, 150–2, 166, 216, 241
personal developmental work 145
person of color 145
persuasive dialogue 86
PittEnrich tutoring program, for elementary-aged youth 226
Pitt Pandemic Service Initiative (PPSI) 218–19
Pittsburgh Public School 223–4
"Pittsburgh's Inequality across Gender and Race" report (2019) 215
PittWire news service 229
place-based community engagement (PBCE) 135 –6, 214
place-based engagement partnerships 218
Place-Based Justice Network 136
police brutality, against Black people in America 1, 12
political advocacy 198
PolitiFact 79
Pomona Unified School District 169

Predominantly White Institutions (PWIs) 185, 222, 215; place-based engagement center 222
presidential leadership, in higher education 104, 134, 136, 140, 143–4, 150–2; American Council on Education study of 134–5; data collection for study of 137–8; diversity, equity, and inclusion and community engagement 147–50; evolution of 134–5; findings in analysis of 139–40; funding incubator and donor engagement opportunity 143–4; implications of 150–1; limitations of 152; personal 144–6; place-based community engagement 135–6; in Seattle University 139–40; in times of crisis 146–7; in University of San Diego 139–40
presidential task force, creation of 107
problem-based learning 102
problem-solving 60–1, 68, 70–1, 81, 162, 186; deliberative 68
professional development 32, 37, 40–1, 48, 50, 103, 107–8, 113–4, 129, 179, 182, 119, 221
professional learning communities 44
professor of color 185
Program Coordinator of Engaged Civic Learning 172
project-based learning (PBL) 60, 67, 70–1
Project H.E.R.E. (Higher Education Reparations Engagement) 18
project management 238
public and community service 104
public forums, for dialogue 20–1, 24, 81
public school system 39
public service internships 39
public spaces 61, 78

qualitative data analysis 32
Queer Woman of Color 187

racial discrimination 12
Racial Equity and Justice Institute (REJI) 15
racial healing 11, 14, 16– 8, 20, 25–6; and transformation 11
racial inequity, cycle of 23

racial justice xiii, 14–5, 18, 22–6, 115, 140; scholarship focused on 18, 22–3, 26
racial profiling, in higher education 1
racial unrest 63
racial violence 11–3, 26; acts of 23; and social injustice 12–13
Reconciliation Pyramid 16
Reddit 79
Reflective Practitioner Model 45
relationship management 218
relationships, building of 3, 66, 108–10, 164, 170
remote learning 68
Repair the World Program 192, 205
reparative justice 16
restorative justice 16, 18
Rock-the-Vote dance party 59
Roosevelt, Franklin Delano 125

Sac State (Hispanic-Serving Institution) 163–4
San Diego County of Linda Vista, California 137
Sandy, Marie 177, 189, 201–5, 243
San José State University (SJSU) 4, 77, 80, 123, 126, 197–201, 242; #CaliforniansForAll College Corps 120–1, 123, 130, 242; Cyber Spartans program 127; service-learning 127, 130
"Say Her Name! Working for Social Justice at the Intersection of Race and Gender" 21
scholars of color, community-engaged 188
Scratch computer programming language 127
Seattle University 137–40, 142–4, 146, 148, 242–3; campus-wide PBCE strategy 142; Carnegie Classified Community Engaged University 140; Center for Community Engagement 138- 9, 158–9, 166, 169, 230, 242–3; COVID-19 vaccine clinics on campus 146; presidents of 139–40; reputation for empowering leaders 139; Youth Initiative 140, 142, 148
self-awareness, need for 145–6
sense of belonging 3, 12, 46, 131, 165
service fellowship, benefits and challenges of participating in 129–31

service-learning programs 46, 191, 206; coordinator 159; development of 102, 193; experiences of 172; in higher education 193; in the Jewish community 192; movement 177, 203; pedagogy 7, 108; within public service centers 46; "Service-Learning 101" workshops 111; social justice-oriented 11, 18, 21–2, 26; use of 108, 193
service-learning schools 141
Smithsonian's National Museum of American History 160
Snopes 79, 95
social-ancestral identities 81
social entrepreneurism 66, 71–2
social identities 14, 19, 139, 171
social injustice 11–2; racial violence and 11–2
social innovation 151, 183
social justice 3, 5, 11, 14, 17– 9, 21–2, 26, 30–2, 35–7, 39–40, 44, 46–9 65, 113, 131, 137, 150, 161, 171, 174, 178, 180, 192, 194–197, 201–3, 206, 214, 225, 238–9
socially marginalized groups 185
socially responsible leadership 173
social media: affordances of 89–90; and climate action 82–4; importance of 76; innovating uses of 76; making a difference through civic engagement 77–9; positionality and motivation for using 79–82; posts about climate change 95; problem of fake news 79; and social issues 77–9; structuring a unit around 82–4; as tool for activism 76; as tool for community engagement and civic action 86; use in civic engagement 89
social movement organizations 89–90
Society of Jesus (the Jesuits) 139
South Florida People of Color: Awkward Dinners 24–5; Critical Race Film Series 20; IDEAS (Inclusivity, Diversity, Equity, Accountability, and Sustainability) curriculum 24; workshops 24–5
Stanford Design School (Stanford d.School) 66
story sharing 66, 68, 71; for building relationships 66, 68; personal 68
storytelling 25, 66, 71, 158, 162

Index

"strategic philanthropy" movement 196
Student Civic Engagement and Voter Empowerment Act 70
students of color 12, 19, 22, 61, 65, 131; barriers to social justice engagement 22; hostility against 12
substantial endowment 135
Sundborg S.J., Emeritus Stephen 137–9, 141–150
sustainability, issue of 225
S.W.O.T. Analysis 58

Tafolla, Andrea 158, 162–6, 173–5, 243
Taylor, Breonna 12
teaching, community-engaged xii, xiv, 181, 196, 213
theory of action 82, 86– 90, 110, 221, 229
Thunberg, Greta 90
Tierney, William G. 237
Tikkun Olam 191–7, 207n3
tobacco tax (California) 159
Tomé, Daniel Fidalgo 158, 170–5, 242
Traditional vs. Critical Service-Learning: Engaging the Literature to Differentiate Two Models (2008) 160
transdisciplinary teaching and learning 66
transparency, issue of 224
TRIO program 42
Truth and Reconciliation Commission 14, 16
Truth, Education, and Reconciliation (TEAR) Initiative 23–4; Steering Committee 23
Truth, Racial Healing & Transformation (TRHT) Campus Centers (W.K. Kellogg Foundation) 17
truth-telling xiii, 14, 16– 8, 23, 26
Tuck, Eve 40
Tufts University: National Study of Learning, Voting, and Engagement (NSLVE) 70
Tully, Andrea xiii, xiv, 3, 4, 5–6, 121, 126–9, 243

Uberification of the university 188
UC San Diego's Global Teams in Engineering Service (TIES) 183
UCSD Changemaker Institute 183
UCSD Jacobs School of Engineering: Center for Global Sustainable Development 183
UMass Amherst Office of Community Service-Learning 171
United Nations High Commissioner for Refugees 182
United Nations Sustainable Development Goals (SDGs) 169
Uniting Californians in Service 122
university-community partnerships 4, 216
University of California, Los Angeles (UCLA) 7, 111, 165; Cooperative Institutional Research Program's (CIRP) Freshman Survey 101
University of Colorado 14, 179
University of Massachusetts–Amherst 171
University of Pittsburgh 213–1 5, 217–21, 227–8, 241; Community Engagement Centers (CECs) 213, 218, 227; School of Social Work 222–3
University of San Diego (USD) 137, 139–140, 148, 242; presidents of 139–40
University of Southern California Joint Education Project 112
Upward Bound Program (2023) 170
Urban Education 215–16, 241
urban immigrant community 171
Urgency and Relevance of Community Engagement, The 115
U.S. News & World Report 140

Verdis, story of 59–60
Victims of Criminal Activity Visas 164
Violence Against Women Act 164
Voice of Witness 46
voter engagement 62, 70, 168

The Way Forward grant 70
Western Region Continuums of Service Conference (1998) 116
Wheatley, Margaret 118
White immunity 145
White nationalist movement 12
whiteness, pedagogy of 22
Woman of Color (WOC) 184, 187–8, 201

workforce training 65–6, 69
WPI Project-Based Learning Institute 70

Yale Program on Climate Change Communication 82

Yamamura, Erica xiii, 3, 103, 136, 139, 221, 243
youth civic engagement 79–83
youth-led movements 76

Zarate, Rosa Martha 189, 206n1